THE BEST SHORT PLAYS *1970*

BOOKS AND PLAYS *by Stanley Richards*

BOOKS:

The Best Short Plays 1969
The Best Short Plays 1968
Modern Short Comedies from Broadway and London
Best Plays of the Sixties
Best Short Plays of the World Theater: 1958–1967
Canada on Stage

PLAYS:

Through a Glass, Darkly
August Heat
Sun Deck
Tunnel of Love
Journey to Bahia
O Distant Land
Mood Piece
Mr. Bell's Creation
The Proud Age
Once to Every Boy
Half-Hour, Please
Know Your Neighbor
Gin and Bitterness
The Hills of Bataan
District of Columbia

Chilton Book Company

PHILADELPHIA / NEW YORK / LONDON

THE
BEST
SHORT
PLAYS *1970*

edited and with an introduction by

STANLEY RICHARDS

The Margaret Mayorga Series

Copyright © 1970 by Stanley Richards
First Edition
All rights reserved
Published in Philadelphia by Chilton Book Company
and simultaneously in Ontario, Canada,
by Thomas Nelson & Sons, Ltd.

ISBN 0-8019-5524-6
Library of Congress Catalog Card Number 38-8006
Designed by Adrianne Onderdonk Dudden
Manufactured in the United States of America by
Vail-Ballou Press, Inc.

Acknowledgment is made to Doubleday & Company, Inc.
for permission to use, in the Introduction,
the excerpt from A Talent to Amuse,
A Biography of Noel Coward, by Sheridan Morley.
Copyright © 1969
by Sheridan Morley.

for Nan A. Talese

"the light behind the stars"

CONTENTS

TERRENCE MCNALLY
Next   *3*

KENDREW LASCELLES
The Trophy Hunters   *29*

JOHN BOWEN
Trevor   *67*

ADRIENNE KENNEDY
Funnyhouse of a Negro   *127*

WILLIAM SAROYAN
The New Play   *151*

JOE ORTON
The Ruffian on the Stair   *183*

ISRAEL HOROVITZ
Acrobats   *217*

ED BULLINS
The Gentleman Caller   *235*

TERENCE RATTIGAN
All On Her Own   *251*

BENJAMIN BRADFORD
Where Are You Going, Hollis Jay?   *265*

JOHN GUARE
A Day for Surprises   *285*

A.R. GURNEY, JR.
The Love Course   *297*

MARTIN DUBERMAN
The Recorder: A History   *327*

BRIAN GEAR
A Pretty Row of Pretty Ribbons   *351*

MARTIN SHERMAN
Things Went Badly in Westphalia   *373*

INTRODUCTION

Shortly after the seventies swung into its decadal position, Noel Coward—one of the giants of the twentieth century theatre—garnered more international news coverage than any other dramatist within recent memory. The occasion: the knighthood conferred upon him by Queen Elizabeth II in recognition of his notable contributions to the stage. To those who already had erased the master off the slate, the royal honor came as somewhat of a second blow. The first occurred in 1964 when Sir Noel (a frequent, favorite target of some pelting disciples of the "new wave" for persistently clinging to "traditional" forms in the theatre) reconfirmed his undeniable status as a master dramatist when Britain's celebrated National Theatre Company, under the leadership of Sir Laurence Olivier, triumphantly revived his 1925 comedy *Hay Fever* with Dame Edith Evans as star. Not only did the revival score a resounding success with audiences, but it also managed to pop quite a few pairs of eyes among the critical fraternity who hitherto had relegated him to the back of the omnibus. To compound the situation, the resurrection of *Hay Fever* also generated an exceptional resurgence of interest in Sir Noel's other works and soon the West End was festooned with distinguished revivals of his comedies, eclipsing most of the more contemporary product then available to London playgoers.

Ironically—and this may strike something of a further blow to the Coward detractors—Sir Noel scarcely could be termed "traditional" if one took the pains to dig into the records, for on more than a few occasions the author's (then) daring themes (nymphomania, drug addiction, bestiality, the delights of a *ménage à trois*) and his forthright treatment of his material rattled journalists, guardians of public morals and even the Lord Chamberlain's office. Such noisy and embattled encounters hardly could be triggered by one accused of being a placid traditionalist.

What Sir Noel was and remains—admittedly, in spite of the featherweight texture of several of his lesser plays—is a supreme craftsman with an immutable respect for both his craft and his audience.

In recent years we have been served up all sorts of theatrical stews that have passed for dramatic art. We also have been fed a lot of nonsense about the conceptual autonomy and moral neutrality of art, and in many of our leading experimental playhouses we have been asked to endure a self-wallowing infantile narcissism as well as pretentious obscurities. Yet some of these amorphous and pointless exercises have been loudly hailed in certain areas of the press, a singular manifestation that today's reviewing is little more than an expression of faddism. When glorification of mere innovation becomes a fetish, without regard to quality or actual substance, and extreme avant-garde gaucherie is proclaimed an authentic reflection of our social, cultural and political life, then drama criticism indeed has lost touch with reality for the average intelligent playgoer who attends the theatre for personal enlightenment and entertainment that *only* can be achieved when there is a direct line of communication between stage and audience. In the "trendy" atmosphere of today, too often it is only the actors who are being edified and amused by the convolutions on stage, and unquestionably there is something arrogant, condescending and self-indulgent about these exercises. The audience seems to have become the forgotten man in some of these bizarre byways of the theatre where a play that tries desperately hard to be "trendy" eventually fails to be a play.

Thoroughly mindful that no form of art attains total fulfillment until it embraces the spectator or listener, Sir Noel prophetically set down these words of advice more than a decade ago: "Consider the public. Treat it with tact and courtesy. It will accept much from you if you are clever enough to win it to your side. Never fear or despise it. Coax it, charm it, interest it, stimulate it, shock it now and then if you must, make it laugh, make it cry and make it think, but above all, dear pioneers, in spite of indiscriminate and largely ignorant critical acclaim, in spite of awards and prizes and other dubious accolades, never, never, never bore the living hell out of it."

As editor of *The Best Short Plays* annuals and other related volumes, I strongly share Sir Noel's precepts, for a collection of printed plays, too, must consider the reader as an integral member of the audience, involve, absorb and entertain him, just as does the staged work. This, of course, does not imply that an editor must slant his own judgement in making his selections or rearrange his personal standards and esthetics to fit into a wider, more general mold of acceptance. On the contrary, it is an admission that he respects his readers and is eager to share with them the pleasures of the dramatic experience that he encountered while making his selections.

Quite naturally, not all will agree completely with an editor's choices, for tastes are as variable as the weather and as inconsistent as the efficiency of our metropolitan utility systems. More variable and inconsistent, of course, are those journalistic triggermen who've suddenly been sprung from cryptic closets or basement catalog rooms to reveal publicly their ineptitude as "authoritative" critics. This faction should be of minor or no concern to the editor as he prepares his collection, for they are merely the servants at the wedding feast; the readers are the guests, the essential participants, the primary concern of the host at the head table. Of course if the "hired" contingent somehow shares in the pleasures of the occasion, too, all well and good.

Undeniably, form has to be broken, fresher visions pursued, more pertinent advancements made in the theatre just as in any other facet of modern life and culture. Since the stage mirrors the times, it is obligatory that it keep tempo with its period in history. Yet, and again, no matter how progressive the format, no matter how radical the concept and approach, it is both fundamental and peremptory that one never discount or lose sight of the audience, for whatever one's personal theories, however brisk the march forward, the constant remains as steadfast as it has through the centuries—without an audience there is no theatre.

STANLEY RICHARDS
New York, New York
March, 1970

THE BEST SHORT PLAYS *1970*

Terrence McNally

NEXT

Terrence McNally

A notable Off-Broadway success, *Next* (paired with Elaine May's *Adaptation*) opened at the Greenwich Mews Theatre on February 10, 1969. Clive Barnes of *The New York Times* proclaimed the presentation as "just plain marvelous—funny, provocative and touching" while his Sunday colleague Walter Kerr counseled, "You mustn't miss it!" *The New Yorker,* in a somewhat rare moment of accord with most of the newspaper contingent, reported that it was "the funniest evening imaginable . . . Terrence McNally is in top form."

The dual bill became an instant smash hit and within months of its Manhattan premiere, companies were dispatched to present the show in Boston (Kevin Kelly of the *Boston Globe* called it "the highlight of the year") and Los Angeles where dedicated readers of the *Hollywood Reporter* were enjoined to "hasten immediately to this rare and precious evening of theatre."

Under the direction of Miss May, *Next* was superbly performed by James Coco (who since has become a Broadway star in Neil Simon's *Last of the Red Hot Lovers*) and Elaine Shore as the granitic female sergeant. The play (and its stage-mate, *Adaptation*) was chosen as one of the "ten best plays of the New York theatre season, 1968–69" by Otis L. Guernsey, Jr., editor of the theatre yearbook.

Few of his contemporaries would contest the fact that Terrence McNally was one of the most reviewed young dramatists of the departing Sixties. Within one season alone (1968–69), six of the author's plays occupied Manhattan stages: *Next;* the double bill, *Sweet Eros* and *Witness,* Gramercy Arts; *¡Cuba Si!,* with Viveca Lindfors, Theatre de Lys; *Tour,* a highlight of *Collision Course,* Café au Go Go; and *Noon,* included in the tripartite *Morning, Noon and Night,* Henry Miller's Theatre.

Additionally, the author enjoyed wide praise for his 1968 television production, *Apple Pie. The New York Times* lauded the three short plays in the overall work as "a bitingly original look at some American attitudes toward the war in Vietnam." Mr. McNally continued his exploration of the same theme in

Bringing It All Back Home which was introduced in *The Best Short Plays 1969.*

The author was born (1939) and raised in Corpus Christi, Texas, and came to New York to attend Columbia University, where he took a B.A. degree in English in 1960. On graduation he was awarded the Harry Evans Traveling Fellowship for work in creative writing and in 1967 he received a Guggenheim Fellowship.

On March 20, 1963, Mr. McNally made his Broadway debut as playwright with a new adaptation of *The Lady of the Camellias,* designed and directed by Franco Zeffirelli. Two years later, the author again was represented on Broadway, this time with an original work that had had its premiere (1964) at the Tyrone Guthrie Theatre, Minneapolis—*And Things That Go Bump in the Night.* The New York presentation (1965) was directed by Michael Cacoyannis and starred Eileen Heckart.

The author presently is at work on a new full-length play, *Where Has Tommy Flowers Gone?* described as a "comedy about a writer-magician and his retirement from magic." Though the play still is dominating Mr. McNally's typewriter, there is more than an even chance that it will be sponsored on Broadway (after a possible summer hearing at the Berkshire Theatre Festival, Stockbridge, Massachusetts) by Lyn Austin and Oliver Smith, who are among the co-producers of *Adaptation/Next.*

A collection of Terrence McNally's work, *Sweet Eros, Next and Other Plays,* was published in 1969 and his aforementioned *Noon* is included in this editor's volume of *Modern Short Comedies from Broadway and London.*

Characters:

MARION CHEEVER

SERGEANT THECH

Scene:

An examination room decorated in neutral colors; anonymous-looking. Stage left there is an examination table, a scale and a cabinet filled with medical equipment. Stage right there is a desk and two chairs. The only bright color in the room is the American flag, center stage.

As the curtain rises, the room is empty.

SGT. THECH: (*Offstage*) Next!

(*Marion Cheever enters. He is a fat man in his late forties and he is nattily dressed. He carries a brief case.*)

MARION: Hello? I'm next!

(*He looks around, puts down his brief case, takes out a cigarette case, lights one up, sits in front of the desk and waits somewhat impatiently.*)

SGT. THECH: (*Entering*) No smoking.

MARION: (*Rising*) Good morning. Good morning! (*Briskly*) Well! I think we can get this over with rather quickly.

SGT. THECH: No smoking.

MARION: (*Snuffing out his cigarette*) I'm sorry. Filthy habit. (*He's put his hat on her desk. Sgt. Thech hands it back to him*) Oh my hat! I'm sorry!

(*He looks for a place to put it. There is none, so he puts it on the floor.*)

SGT. THECH: (*Already busy at her desk with papers and forms*) Your card and bottle, please.

MARION: (*Rummaging in his brief case*) As I was starting to say, I think we can get this over with rather quickly. There's obviously been a mistake. (*He laughs*) I mean I—

SGT. THECH: The government does not make mistakes. If

your country has called you it has its reasons. May I have your card and bottle, please?

MARION: (*Still going through his brief case*) I thought to myself, "My God! They can't mean me."

SGT. THECH: That's it.

MARION: Is that it? (*Hands her the card. She begins to type*) I thought to myself there must be someone else in my building with the same name because why else would I get a card to come down here?

SGT. THECH: Is your name Marion Cheever?

MARION: Yes, it is. But you know I just had a fortieth birthday and I thought to myself nobody sends a card like this to a man like me.

SGT. THECH: They're taking older men.

MARION: How old exactly?

SGT. THECH: It's inching up all the time. May I have your bottle, please?

MARION: (*Looking in brief case*) Inching up all the time, is it? The bottle, yes, here it is!

(*He hands her his urine specimen*)

SGT. THECH: Strip.

MARION: I didn't know that . . . the inching up all the time.

SGT. THECH: Remove all articles of clothing including your shoes and socks.

MARION: Who are you?

SGT. THECH: Your examining officer, Sergeant Thech. And by the authority vested in me by this government, I order you to strip.

MARION: A lady examining officer! Oh that's funny! They must be pretty hard up these days.

SGT. THECH: And if you have not begun to strip in the next ten seconds I will complete these forms without further examination and report you to the board of examiners as fit for duty.

MARION: (*As if coming out of a trance*) Oh my God,

I'm sorry. I didn't hear one word you said. I don't know what I was thinking of. What did you say? That if I hadn't . . .

SGT. THECH: Begun to strip in the next ten seconds . . .

MARION: You will complete those forms . . .

SGT. THECH: Without further examination . . .

MARION: And report me to the board of examiners? . . .

SGT. THECH: As fit for duty.

MARION: (*Biting his lip*) Do you think that's fair?

SGT. THECH: Would you prefer not to strip?

MARION: Indeed I would!

SGT. THECH: Very well, then I will stamp these forms . . .

MARION: No, don't do that!

SGT. THECH: Then you have ten seconds. (*Timing him*) One one-thousand, two one-thousand . . .

MARION: I'm going to strip! (*While Sgt. Thech counts*) I'm going to let you do it because not only am I over forty, I am not a healthy over forty and . . .

SGT. THECH: Seven one-thousand.

MARION: (*To make her stop*) Where do I go?

SGT. THECH: (*Points to the center of the room*) Right over there.

MARION: Right over there. Well! Everybody else is doing it, why not?

SGT. THECH: (*Filling out a questionnaire*) Your name.

MARION: Do you have a little hanger?

SGT. THECH: Use the stool. Your name.

MARION: Cheever. Marion Cheever.

SGT. THECH: Do you spell Marion with an *o?*

MARION: I do, yes.

SGT. THECH: Age.

MARION: Forty . . . eight! Forty-eight.

SGT. THECH: Sex.

MARION: Did you put that down? I'm forty-eight years old.

SGT. THECH: Sex.

MARION: Well what do you think I am?

SGT. THECH: Color of hair.

MARION: Brown. Black. Blackish brown.

SGT. THECH: Eyes.

MARION: Two.

SGT. THECH: Color of eyes . . .

MARION: I'm sorry! Blue. Blue-green. Aqua.

SGT. THECH: Occupation.

MARION: (*Still apologizing for the eyes*) You rattled me.

SGT. THECH: Occupation.

MARION: I don't know what's the matter with me.

SGT. THECH: Your occupation, Mr. Cheever.

MARION: I'm a dancer.

SGT. THECH: Toe or tap.

MARION: Oh really! Toe or tap! I'm the assistant manager of the Fine Arts Theatre, 58th Street and Park Avenue. You've probably heard of us. Toe or tap! I was funning!

SGT. THECH: How long.

MARION: Is what?

SGT. THECH: How long have you been the assistant manager of the Fine Arts Theatre?

MARION: I'm sorry. How long have I been assistant manager of the Fine Arts Theatre? About twelve years.

(*He has removed his shirt by now. His undershirt is torn and dirty. He's trying to find something to hide behind*)

SGT. THECH: Marital status.

MARION: (*Eying the American flag*) Single. Single now. Divorced I guess is what I'm supposed to say.

(*He will use the flag to cover himself as he continues to strip. Sgt. Thech doesn't see all this, as he is behind her and she is busy typing in the questionnaire*)

SGT. THECH: How many times.

MARION: Twice.

SGT. THECH: Number of dependents.

MARION: Three girls.

SGT. THECH: Sex.

MARION: I said three girls!

SGT. THECH: Ages.

MARION: Fourteen, twelve and two. Two with my first wife and one with my second.

SGT. THECH: Did you finish grammar school?

MARION: I certainly did.

SGT. THECH: High school.

MARION: You bet.

SGT. THECH: College.

MARION: No, I never got to college. I meant to but I never . . .

SGT. THECH: Do you belong to a church?

MARION: I just never got there. You know what I mean?

SGT. THECH: Do you belong to a church?

MARION: Oh yes!

SGT. THECH: Which denomination.

MARION: The Sacred Heart of Jesus.

SGT. THECH: Which denomination.

MARION: Roman Catholic. What do you think with a name like that? It's a temple?

SGT. THECH: Do you attend church?

MARION: You bet.

SGT. THECH: Regularly or occasionally.

MARION: Yes, unh-hunh, unh-hunh!

SGT. THECH: Regularly or occasionally.

MARION: Yes, regularly on occasion.

SGT. THECH: Is your father living or deceased?

MARION: Living.

SGT. THECH: His age.

MARION: Seventy-two.

SGT. THECH: Is your mother living or deceased?

MARION: Deceased.

SGT. THECH: Age of death.

MARION: Thirty-one.

SGT. THECH: Cause of death.

MARION: Natural causes.

SGT. THECH: Be specific.

MARION: Heart.

SGT. THECH: Any brothers.

MARION: Yes.

SGT. THECH: How many?

MARION: One. He's alive.

SGT. THECH: Sisters.

MARION: Two. They're both alive. Both living.

SGT. THECH: Do you live alone?

MARION: At the present time I do. I get a lot of company, of course, but unh, officially, for the record, I live alone.

SGT. THECH: Do you own your own home?

MARION: No. It's a . . . you know . . . residential hotel for . . . unh . . . men. Single men.

(Marion has undressed now and is sitting on a low stool. The flag is draped across him)

SGT. THECH: *(Turning to a new page)* Measles.

MARION: What?

SGT. THECH: Have you ever had the measles?

MARION: Oh measles! No, no I haven't.

SGT. THECH: Chicken pox.

MARION: No, I never had chicken pox.

SGT. THECH: Whooping cough.

MARION: I think it *might* have been. I was coughing an awful lot and I was very sick.

SGT. THECH: Yes or no.

MARION: No. It wasn't *exactly* whooping cough but . . .

SGT. THECH: Rheumatic fever.

MARION: *(Thinking hard)* Unh! Did I have rheumatic fever? Is that what it was? No, no I don't think so.

SGT. THECH: Mumps.

MARION: *(Jumping at this)* Yes! Yes, yes, yes! Now just a minute on the mumps.

SGT. THECH: Tuberculosis.

MARION: They weren't your ordinary mumps!

SGT. THECH: Jaundice.

MARION: Will you please let me tell you about my mumps! I was in bed for months. I practically had last rites!

SGT. THECH: Venereal disease.

MARION: I don't think you realize how serious my mumps were.

SGT. THECH: Venereal disease.

MARION: Not yet! I just wish you'd let me tell you about my mumps.

SGT. THECH: Allergies.

MARION: What about allergies?

SGT. THECH: Are you allergic to anything?

MARION: Yes, yes, as a matter of fact I am.

SGT. THECH: Go on, explain.

MARION: I know this sounds silly but I'm allergic to peach fuzz. I swell up like a balloon.

SGT. THECH: Anything else?

MARION: No, but I can't even go *near* a fruit stand. All I have to do is look at a peach and . . .

SGT. THECH: Any history of epilepsy.

MARION: Me and peach fuzz is no joke!

SGT. THECH: Have you a family history of diabetes?

MARION: Diabetes? Well why not. Somebody must have had it.

SGT. THECH: Heart attacks.

MARION: I told you about that.

SGT. THECH: Cancer.

MARION: Bite your tongue!

SGT. THECH: Nervous or mental disorders.

MARION: I'm a nervous wreck!

SGT. THECH: Do you smoke?

MARION: You saw me. Remember? When you came in here, the first thing you said . . .

SGT. THECH: How much.

MARION: Three packs a day. Twenty cigarettes to a pack, that's sixty cigarettes. That's a lot of smoking.

SGT. THECH: Do you drink?

MARION: That, too, oh yes!

SGT. THECH: How much?

MARION: Whenever I smoke. Smoking makes me want to drink, and drinking makes me want to smoke. It's a vicious circle.

SGT. THECH: Do you take any drugs?

MARION: Anything! Give it to me and I'll take it.

SGT. THECH: Name the drugs.

MARION: Aspirins and bromo seltzers for the hangovers, Nikoban for the smoking. And Miltown! I take lots of Miltown.

SGT. THECH: For what purpose?

MARION: Because I am a nervous wreck. For what purpose!

SGT. THECH: All right, Mr. Cheever, on the scale now, please. (*She turns and sees him draped in the American flag*) Drop that flag.

MARION: I was just admiring it! I have one just like it at home. (*Sgt. Thech returns the flag to its proper place. Marion all the while walks along with it, unwilling to give up its protection*) The same colors, the same shape. It's amazing how similar they are! (*Sgt. Thech is pulling the flag away from him*) Then could I have a little robe or something? I mean I don't know if it's of any interest to you, but I'm right on the verge of another bad cold. (*Sgt. Thech hands him a sheet*) Thank you. Thank you. (*Sgt. Thech salutes the flag, then makes ready to examine Marion*) I'm going to write somebody a letter about this.

SGT. THECH: On the scale.

MARION: (*Wrapping the sheet around himself*) I'll refuse to go, you know. You're just wasting your time, I hope you understand.

SGT. THECH: On the scale, Mr. Cheever.

(*Marion gets on the scale and plays with the weights*)

MARION: You know something? It's wrong. At least ten pounds off. Easily that.

SGT. THECH: Don't tamper. (*She is washing her hands*)

MARION: What are you going to do? Operate? (*Sgt. Thech comes to the scale and weighs him. Next, she makes ready to measure him. When she raises up the measuring pole, Marion starts and backs off the scale*) Would you warn someone before you do that? You know you could put someone's eye out with that thing.

SGT. THECH: Step back onto the scale.

(*Marion gets back onto scale while Sgt. Thech measures him. When she swings the pole back into place Marion jumps off again*)

MARION: You missed me by *that* much!

SGT. THECH: (*At the examining table*) Sit at the edge of the table.

MARION: (*Under his breath*) I hate this whole day! It's goddamn humiliating, that's what it is. Calling a man in here and . . .

SGT. THECH: On the table, Mr. Cheever.

MARION: (*Trying a new approach*) I'm sorry I'm not cooperating. You have your job to do, and I'll try to help in every way I can.

SGT. THECH: (*At his back, listening with a stethoscope*) Breathe. In, out. In, out.

MARION: In, out. See when you ask me how simple it is? (*Sgt. Thech's stethoscope is at his chest now. Marion is very ticklish*) Don't do that!

(*He laughs while Sgt. Thech listens to his heart*)

SGT. THECH: Unh-hunh!

MARION: What did that mean? "Unh-hunh?" You heard something you didn't like?

SGT. THECH: Open.

(*She has a tongue depressor down his throat*)

MARION: Just ask me and I'll open! You don't have to lunge at me like that! (*Sgt. Thech checks his eyes with a light*) It's on, it's on! (*Sgt. Thech looks into his ears with a light*) I hate this. I hate it a lot. (*While Sgt. Thech checks his ears*)

When you were examining my heart, did you hear something I should know about? It wasn't very subtle, going "unh-hunh" like that. It's my ticker, so if there's anything wrong I'd like to know about it. (*Sgt. Thech has crossed the room. She turns to face him and speaks very softly. We just see her lips moving*) What? What did you say?

SGT. THECH: Your hearing is perfect.

MARION: Now just a minute. I will not be railroaded.

SGT. THECH: (*Holding up an eye chart*) Read this chart.

MARION: All of it?

SGT. THECH: The third line.

MARION: (*Running all the letters together*) TOZDY!

SGT. THECH: The second line.

MARION: The second line's a little fuzzy.

SGT. THECH: Try the top line, Mr. Cheever.

MARION: (*With much squinting*) The top line's a real problem. Let's see . . . it's a . . . no . . . Z!

SGT. THECH: Excellent.

MARION: Now just a minute. It's an *E*. I said it was a Z. Now I failed that test. You give me credit for failing.

SGT. THECH: Failure is relative in any case, private.

MARION: Private?

SGT. THECH: (*Back at the examining table*) Lie down.

MARION: You called me private.

SGT. THECH: Lie down.

MARION: You've got me inducted already when I haven't even been given a full opportunity to fail yet.

SGT. THECH: This is your opportunity, Mr. Cheever, don't pass it up. (*Timing him until he obeys*) One one-thousand, two one-thousand . .

MARION: (*Getting onto the table*) All right, I'm lying! Just stop all that counting. (*Sgt. Thech begins to take his blood pressure*) I've heard of shanghaiing but this little episode is really a lulu. It's white slavery if you think I'm passing this test. Out and out kidnapping. I simply won't go. You can't just take a man out of civilian life and plop him into the army. So there's a war on, I didn't start it. (*Lifts his head up a moment*) I think you'll find I have a labile blood pressure. It can rocket at a moment's notice.

SGT. THECH: Keep your head down.

MARION: What do they want with me anyway? I'm on the verge of my big break. Do you know what that means to a civilian? I've stood in the back of that lousy theatre for eleven years, and they are going to promote me next winter. I am going to be *the* manager at quite a substantial raise in salary, thank you. Unh-hunh, sergeant, I'm not going into any army, war or peace!

SGT. THECH: (*While she makes ready to take a blood sample*) I want you to close your eyes and count to ten slowly and then touch the tip of your nose with your left index finger.

MARION: Oh, all right, that sounds easy. I don't mind this part at all. One, two, three, four . . . this is very restful . . . five, six—(*Suddenly sitting up*) Wait! Wait, wait, wait, wait, wait! I saw it. (*Sgt. Thech is holding a syringe*) I hate needles. I'm not afraid of them, I just don't like them.

SGT. THECH: Shall I complete the forms, Mr. Cheever, or will you let me continue with the examination?

MARION: I know you must do your job, but please be very careful. I have very small veins. Don't be nervous.

SGT. THECH: Lie down.

MARION: You have all the time in the world. And no air bubbles! (*Sgt. Thech is drawing blood*) Oh my God! I'm going to have a heart attack right on this table. (*Sgt. Thech finishes, empties his blood from the syringe into a test tube*) I'm bleeding. Look at this, I'm bleeding. (*Sgt. Thech's hands go under the sheet as she checks his spleen, liver, kidney, etc.*) Just tell me what it is you're looking for and I'll tell you where it's at!

SGT. THECH: In.

MARION: In!

SGT. THECH: Out.

MARION: It's out!

SGT. THECH: In.

MARION: In! In! Oh my God, oh!

SGT. THECH: On your feet.

MARION: On my feet! Bleed someone to death and tell him on his feet. Sure, why not? Here I go, sergeant, on my feet!

SGT. THECH: Drop your shorts.

MARION: What?

SGT. THECH: You heard me. (*Timing him*) One one-thousand, two one-thousand . . .

MARION: Drop my shorts? Oh no, sergeant, that I flatly refuse.

SGT. THECH: You are a candidate for national service. I am your examining officer and I am ordering you to drop your shorts.

MARION: (*While Sgt. Thech counts*) Now wait just a minute. Let me explain something. I'm not wearing shorts. I have this . . . well, *problem* . . . and I have to wear this . . . well sort of a *girdle* and . . .

SGT. THECH: Drop your girdle.

MARION: (*As Sgt. Thech is nearing the count of ten*) Yes! Yes, of course, I'll drop it. I just thought I should explain about my back problem and the abdominal muscles. I thought you'd want to know about them. (*Marion has worked off the girdle. It drops to the floor. Sgt. Thech is approaching him*) It's off! I swear to God it's off!

(*Sgt. Thech has her hand under sheet and at his groin*)

SGT. THECH: Turn your head and cough.

MARION: Oh really!

SGT. THECH: Cough.

MARION: Cough!

SGT. THECH: Again.

MARION: Cough!

SGT. THECH: Again.

MARION: How many hernias are you checking for? Two's about average, you know. Cough!

SGT. THECH: Well done, Cheever. Now sit.

MARION: (*Sits on the edge of the examining table while Sgt. Thech checks him for reflexes*) You're terrific you are! You and Pegeen ought to team up. She was my first wife. Talk about your lady wrestlers and roller-derby queens! But next to you, she was Snow White. But I foxed her. Just when she thought she had me where she wanted me, I sprang the divorce on her. "On what grounds, may I ask?" she growled, fat hands on her fat hips . . . Dutch Cleanser I used to call her. "On exactly what grounds?" (*Sgt. Thech is busy completing some forms*) "Mental cruelty," I smiled, and boy did that answer ever throw her for a loop! She begged me to change it to adultery but I held firm. You should have seen the look on that judge's face in Juarez when I dropped that little bombshell. Mental cruelty!

SGT. THECH: All right, Mr. Cheever, you can get dressed now. Your physical examination is over.

MARION: (*Caught in midair*) Oh. It's over. Well that wasn't so bad. How did I do? Am I 4-F?

SGT. THECH: You have nothing to worry about. I found no evidence of physical abnormality.

MARION: (*Aghast*) You found no evidence of physical abnormality? Now wait a minute. What about my labile blood pressure? Oh no, sergeant, I'm not done in here. Not yet. I want more testing. You're not convinced. I'm not leaving until I get a better verdict. What about my sinus condition? Did you know I had one? Of course not, you didn't look up my nose. What kind of examination is it without looking up a person's nose? A lot of things could be wrong up there. I can't breathe seven months out of the year. Would you write that down, please? And what about my eye test? I know I failed my eye test!

SGT. THECH: (*Busy at her desk tabulating the examination results*) If you won't cooperate, I have to judge you on the basis of objective evidence. You do not squint, you do not wear glasses and you saw my lips moving at a distance of over fifteen feet away. We have ways of evaluating the condition of a subject whether the subject cooperates or not. You'd have to be a lot smarter and better rehearsed than you are to fool an examining officer.

MARION: (*Triumphant*) All right, then what about my feet? You didn't even make me take my socks off. That's all right, I'll do it myself. Here. Now look at this. They're flat. I'm not ashamed. See how flat they are? Do you see any arch? Of course you don't. You call that normal? And see, see all those corns? My feet are covered with corns. And I'll tell you something, something highly abnormal: I was born with all these corns. That's right, sergeant, I was born with corns. They are hereditary. Ask yourself, is that normal? (*Sgt. Thech continues working at desk*) And look! (*He shakes his arms in front of her*) No muscle tone. All flab! See how the skin just hangs there? And it's not a question of diet. I've dieted all my life. I simply don't burn fat! (*Now showing her his teeth*) And teeth! My teeth. They're full of decay. If I have a candy bar I have to have an inlay. I swear to God I do. My gums are very spongy. I mean I'll probably have a coronary in five years . . . if I live very carefully. (*Desperately trying to attract Sgt. Thech's attention*) And sergeant, here, watch this, look now, sergeant, over here, see this? . . . (*He removes his toupee*) You didn't know that, did you? It fools lots of people but there it is. I lost all of my hair in a period of thirteen months after my last divorce. It just went! Right out by the roots it came. Is that normal, to lose so much hair in thirteen months? And that's not hereditary, sergeant. My father still has every hair in his head. You know what my kind of hair loss is? Nerves, sergeant, plain old-fashioned nerves! It's highly irregular he should have all his and I don't have mine! And what about my mind? You haven't asked me one single question about my mind. For all you know I could be a raving lunatic. I could be a . . .

SGT. THECH: (*She's into the psychological and intelligence tests*) I have twelve apples.

MARION: (*Thrown*) You have what?

SGT. THECH: You have twelve apples. Together we have

. . .

MARION: (*Involuntarily*) Twenty-four apples.
(*He realizes what he's done and groans*)

SGT. THECH: I have a pie which I wish to divide as follows: one-fourth of the pie to Fred, one-fourth of the pie to Phyllis, one-fourth of the pie to you. How much pie will I have left for myself?

MARION: (*Thinks a moment*) Who are Fred and Phyllis? I mean maybe Phyllis didn't finish all her piece and then there'd be more for you. A quarter and a half!

SGT. THECH: You are on a train going sixty miles an hour. Your destination is a hundred and twenty away. How many hours will it take you to get to your destination?

MARION: I would say three days. But then I don't take trains. I really wouldn't swear to that answer.

SGT. THECH: Who was the first President of the United States?

MARION: George Washington. Was that right?

SGT. THECH: Who were the allies of the United States in the Second World War?

MARION: The good people.

SGT. THECH: Who were its enemies?

MARION: No one. We had no enemies.

SGT. THECH: Who are the allies of the United States now?

MARION: Just about everyone.

SGT. THECH: Who are its enemies?

MARION: Who can tell?

SGT. THECH: Name three of the twelve Apostles.

MARION: Joseph . . . and his brother . . . and his sister!

SGT. THECH: In what year did Columbus discover America?

MARION: 1776. No, wait, it was 1775!

SGT. THECH: What is the great pox and how does it differ from the small pox?

MARION: The great pox is greater than the small pox. However, both are poxes.

SGT. THECH: If you found an unopened letter lying on the sidewalk, fully addressed and stamped, what would you do?

MARION: I would probably step on it. I mean who wouldn't? You're walking along, you'd be surprised what you step on!

SGT. THECH: If you were seated in a theatre and you saw a fire break out nearby before the rest of the audience noticed it—what would you do?

MARION: That one's right up my alley. As a theatre manager I know about this. The main thing is I wouldn't want to start a panic. So I'd very quietly leave and go home.

SGT. THECH: If you found a wallet lying on the sidewalk —what would you do?

MARION: I'd be delighted. I never find anything.

SGT. THECH: What is the similarity between a chair and a couch?

MARION: A chair and a couch? You can sit on them.

SGT. THECH: A rabbit and a squirrel.

MARION: (*Reasonably*) You could sit on a rabbit and a squirrel. The rabbit might even like it.

SGT. THECH: What is the difference between a giant and a dwarf?

MARION: The difference? I see the similarity all right but the difference is tricky.

SGT. THECH: A profit and a loss.

MARION: A profit is when the loss is greater than the sum. It's exactly like giants and dwarfs.

SGT. THECH: A man and a gorilla.

MARION: Hair. Lots of hair.

SGT. THECH: Complete the following sentences. People obey the law because . . .

MARION: Because! Because they have to obey it.

SGT. THECH: I am happiest when my family is . . .

MARION: Yes! I think we all are. Well aren't you?

SGT. THECH: What is the meaning of the following proverbs. He who laughs last laughs best.

MARION: Yes . . . well . . . that means that *he* who laughs *last* laughs *best*.

SGT. THECH: A rolling stone gathers no moss.

MARION: That's one of my favorites. It means that a rolling *stone* . . . gathers no *moss!*

SGT. THECH: I am going to say a word.

MARION: Did I get that one right?

SGT. THECH: After I say it I want you to say the first word that comes to your mind without thinking.

MARION: Are you sure?

SGT. THECH: You have one second. Tree. Tree!

MARION: I'm sorry. I was thinking. I couldn't help myself.

SGT. THECH: House.

MARION: House. The first word that comes to mind when you say house is house.

SGT. THECH: Father.

MARION: (*Drawing a blank*) Father . . . father . . .

SGT. THECH: Grass.

MARION: Green. There, I got one!

SGT. THECH: Shower.

MARION: Tree. When it showers you stand under a tree with your father.

SGT. THECH: Snake.

MARION: Juicy. Juicy snake.

SGT. THECH: House.

MARION: Whores. No, no! that's not right.

SGT. THECH: Mother.

MARION: None. I mean . . .

SGT. THECH: Green.

MARION: Colors. Green colors.

SGT. THECH: Floor.

MARION: Me. Really! I'm on my feet all day.

SGT. THECH: Purse.

MARION: Snatch. Purse snatcher.

SGT. THECH: Have you ever suffered from night terrors?

MARION: Terribly.

SGT. THECH: Insomnia.

MARION: Of course insomnia! Because of the night terrors.

SGT. THECH: Sleepwalking.

MARION: Absolutely! In the morning my ankles are so swollen!

SGT. THECH: Anxiety states.

MARION: This is so good in here this part! Keep on.

SGT. THECH: Hallucinations.

MARION: Of grandeur. Of course terrible grandeur!

SGT. THECH: Delusions.

MARION: They're not the same thing? Listen, can't we go back to the anxiety states?

SGT. THECH: Compulsive eating.

MARION: No, I've never been bothered by that. About my anxiety states . . . !

SGT. THECH: Have you ever indulged in homosexual activities.

MARION: They have been very good to me.

SGT. THECH: When did you stop?

MARION: Who said anything about stopping? They're a small but vital minority. The Fine Arts Theatre welcomes them.

SGT. THECH: Did you have a normal relationship with your mother?

MARION: I'm sure she thought so!

SGT. THECH: Did you have a normal relationship with your father?

MARION: After we stopped dating the same girl, everything was fine.

SGT. THECH: Do you have any history of bedwetting?

MARION: Even my top sheet is rubber.

SGT. THECH: Have you ever attempted suicide?

MARION: No, but I've thought of murder.

SGT. THECH: Are you now or have you ever been a member of the Communist party?

MARION: I wouldn't be surprised. I mean you join anything nowadays and next thing you know it's pinko.

SGT. THECH: What is your responsibility to your community?

MARION: Unh . . . to shovel the snow.

SGT. THECH: What is your responsibility to your family?

MARION: To be there.

SGT. THECH: What is your responsibility to your country?

MARION: To be there.

SGT. THECH: (*Abruptly*) All right, Mr. Cheever, you may go now. The examination is over.

MARION: The whole thing?

SGT. THECH: That's right.

MARION: Well? How did I do? Am I 4-F yet?

SGT. THECH: I don't think you have anything to worry about. I doubt if they would find someone like you acceptable.

MARION: (*Stung, but hiding it*) Oh well good. Good. Based on what? The last two answers?

SGT. THECH: The entire psychological examination.

MARION: I see. Well, then I *am* 4-F?

SGT. THECH: You'll get your classification in the mail.

MARION: I can hardly wait.

SGT. THECH: You may go now. I'm through with you. (*Sgt. Thech turns her back to him and begins typing up his test results*)

MARION: (*Beginning to dress*) Oh don't worry, I'm going. Nothing in the world could make me stay here. Granted, I've enjoyed all this. I mean you've been just wonderful. It must be difficult examining someone while they're still alive and breathing! And your attention has been so flattering. I'm not used to so much fuss. You're great, just great. The way you concentrated on me. I never distracted you from me once. I'm sure you have a big future ahead of you. (*Sgt. Thech types*) Now you're through with me and would like me to go. You have taken my time, you have taken my blood, you have taken my urine, you have taken my secrets and now you would like me out of here so you can digest them in private. Isn't that right? Well I'm not going. If I go I take *all* of me with me. I'd like my blood and my urine back! I mean I'm 4-F, you can't have any use for them. (*Sgt. Thech types*) You know I am not simply the sum total of my parts. I am someone. I am a citizen. I have my rights. I pay my taxes, I serve my jury duty, I buy American. I don't make trouble. I support the administration. I keep my mouth shut. I believe everything I read. I do all that and that gives me rights! I want my blood and my urine back and I . . . I demand an apology! I have given everything to everyone and now I want something back! Don't tell me about responsibilities. I visit my kids, I bring them presents; I visit my father, I bring him presents; I visit my sisters, their kids get presents, too. I pay my rent; I pay my alimony; I meet my car payments—a hot red Mustang I can hardly fit behind the wheel of, but I'm meeting those payments! I do everything I'm sup-posed to do . . . I'm never late for work . . . and now I demand a reward! I want a reward. You owe me something. My country owes me something. Somebody owes me something. Because I have nothing! My big break? A lousy twenty-bucks raise. Big deal, crap! My children don't give a damn. What do I get on Father's Day? A lot of crap from Woolworth's their mothers picked out. My father doesn't recognize my voice on the tele-phone. My mother is dead. I've been married twice. You think it's fun, a man my age going home alone at night? Who looks at men like me after a while? I know what I look like! I'm no fool! (*Sgt. Thech continues typing*) You know what the ushers at the theatre call me behind my back? Fatso. Yeah! that hurts. But when I become *the* manager I am going to fire those ushers and hire new ushers and *they* will call me Fatso behind my back. Because that is exactly what I am. A fatso. I am nothing but what I eat. But I feed myself. Nobody feeds me. And I eat everything I want. When I want candy, I eat candy. When I want a pizza at two A.M., I call up and order pizza. I'm going to get older and fatter and someday I'm going to die from over-weight and smoking. But when I go, I'm paying for my own funeral and I'm going to give myself the best funeral that money can buy. Because dead or alive I pay my own way! Those niggers on relief, can they say that? They cannot! And they get to do everything. They get to riot, they get to loot, they get to yell, they get to hate, they get to kill! They get in the papers, they get on television and everybody pays attention. Everybody cares. And what do I get? There's nothing on television about me. My name's not in the Sunday papers. And I'm the one who does everything he should. I'm the one who never makes trouble. I'm the good citizen. But everybody else gets to do everything! You see those teen-age girls with their skirts up to here strutting around with their hair all piled up and driving a man crazy. And those men all like fags with that hair and those pants. They do anything they want. They have anything they want. And I get shit! (*He bangs on Sgt. Thech's desk with his fist. Sgt. Thech goes on typing*) How dare you call me in here, examine me, ignore me, dismiss me and tell me I'm not accept-able. *You* are not acceptable! I want my orange juice. You took my blood and I want my orange juice. I know my rights. I want my radiator fixed. I want those people next door to turn their radio down when I bang on the wall. I want quiet. I want my sleep. I want them to stop all those parties upstairs. I want people to listen to me when I call up and make complaints. Not just sit there and type. Stop it! And listen to me! (*Sgt. Thech has finished typing up her report*) I said stop! (*He puts his hands over the typewriter keys*) Good. Very good! (*Now Marion will describe everything Sgt. Thech does while she is doing it—as if he were giving her the orders to do it*) That's right. Fold the paper. Open the drawer. Put it away. Close it. Now you're doing exactly as you're told. Get up. Fold the sheet. Check the instru-ments. Make sure you've got everything. One final check now. Excellent. Now out you go. Close the door. There! (*Sgt. Thech has left the room, closing the door behind her*) All right, on the scale now, Cheever! Do I have to? Why not? There's nothing to be afraid of. (*Marion gets on the scale*) You're the perfect weight, just right for your height. You're an excellent physical specimen, Cheever. Am I? You're in very good shape. You're very acceptable. (*Marion steps off the scale*) On the table now. (*Marion crosses to the examination table*) Lie down. (*Marion obeys*) Give me your arm. Will it hurt? Not you, Cheever. You're very brave. (*Marion moves his lips silently: "Can you hear what I'm saying?"*) Yes, you said, "Can you hear what I'm saying?" Your hearing is perfect. I know. Now read the chart. The last line, the smallest letters. "A-W-G-H-L." Excellent, you have perfect vision. Rest now. Thank you. (*Marion lets his head drop on the table*) Tell me about it. I was thirteen years old. Yes, go on. I came home and she wasn't there. Yes. It was so sudden. None of us knew. We all thought she would always be there and then when she wasn't . . . (*His voice trails off in tears*) You must have been very sad. I was, I was. I felt so cold. Didn't you tell anyone how you felt? Nobody asked me. I'm asking you. I never got to say good-bye. I understand. (*Short pause*) On your feet now. I don't think I can. Yes, Cheever, you can do it. You're very strong now and very brave and very acceptable. (*Marion gets up off the table*) Up now, shoulders back, walk tall. That's it. You're doing fine. (*Marion goes to Sgt. Thech's desk, puts on her white examination coat which she has left over her chair, sits, types a moment, then looks up*) You have ten seconds to strip. By the power vested in me by the United States government I order you to remove all articles of clothing. One one-thousand, two one-thousand, three one-thousand, four one-thousand. Sorry. You are not acceptable. (*His head spins around as he looks straight ahead into the audience*) NEXT!

(*The lights snap off*)

Curtain

Kendrew Lascelles

THE
TROPHY HUNTERS

Kendrew Lascelles

One of the most rewarding joys of being an editor is the discovery of a play of exceptional quality and originality, and if it comes from an unexpected source the joy is compounded.

Kendrew Lascelles, the co-author and one of the leading players in the celebrated South African musical entertainment, *Wait a Minim!,* of course was familiar to this editor but primarily as a gifted comedian whose presence in that revue remains steadfast in memory. *The Trophy Hunters* now emphatically reveals that Mr. Lascelles is exceedingly more than a comic sprite. He also is an exceptional serious dramatist who, authentically and provocatively, has evoked a mood of the South African bush country and its inhabitants.

Wait a Minim!, the revue that brought Mr. Lascelles to international success, originated in 1962 at a small Johannesburg theatre. It toured South Africa and Rhodesia in three editions for two years, then was presented at the Fortune Theatre in London, where it ran for another two years. In 1966 it opened at the John Golden Theatre, New York, and played 456 performances.

Leon Gluckman, who devised and directed *Wait a Minim!* has said of Mr. Lascelles, "I enlisted the highly professional services of a good friend and determinedly inarticulate comic who could not sing a note. Kendrew Lascelles, among other things, had played the mute in a production which I had directed of Jean Anouilh's *Bal de Valeur.* Like all good comics, Kendrew is a sad, funny man, with a melancholic, almost neurotic absorption with the effectiveness of his comic business."

Unlike most of his performing colleagues, Mr. Lascelles also happens to be somewhat diffident when the occasion relates to himself. In response to a request for biographical data, he complied (providing both questions and answers) with what well may be the least voluble personal chronicle in theatre history:

Born: Gatley, Chester, England. 1935.
Raised: South Africa. 1938–51.

> *Educated:* Sporadically, with final incompletion at Kears-
> ney College.
> *Degrees:* None.
> *Occupation:* Theatrical.
> *Number of Years in Occupation:* Seventeen.
> *Years Writing:* Not enough. Yet.
> *Addenda:* International harbinger of joy and deep purple
> glimpses of cosmic significance and the muscles between
> my ears!

The Trophy Hunters is published for the first time anywhere
in *The Best Short Plays 1970* and, recently, Mr. Lascelles completed another short play, *Tigers.*

Characters:

STUBB

HELLALOOYA

LANG

Scene:

The action takes place in what is called the front room, or living room, of an owner-built house in the middle of the African bush.

The essential qualities of the set are: no African curios or objects des "primitive" arts. Pictures, if any, should depict British Cavalry charging into battle, prints. The furniture is sparse and drab. One easy chair. Stubb's chair.

There are two doors; one leading to the interior of the house, the other leading to the exterior of the house. We should have the impression that there are large windows downstage in the proscenium wall.

The essential props are a rifle in a rifle rack; a portable hand-winding type gramophone and a 78 RPM single record of a brass band rendition of "I Do Like to Be Beside the Seaside," or something similar with a brass band military romping flavor. The gramophone is on a table beside the chair Stubb occupies. Both chair and gramophone are near to one of the downstage windows.

Hellalooya, a middle aged black man, is seated upstage, reading. Stubb, an old white man, is seated in the easy chair. He is leaning forward, peering directly up at a sharp angle through the window. He also looks directly out, once or twice, as if watching something approaching.

Stubb winds the gramophone, plays the record. The record stops playing. We can hear the approach of a vehicle. Hellalooya looks up. Stubb remains impassive, removes the needle from the record, goes back to peering out the window.

Truck doors slam off. Lang, a younger white man, enters exterior door.

Note: Both Stubb and Lang wear bush outfits. Lang may wear short pants and rolled down socks. Hellalooya: bush jacket top, Sam Brown and sarong type skirt. Barefoot. Stubb wears slippers.

LANG: Hello Stubb. Howzit hey?
How are things, hey?
I said hello. How iz it with you?
What's the matter?
Hey! What's the matter with him, hey?
       (*Hellalooya looks toward Stubb, shrugs and looks back into his book*)
LANG: Hey Stubb, man!
STUBB: No need to shout. I know you're here. I've been watching you.
LANG: Well I thought you'd gone deaf or something.
STUBB: I haven't gone deaf.
LANG: Well, how the hell was I supposed to know that if you just sit staring up in the sky.
       (*Stubb looks up out the window. Lang extends his hand. Stubb and Lang shake hands*)
LANG: How was I supposed to know you hadn't gone deaf in the last four months or something, hey?
STUBB: Four months? Has it been as long as that?
LANG: June, July, August, September. Four months.
STUBB: Is it September already?
LANG: It's October already, never mind about September. October.
STUBB: October?
LANG: Ja, man, October.
STUBB: Is it really?
LANG: Ja. Definitely.
STUBB: Incredible. Oh I do love October.
LANG: Hey?

STUBB: I said October.

LANG: That's it, man.

STUBB: I'm very fond of October.

LANG: What's the difference, man.

STUBB: Lots of things.

LANG: They're all the same.

STUBB: Oh no, no, no, old boy. October's different.

(*Pause*)

LANG: You all right?

STUBB: Couldn't be better.

LANG: Hey! Is he all right? I asked you a question, hey.

HELLALOOYA: There is nothing the matter with him.

STUBB: You have those gusty winds . . .

LANG: Are you watching out for him, man?

STUBB: Chasing right down the mall . . .

HELLALOOYA: He has my undivided attention.

STUBB: And ripping away at those old flags . . .

LANG: I just hope so, hey? I hope you are giving him your undivided attention, hey.

STUBB: Brrrr! The best time of all. Autumn.

HELLALOOYA: Twenty four hours a day.

STUBB: Chestnuts frying.

LANG: He's been blarry good to you, man. That's all I can say.

STUBB: You could take a lovely walk through the park.

HELLALOOYA: I know what he has done for me.

STUBB: Oh, it's so beautiful.

LANG: Hey?

STUBB: I said it was so beautiful.

LANG: October?

STUBB: No. St. James.

LANG: Hey?

STUBB: St. James Park. London.

LANG: Oh.

STUBB: I love Autumn.

LANG: It's spring, man.

STUBB: It's the best time of all actually, everything turning to gold . . .

LANG: It's spring, man.

HELLALOOYA: He's referring to the northern hemisphere.

LANG: What? Hey?

HELLALOOYA: It is Autumn in London, England.

LANG: Is that so, hey? Well I don't need you to tell me.

STUBB: Do you have to shout? (*Pause*) Every time you walk into my house you start shouting at him and, if you don't mind me saying so, it's getting a bit of a bloody bore.

(*Pause*)

LANG: Well, if that's how you feel about it, hey, I'll blarry well go. I don't have to stand here listening to him, man.

STUBB: I'm sorry, Evvie. I didn't mean to shout.

LANG: Ja, well, hey?

(*Pause*)

STUBB: I do apologize.

LANG: Ja. Well, man, what do you think it's like for me, hey? Driving all this way out here to see you and everything and you just sit there staring up in the sky. What do you think it's like for me, hey? Driving out here like a blarry grocery boy or something.

STUBB: You don't have to.

LANG: What?

STUBB: Drive out.

LANG: Is that so, hey? And who would if I didn't, hey?

STUBB: One of the chaps.

LANG: Which one? (*Pause*) No, come on, hey, you tell me which one of the blokes is going to drive out with your blarry provisions if it wasn't me, hey? (*Pause*) Come on.

STUBB: Johnson.

LANG: Johnson, hey?

(*Pause*)

STUBB: Yes. Why not? (*Pause*) Well if he's too busy. Young Whittaker.

LANG: Whittaker, hey?

(*Pause*)

STUBB: Well, Boyo, or one of the fellows. One of the fellows would come. (*Pause*) Wouldn't they? (*Pause*) Wouldn't they, Evvie?

LANG: Of course they would, man. Of course they would. What the hell makes you think they wouldn't, man? Of course they'd come out, man, but well you see how it is, man, it's the start of the season, hey? That's what I mean, it's the start of the season, is what I mean and all the blokes are busy, man. You know how it is in Spring, hey? With all the tourists coming in, man. They're all helluva busy, hey. Me too, I'm busy myself, man.

STUBB: I haven't seen any of the other chaps. Do you know that?

LANG: As a matter of fact I've got a party to take out on Thursday. Americans.

STUBB: You're the only one, Evvie. The other chaps never come.

LANG: Rich Americans, man. What do you think about that, hey? Isn't that a nice account?

STUBB: Why don't they come out?

LANG: Hey Stubb, man, guess what?

STUBB: I can't understand why they don't come out.

LANG: You'll never guess what they blarry did.

STUBB: Do you have to shout?

LANG: You'll never, never guess what those Americans did, man.

STUBB: Which Americans?

LANG: Hell, man, of course you don't know about it, hey? You haven't heard the news.

STUBB: What news?

LANG: You'll never blarry guess, man.

STUBB: What? (*Pause*) Come on, what?

LANG: They did it.

STUBB: Who did what?

LANG: You see. I knew you'd never guess.

STUBB: Oh, come on.

LANG: Are you ready, hey? (*Pause*) They walked on the moon. (*Pause*) Did you hear me, hey? They walked on the moon.

STUBB: Who?

LANG: Those Americans, man.

STUBB: Which Americans?

LANG: Those astronauts. Armstrong, Aldrin and what's his name.

STUBB: Who's that?

LANG: Collins, man.

STUBB: Never heard of him.

LANG: They're those blarry astronauts, man. They go off in rocket ships and walk on the moon.

STUBB: Twaddle.

LANG: Hey?

STUBB: Twaddle.

LANG: Twaddle?

STUBB: Yes. Twaddle and bloody hogwash.

(*Pause*)

LANG: It was all round the world on blarry radio, television, the newspapers and everything . . . Wait, just you wait right there, hey.

(*Lang exits through flyscreen door. Hellalooya looks up from his book. He stares at Stubb. Stubb turns slowly in his chair. Hellalooya looks down at his book. Stubb looks at Hellalooya. Lang returns at a run. He has a stack of newspapers*)

LANG: Twaddle, hey. Twaddle and blarry hogwash, hey? (*Lang presents the newspapers to Stubb*) Look at that, hey. Look at that photograph, hey. That's Armstrong inside that spacesuit, man, and that's the moon he's walking on. Now what's twaddle, hey?

(*Pause*)

STUBB: Do you know what he does?

LANG: What about those craters and things, man. Look at that, hey. Craters.

STUBB: Every night? Every single night without fail?

LANG: What about this one here, hey? There's both of them, man, Armstrong and Aldrin, man. Old Neil and old Buz, man, walking on the blarry moon, hey.

(*Pause*)

STUBB: Do you know what he does.

LANG: All right, man, what?

STUBB: He steals my underpants. Steals them off my body, sir. While I'm asleep.

LANG: Hey?

HELLALOOYA: I do not steal them.

STUBB: It's bloody humiliating waking up and finding yourself debagged every morning.

LANG: What's the matter with you, hey?

HELLALOOYA: What?

LANG: Why'd you steal his underpants, hey?

HELLALOOYA: What do you suggest I do? Leave him to sleep in wet ones all night?

LANG: Give him a dry pair, man.

HELLALOOYA: I give him dry ones in the morning, at midday and in the early evening.

LANG: Well give him another pair when he goes to sleep, stupid.

HELLALOOYA: I cannot do that, Mr. Lang, because he has only got two pairs.

LANG: So wash them as you change them, man.

HELLALOOYA: I do.

LANG: Then why should he sleep without any, hey?

HELLALOOYA: Because the pair I wash in the early evening do not dry by the time he goes to sleep.

LANG: Why?

HELLALOOYA: Because the sun sets. (*Pause*) That pair

does not dry until morning and the pair he puts on in the
evening are soaked through by the time he goes to bed but he
refuses to remove them.

LANG: All right, man, let him keep the blarry things on.

HELLALOOYA: Wet through?

LANG: Ja, if he likes, man. If he likes.

HELLALOOYA: If he likes? What about his skin? Acid
causes skin rash. Festering, open, scabby sores!

LANG: All right, man.

(*Pause*)

STUBB: Did the queen make a comment?

LANG: How come he's only got two pair, hey?

HELLALOOYA: The others have been washed to pieces.

STUBB: I'm sure she must have made an eloquent comment.

LANG: You mean washed full of holes, hey?

HELLALOOYA: Yes, full of holes.

LANG: Why don't you sew them up?

HELLALOOYA: There was nothing left to sew. I threw
them away.

STUBB: The president of the United States made a comment. The queen must have said something.

LANG: Stubb, man. I think he's right, hey. It's better than
getting festering, open, scabby sores all over, hey?

STUBB: Was there or was there not a Royal Comment
over this moon business?

LANG: A royal what?

HELLALOOYA: He wants to know if the queen had something to say.

LANG: How the hell should I know, man?

STUBB: Well you read the damn things, didn't you?

LANG: Not properly, man.

STUBB: Then what the devil did you get them for?

LANG: For you, man.

(*Silence. Stubb looks through the papers. Hellalooya reads
his book. Lang stands at the window looking out*)

STUBB: Evvie?

LANG: Ja?

STUBB: How are you?

LANG: Fine, man. Just fine, thanks.

STUBB: How are things? In Mwanza? With the fellows?

LANG: Fine, man. Just fine.

(*Pause*)

STUBB: Haven't seen Boyo, Johnson, Sharps.

LANG: Well they're all busy, man. I told you that. (*Pause*) It's just that everyone's busy now, hey.

STUBB: Yes.

(*Pause*)

LANG: That's all it is, man. They're all busy you see.

STUBB: Yes. Quite. Do they, well, do they ever ask after me?

LANG: Hell yes, of course they do, man.

STUBB: Do they?

LANG: All the time, man.

STUBB: Really?

LANG: Positive, man. That's all they talk about.

STUBB: What?

LANG: You.

STUBB: Me?

LANG: Ja, man, they talk about you all the time, hey.

STUBB: What do they say?

LANG: All sorts of things, man. They say all sorts of things.

STUBB: Such as? What sort of things?

LANG: Oh, you know, nice things.

STUBB: Do they really? (*Pause*) Do you still gather at Sarrel's?

LANG: That's it, man, we all get together at Sarrel's.

STUBB: Every night?

LANG: Right.

STUBB: Just as we used to?

LANG: Now you're saying it, old chum. Every night.

STUBB: And you talk about me?

LANG: That's it, hey.

STUBB: Did they ask you about my attack?

LANG: Ja, man. They ask me everything about you. How you looked and everything, and how you were feeling.

STUBB: I suppose you must be the center of attention.

LANG: Hey?

STUBB: Well, other than the doctor and Hellalooya, you're the only one who's seen me.

LANG: Ja, that's right, hey.

STUBB: So you must be the center of attention when it comes to the questions.

LANG: That's it, hey. I'm right smack in the middle of the attention.

STUBB: Evvie?

LANG: Ja?

STUBB: Do me a favor, old boy.

LANG: Just name it, man.

STUBB: Don't tell them.

(Pause)

LANG: What?

STUBB: That I wet my pants.

LANG: No, man, of course not. I'll never tell them that, man.

STUBB: That part of my brain's gone dead, you see. (Pause) You see what happens is I can't feel that sensation. You know that sensation when you want to go to the lav?

LANG: Ja.

STUBB: Well I get that sensation but the part of my brain which is supposed to register that has gone dead. So I wet my pants.

LANG: Ja.

STUBB: So. You still gather at Sarrel's?

LANG: Ja.

STUBB: And look out across the Vic?

LANG: Just sit there and look out across the lake is right, hey.

STUBB: And my name comes up?

LANG: All the time, man.

STUBB: Tell me what they say about me.

LANG: Well let's see now. Well for instance, for instance old Boyo.

STUBB: Boyo?

LANG: Old Boyo, yes.

STUBB: What?

LANG: Well he'll say something like, "Hey Evvie, old chummie?" And I'll say, "Ja?" and he'll say, "When's old Stubb coming in to see us?"

STUBB: Does he really say that?

LANG: True as God. Cross my heart and everything, man. He says it all right.

STUBB: He actually asks when I'm coming into Mwanza?

LANG: Just like that, hey. Just like I said. "Hey Evvie, old chummie, when's old Stubb coming in to see us?"

STUBB: What do you say?

LANG: Me?

STUBB: Yes. How do you reply to that?

LANG: Well, you see . . . I say . . . Aha!

STUBB: Aha?

LANG: Ja. Aha.

(*Pause*)

STUBB: And then?

LANG: And then I point.

STUBB: Point?

LANG: Ja. Like this. Way off up the road.

STUBB: Which one?

LANG: There's only one road into Mwanza.

STUBB: I mean which way do you point. Up the road this way or . . .

LANG: This way, man. To the west, man. I point west and you know what I say?

STUBB: What?

LANG: I say, "Just you watch, hey chummies. Just you watch because one day you're going to see him, hey."

STUBB: Do you, really?

LANG: "One day, hey!" I say, "One day you're going to see that old bastard, hey! You're going to see him coming with a blarry rifle in his hand . . ."

STUBB: Do you say with a rifle?

LANG: Damn blarry right I do, man. "You're going to see him coming with a blarry rifle in his hand, old Hellalooya walking just behind him, hey, and he'll come right over that blarry hill there," I say, "right over that hill, straight on down the road, then right through this door here, my chummies, right through this door and he's going to hand his rifle back to Hellalooya and you know what he's going to do then, my chummies? He's going to bang that blarry old fist of his right down on your bar here," I say to Sarrel, "bang his blarry old fist right down on your blarry bar here, hey, and order blarry drinks all round for one and all." That's what I tell them.

(*Pause*)

STUBB: Drinks all round for one and all. What do they do when you say that?

LANG: They look off to the west, right into the sunset where I am pointing.

STUBB: Up the road.

LANG: Off up the road, ja.

STUBB: Can you imagine their faces if I did?

LANG: Hell, man, imagine that, hey?

STUBB: If I came walking in one evening, right smack out of the bloody sunset.

LANG: Just see it, man. Here you come over the hill.

STUBB: Ha. Smack out of the bloody sunset, a bloody rifle in my hand. Hellalooya at my bloody shoulder. Can you picture it?

LANG: Christ!

STUBB: Tramping right on in over that bloody hill, right

down the road, in through that bloody flyscreen door of his, hand my rifle back to Hellalooya, bang my fist down on that bloody bar and . . .

HELLALOOYA: Wet your trousers.

(*Pause*)

LANG: Why the hell did you say . . .

HELLALOOYA: Because he is not supposed to be excited.

LANG: It was just a little fun thing . . .

HELLALOOYA: The heart responds to mental stimulation.

LANG: Well for hell's sake, man . . .

HELLALOOYA: The doctor gave me instructions, Mr. Lang.

LANG: Don't give me any of your blarry lip, man . . .

HELLALOOYA: Go on shouting, Mr. Lang, and be responsible for an attack.

(*Silence*)

LANG: What? (*Pause*) What you staring at all the time, hey?

(*Pause*)

HELLALOOYA: Vultures.

LANG: What vultures?

HELLALOOYA: Up there. They have been up there since early this morning.

LANG: Oh, ja, I see them now. So that's what you've been staring at, hey? That's what you were staring at when I came in, hey?

STUBB: Yes.

LANG: Hell, man, they're pretty high.

STUBB: Not as high as they were yesterday.

HELLALOOYA: Yesterday? Were they here yesterday?

STUBB: Yes. And the day before.

(*Pause*)

HELLALOOYA: You did not tell me.

STUBB: No.

(*Pause*)

LANG: Something's out there. Dying. As a matter of fact, if you look at the angle, hey, whatever it is is pretty nearby, man.

Just look at that angle, hey, you can see for yourself that whatever it is is pretty nearby, hey? Hey? (*Pause*) Ja, man, something's come to die all right. (*Pause*) P'raps it's an old stray, hey?
An old stray or something hey, Stubb?

STUBB: Yes. (*Pause*) We found an old stray one day.

LANG: Is that so?

STUBB: Yes. Do you remember that?

HELLALOOYA: I remember.

LANG: What was it, hey?

STUBB: A wildebeest.* An old cow wildebeest. She had
a worm in her brain.

LANG: She had a what?

STUBB: One of those worms in her brain.

LANG: Which worms?

STUBB: You know them?

LANG: No.

STUBB: What are they called? Hellalooya? What are
those little grubs called? That hatch out in an animal's brain?

HELLALOOYA: I don't know.

STUBB: Well they're little egg things, or something, that
hatch out in an animal's brain.

LANG: How?

STUBB: They come from a wasp or something, the animals gets stung and this sting thing carries the egg through
the bloodstream to the brain, one of the little capillaries in the
brain. The egg hatches out into a little grub and off it goes eating
its way through the brain. Cell by cell. Thought by thought.
Imagine having something nibbling away at your thoughts,
your thinking, until all your conscious ends up in the stomach
of a slimey little yellow grub.

LANG: I didn't know about them.

STUBB: Neither did I at first.

(*Pause*)

LANG: What do they look like? (*Pause*) Stubb?

STUBB: Yes?

* Pronounced vildabees (Vilda as in Hilda. Bees as in peace.

LANG: What do they look like?

STUBB: What?

LANG: Those worm things, man?

STUBB: Oh. I don't know.

LANG: You said they were sort of yellow, man.

STUBB: Perhaps they are. I don't know for sure. I've never actually seen one.

LANG: Then how do you know about them if you've never seen one, hey?

STUBB: Oh, I know about them, all right. I mean everyone who knows the country and the animals and things knows about them, old boy.

LANG: Well I don't know about them, man.

STUBB: You will. You'll learn to recognize them.

LANG: What the hell do you think I'm going to go round looking for worms, man?

STUBB: You'll learn to recognize their effects. What I mean is you'll be able to tell whether an animal's got one or not.

LANG: How?

STUBB: Well they stray for a start and then they sort of cease to act, or react.

LANG: Hey?

STUBB: Well they don't act properly. This old cow wildebeest, for instance, I mean you could tell she was senseless. You could tell.

LANG: How, man?

STUBB: She didn't do anything. I mean there she was. A wild wildebeest, wild, absolutely wild. I mean she didn't react properly. We came right up and she didn't run. She just lay there, in the grass. Quite still. I went right up to her. I did. Ask him. He was there. I did. Went right up to her. Very slowly. She didn't move. And then, I got from about here to there and I put my hand out, like this, went up a bit closer, stretched out like this and then . . . Do you know what I did?

LANG: What?

STUBB: I chucked her, sir. I actually chucked her.

LANG: Chucked her? How?

STUBB: You know. Chuck, chuck, chuck, chuck chuck!
Like that. Under the chin.

LANG: What? A wild blarry wildebeest?

STUBB: Precisely.

LANG: Just chucked it, hey? Like a dog or a cat, man?

STUBB: Precisely, like a dog or a cat.

LANG: Christ, hey? What the hell did she do then?

STUBB: Nothing.

LANG: No, what I mean, man, is did she give a sign?

STUBB: A sign? What sort of sign?

LANG: You know like a dog gives a sign when it's happy.
You know. A dog wags its tail to show it's happy, man.

STUBB: Yes?

LANG: Well did she give a sign when you chucked her,
hey? Did she wag something or do something to show she was
happy?

STUBB: No. No, she couldn't, Evvie. How could she give
a sign when she didn't have any brain left to know anything.

LANG: You mean she didn't even know you were there,
hey?

STUBB: That's what I'm trying to tell you. She didn't
know whether *I* was there, *she* was there or *anything*. She
didn't know anything.

(*Pause*)

LANG: So there was no way of telling, hey?

STUBB: Telling what?

LANG: That she was happy, or anything, that you were
chucking her?

STUBB: No. There was no way of telling.

(*Pause*)

LANG: So? What did you do?

STUBB: I went on chucking her. There was nothing else
I could do, was there?

LANG: No. But in the end? What did you do in the end?

STUBB: The end?

LANG: Ja, man. Did you just go away and leave her to die?

STUBB: No.

(*Pause*)

LANG: Well, what?

STUBB: Well I just went on chucking her.

(*Stubb winds the gramophone*)

LANG: And then? Did you chuck her all night, man?

STUBB: No. He came up behind my back. With my rifle.

LANG: Ja? Well, what happened, man?

STUBB: He blew her head to pieces.

(*Stubb places the needle on the record. "I Do Like To Be Beside The Seaside" blares out*)

LANG: What the hell did you do that for?

HELLALOOYA: What? What did I do what for?

LANG: Blow his wildebeest's head off?

HELLALOOYA: Because we had nothing to eat.

(*Hellalooya returns to his book. Lang stares out the window. Stubb taps in time to the music*)

STUBB: I don't want to bloody die out here.

LANG: Hey?

STUBB: I said I don't want to bloody well die out here.

LANG: You're not going to die, man.

STUBB: The whole bloody continent's gone to pot. Look there. Look at that desolation. (*Stubb rises, moves to the window*) Just look at it.

(*The record plays out. Lang stops the gramophone. Silence*)

STUBB: I've got a good mind to take my savings and go back to London.

LANG: Hey?

STUBB: Yes. Go back.

LANG: To London?

STUBB: Yes.

LANG: It's expensive, man.

STUBB: I'll use my savings. Buy a ticket, get a little flat when I get there.

LANG: What I'm saying is is that it costs lots of money to live over there, man.

STUBB: I could get a comfortable little flat right on the King's Road for a few pounds a week.

LANG: It's just what I hear from tourists and things.

STUBB: I could take my savings and live quite comfortably.

LANG: I had an Englishman and his wife a few weeks ago. He was only here for a few days. He said he used to stay longer before. He said he couldn't afford to anymore because of the cost of living and things in England. (*Pause*) He said that things were expensive in London, man, and now he couldn't afford long holidays anymore.

STUBB: I could get a lovely little place right on the King's Road.

LANG: Things would have changed you see, man. (*Pause*) You see that, hey?

STUBB: Don't talk twaddle.

LANG: Well it's just that things change over a time, hey. I mean it's been what, hey, since you were there? Forty years, hey?

STUBB: Forty-two.

LANG: Well things change you see, man.

STUBB: Nonsense. They couldn't have changed that much. London's traditional. Granted it got a little smashed up in the blitz, but it's all been repaired. I've seen lots of photographs. It's all been built up again. Buckingham Palace, Tower Bridge, Westminster, Waterloo, Covent Garden, Soho, it's all still there. Whipsnade, Hyde Park Corner. The Mall . . . it's all there, sir. Nothing's changed. You can't change bloody tradition, man. Just the same as you can't change those bloody newspapers. I can't find her comment anywhere. (*Pause*) Nothing. Absolutely nothing. I haven't seen a damn thing for years. That wildebeest was the last. Do you know that? That wildebeest was the last thing I saw by way of fauna. I haven't seen an elephant, or a buff, or any of the big five. Haven't seen a herd in years. I haven't seen a herd of zebra . . . I haven't seen a herd of bloody grasshoppers let alone anything else. What's happened to this bloody country?

LANG: The herds are south.

STUBB: What?

LANG: I said the herds are south. (*Pause*) Further south. You won't see any up around here this time of year. You should know that, man.

STUBB: I know that, but what I'm saying is I haven't seen any at any time of year in the last two years. Only that old wildebeest. (*Pause*) I've got a good mind to take my bloody savings, every last penny of them and go back to Britain. (*Pause*) What do you think about that?

(*Hellalooya rises, moves to newspapers, takes them. Reads. Stubb stands with his back to the window and audience*)

HELLALOOYA: Is this the surface of the moon?

LANG: Ja.

HELLALOOYA: And these are men?

LANG: Ja.

HELLALOOYA: It is unbelievable. (*Pause*) This is fantastic. That men have done this.

LANG: White men. Don't forget.

(*Hellalooya looks at Stubb. Lang looks at Stubb. Silence. Hellalooya leads Stubb out through house interior door. Lang winds the gramophone. He puts the needle on the record, exits house exterior door. The record player runs out. Lang enters, lifts the needle. Stubb enters changed into fresh trousers*)

STUBB: Shh! Got a cigarette?

LANG: What's the matter? Why you whispering?

STUBB: Shh! I'm not supposed to.

LANG: All right so you're not supposed to, so why the hell should you whisper, man?

STUBB: Come on, quickly.

(*Lang and Stubb light up*)

LANG: Hell, man, who's whose blarry boss around here, hey? (*Pause*) You act as though he's the boss in your own blarry house, man.

STUBB: He's a good fellow, Evvie.

LANG: You've been blarry good to him, man. (*Pause*) I don't see why the hell you should blarry worry your head whispering over him, hey. (*Pause*) It's your blarry house. Your blarry heart attack. If you want to smoke, man, smoke.

STUBB: It's more than that, Evvie.

LANG: Come on, man, he's your tracker, you keep him and everything, man.

STUBB: You don't understand.

LANG: I do.

STUBB: You do not.

(*Pause*)

LANG: Ag! Let's not argue, man.

STUBB: He doesn't draw a salary. You know that, don't you?

LANG: So what's that got to do with it, man?

STUBB: Everything. There's no need for him to stay on.

LANG: No? What about that thing you told me about?

STUBB: What thing?

LANG: That thing you told me about last time, hey?

STUBB: What?

LANG: That last will and testament thing, hey?

STUBB: Is that what you think?

LANG: That's what I know, man.

STUBB: Is that what you think of him?

LANG: Come on, man. What else?

STUBB: And when he ran those thirty bloody odd miles into Mwanza when I conked . . .

LANG: That was before you wrote the blarry thing, hey?

STUBB: You're annoying me, Evvie.

LANG: And you, man, whispering and everything, man, you've given him plenty, man, all this blarry geography, history, sums, mathematics, science, every damn thing you taught him. The blokes even talk about that, hey, they reckon he's about the smartest bastard in the whole blarry area and you taught it him, man, you don't owe him a blarry thing I can tell you.

STUBB: That aside, I'm talking about friendship, Evvie.

LANG: What?

STUBB: Please. Don't shout.

(*Pause*)

LANG: Friendship? Hey?

STUBB: Yes. If you really put your mind to it and when it comes down to brass tacks, he's the only true friend I have.

LANG: Now I've heard everything, hey.

STUBB: I don't need your South African prejudice.

LANG: Hey?

STUBB: As far as I'm concerned a friend is a friend, and I don't care what color his skin is.

LANG: Is that so hey, and as far as I'm concerned, man, I think you've got friends you don't even blarry know about, man. I think you should think about other friends when you're so blarry busy thinking about brass tacks, hey.

STUBB: I do.

LANG: I think you should think about a thirty mile drive every time you think about brass tacks, hey?

STUBB. I'm grateful. I know what a trek it is.

LANG: And the petrol when it comes to brass tacks, hey.

STUBB: I agreed to pay the petrol.

LANG: That's just what I mean about the brass tacks, hey. You don't know anything about brass tacks, man, because when it comes down to brass tacks, hey, you should just think about everything and I don't mean just changing and washing your blarry underpants, either, hey, I mean the payments and things on petrol and provisions, hey.

STUBB: Johnson's got strict instructions to deduct every penny from my savings and you bloody well know it, so ask him for the money, don't ask me.

LANG: What savings, man?

STUBB: My savings, sir.

LANG: That's what I mean, hey. What savings?

STUBB: What the hell do you mean?

LANG: I mean everything. I mean your stroke. I mean the doctor and the helicopter and everything. Johnson had to pay that for a start.

STUBB: I didn't expect it for bloody nothing, man.

LANG: All right, hey, and what about the savings?

STUBB: What do you mean what about the savings? They're there, man.

LANG: Oh. How much do you think that stroke thing cost you, hey?

STUBB: I don't know. I never saw the bill. It couldn't have cost that much.

LANG: No come on, take a guess.

STUBB: Don't shout!

LANG: Just how much do you think it cost to fly that blarry doctor to you, man?

STUBB: Oh. I'd say, at a rough guess, about fifty pounds.

LANG: How much?

STUBB: Fifty, perhaps a little more.

LANG: Stubb, man.

STUBB: Petrol and oil, about seventy-five.

LANG: Hey, Stubb, man.

STUBB: It's not that long a flight. I'd say . . . At the outside . . .

LANG: Stubb.

STUBB: A hundred at the outside.

LANG: Stubb.

STUBB: Petrol for the flight . . .

LANG: Stubb.

STUBB: A hundred at the outside.

LANG: Stubb. (*Pause*) Just shurrup for one second, hey. Just shurrup! (*Pause*) The pilot, the petrol, the cost of hiring the helicopter, the medicine, doctor's fee, everything. How much? (*Pause*) Eight hundred pounds! With the extras you might as well call it a thousand, hey.

STUBB: Rubbish.

LANG: Blarry fact. Not rubbish.

(*Silence. Stubb sits*)

STUBB: You're lying.

LANG: I am not blarry lying to you, for Christ sake. Look man, Stubb, just open your eyes and think about the world out there today, man. There is ous * walking 'round on the blarry moon and Queen Victoria is dead.

STUBB: I know she's dead.

LANG: Do you?

(*Silence*)

STUBB: Evvie? (*Pause*) A thousand? That's almost half my savings.

LANG: That was the *rest* of your savings, man. You've been paying for your food and stuff for those years before that, man. How long did you think a couple of thousand was going to last, hey?

(*Hellalooya enters*)

HELLALOOYA: The doctor told me specifically not to let him smoke. You know that he is not supposed to smoke.

LANG: Well, he just wanted a little smoke, man, that's all.

HELLALOOYA: It makes his heart race.

LANG: Ag, man, come on.

HELLALOOYA: Smoke congests the lungs, there is a shortage of oxygen, the heart has to pump more blood through.

LANG: All right, hey. All right.

(*Pause*)

---

* ous: A South Africanism. Pronounced O's as if saying you have read off a series of OOOOOOO's.

HELLALOOYA: Why were you shouting before? (*Pause*)
I was told to keep him quiet and calm.

LANG: All right, man. All right.

HELLALOOYA: What is the matter?

LANG: Nothing's the matter. He's all right.

(*Pause*)

HELLALOOYA: What is the matter?

(*Pause*)

LANG: Nothing.

HELLALOOYA: I am talking to *him*.

LANG: Don't get stroppy with me, hey. (*Pause*)
Nothing's the matter that you can do anything about. It's
nothing but his own private business.

HELLALOOYA: What business?

LANG: I told you. His own private business.

HELLALOOYA: I know about all his business. He put it all
into my hands when he had the attack.

LANG: Is that so, smarty pants, then why the hell didn't
you tell him he was bankrupt?

(*Pause. Stubb rises*)

STUBB: *I am not bloody bankrupt!*

LANG: Then how come me, Johnson, Boyo, Whittaker,
Sharps and old Sarrel have to put our hands into our pockets
every month and come up with a little collection to pay for
your blarry provisions, hey? Bankrupt, old chummie, finished
and blarry klaar. Bankrupt. (*Pause. Stubb sits*) Now you think
about the brass tacks, hey. You got blarry friends. Don't worry
on that score, hey. Well there it is, hey. You had to know
sometime, man. (*Pause*) He had to know sometime, hey. You
too, hey. If you're supposed to be in charge of everything there's
nothing wrong with you knowing the facts, hey? (*Pause*) Hey,
Stubb? Hey, Stubb, man. Come on, hey, thing's aren't so bad,
man. You've still got this, man. You can still sell this place,
hey. I know a couple of blokes who'd like to buy it, man.
That's why things aren't so bad, man; you could always sell
this place, pay off your debts. And if you want to know what

we think, me and the other blokes? We think you should do
that. That's what I think you should do, hey, Stubb. Sell this
blarry place while you can and pay off your debts. Hey, Stubb,
that's what I think you should do. Stubb? Hey? You all right?
Stubb!

STUBB: I wish you wouldn't bloody well shout!

LANG: Well, hell man, I thought you'd gone deaf or
something. You all right?

STUBB: Yes. Thank you.

LANG: Well you don't look all right. (*Pause*) How does
he look to you? Hey?

HELLALOOYA: No good.

LANG: What the hell do you mean no good?

HELLALOOYA: I mean in a state of shock, damn it. You
cannot tell a man in his condition that he is bankrupt and
then expect him to look the proverbial picture of health.

LANG: Now you blarry listen . . .

STUBB: Shut up! (*Silence*) If you boys have finished,
Evvie, I think you'd better go.

(*Pause*)

LANG: Well if you feel like that I, hey, I suppose I just
better. If you feel like that about it.

STUBB: Nothing personal. I think you'd better go. That's
all. Nothing personal.

LANG: All right, hey. (*Pause*) If that's how you feel I'll
go. Right now, man.

STUBB: I'm very grateful to you. For telling me. (*Pause*)
I'm glad you told me.

LANG: Well, you see man, I knew you'd like to know.

STUBB: Yes.

LANG: If I was old Stubb, I said to myself, I'd like to
know what's going on. That's what I said to myself.

STUBB: I'm truly grateful.

LANG: It wasn't easy, hey. It wasn't nice for me, you
know that, hey? It was a sort of a duty to be done, man. You
understand, hey?

STUBB: Quite.

LANG: It wasn't easy, man.

STUBB: I'm very grateful. (*Pause*) Truly grateful.

(*Pause*)

LANG: It was nothing, hey. (*Pause*) You don't have to thank me, man. (*Pause*) We're friends, hey?

STUBB: Yes. We're friends.

(*Pause*)

LANG: Ja.

(*Pause*)

STUBB: Goodbye.

(*Pause*)

LANG: Ja. So long, hey. Well. Goodbye, hey.

(*Pause*)

STUBB: Evvie.

LANG: Ja? Yes? What?

(*Pause*)

STUBB: Thank the fellows for me. For the stuff, and everything.

LANG: That's nothing, hey. (*Pause*) That's blarry nothing, man. You don't have to thank us, hey. It's a blarry pleasure. That's all it is, hey. A blarry pleasure, and there's some more where that came from I can tell you. There's a whole lot more where that came from. You should just get up and take a look and see what they've stacked up in that blarry shed, hey. You should just see. Well I'll tell you there's a whole lot more where that came from, and as long as we are in Mwanza, as long as old Sarrel, Whittaker, Boyo, Johnson, Sharps and me are in blarry Mwanza and we've got it to spare you've got blarry nothing to worry about, hey.

(*Pause*)

STUBB: Thank them profusely. And thank you, Evvie. Thank you. You're a wonderful friend. (*Pause*) You've been a wonderful friend to me.

LANG: Hey. Come on man, Stubb. It's all right, hey. (*Pause*) Well, so long, hey? So long. (*Pause*) Hell, man, you know what? Hell, have I got a idea, hey. You know what I am going to do next time? Guess what I'm going to do, I'm going to bring you some more underpants, man. What the hell do you think about that?

(*Pause*)

STUBB: I'm very grateful.

LANG: You bet, hey. You bet what I'm going to do, hey. I'm going to tell all the ous, man, I'm going to tell the ous in Sarrel's, man. You know what I'll do, hey? I'll bang my blarry fist down on the bar and say, "Listen here," I'll say. Bang my fist down and say, "Listen here you blokes, we've got to get old Stubb some blarry underpants." I'll say. You'll see, man. Next time I come you'll have more blarry underpants than you'll know what to do with, and he won't have to pinch them off you in the night, hey. And what the hell do you think about that?

STUBB: Wonderful, thank you.

LANG: I thought you'd like that, man. I thought so.

(*Pause*)

STUBB: Goodbye.

LANG: Ja. Well. Goodbye, hey. See you in a few months, hey? Hey, Stubb?

(*Pause*)

HELLALOOYA: Goodbye.

LANG: Watch him, hey.

(*Lang exits exterior door. Truck doors slam, engine starts, truck sound driving away, etc. Silence. Hellalooya moves to the window, looks up. Looks out*)

STUBB: What do you think it is?

HELLALOOYA: I can't see anything.

(*Pause*)

STUBB: Well that was a bit of a shocker, wasn't it? What? A bit of a shocker.

HELLALOOYA: I had my suspicions.

STUBB: Suspicions?

HELLALOOYA: In the broadest sense.

STUBB: It was the helicopter and the doctor.

HELLALOOYA: Don't think about it.

STUBB: I had no idea . . .

HELLALOOYA: Don't think about it. Think about other things. Pleasant things.

STUBB: I can't help thinking about it.

HELLALOOYA: You'll make yourself ill.

(*Pause*)

STUBB: What do you think I should do? Hellalooya?

HELLALOOYA: In regards to?

STUBB: Those fellows. In Mwanza. Them paying for everything? What? I mean, well, they've been feeding us. Keeping us. That's charity, sir, you understand that, don't you? It's charity. Do you think I should do what he suggested?

HELLALOOYA: About selling the house?

STUBB: Yes. (*Pause*) Would you be very hurt? What I mean is would you, well, would you mind? (*Pause*) I don't mean mind, so much, Hellalooya, as would you help me?

HELLALOOYA: How?

STUBB: Well, reach a decision. I mean I wouldn't sell out unless you agree.

HELLALOOYA: I know that.

STUBB: Quite. Quite. I mean you can appreciate my feeling about accepting charity, can't you? You'd know about that. It's inbred in me. You understand, don't you? You'd know exactly what I'm talking about. Hellalooya? (*Pause*) Well I mean after all, when all is said and done it is your house, really, isn't it, so I'd need your approval. We'd have to do it together, wouldn't we? You'd have to agree to it or I wouldn't do it. It looks as if I might have to. *We* might have to. Pay off those debts. I'd give you the rest. I'd give you every penny of the rest. You understand that? You do see my point, about charity, don't you, well what I'm saying, Hellalooya, is I'd rather be in debt to you than to those chaps. I'd rather tear up the will and take it back.

HELLALOOYA: What?

STUBB: The house. When I say take it back, I mean tear the will up so it doesn't apply anymore. I'd rather be indebted to you than them. I'd rather say, "Sorry Hellalooya old boy, I'm not leaving my house to you after all," than live on charity. Purely because I know the extent and the value of our friendship. You do understand what I'm trying to say.

HELLALOOYA: Yes. I understand.

(*Pause*)

STUBB: Well? What do you suggest? (*Pause*) Hellalooya?

HELLALOOYA: I don't think you should worry about it now.

STUBB: I can't help worrying about it.

HELLALOOYA: Anxiety affects the heart.

STUBB: I'm not talking about my heart, sir. I'm talking about that bloody bombshell. I don't relish being broke and dependent on charity. If we just talked it out, between us. If we could reach a sort of solution. I wouldn't worry half as much.

HELLALOOYA: I suggest we leave it for now and talk about it tomorrow. Sit back. Relax.

(*Stubb rises*)

STUBB: I can't. How can I sit back and relax? I want to get it solved. Now do you or don't you think we should sell out and square up?

HELLALOOYA: It's up to you.

STUBB: It's not. It's between us. That's what I'm driving at, it's between you and me.

HELLALOOYA: I am not prepared to discuss it now. I would much rather discuss it tomorrow.

STUBB: Well I'd rather discuss the bloody thing now and get it off my mind. (*Pause*) It's on my mind. I can't put it aside just like that. It's a thing of honor, man. (*Pause*) That's the only solution. Hellalooya. It's the only solution. We'll have to sell out. Sell out, square the debt, you take the difference and I'll, well, I'll think of something. (*Pause*) That's logical. Isn't it? Isn't it? Well is it or isn't it?

HELLALOOYA: If you think so.

STUBB: Stop being so bloody negative, man! If *I* think so. I'm bloody well asking you. Do you or don't you think that's a logical thought? (*Pause*) Come on, man, commit yourself to an answer. Yes or no? Don't tell me I've been wasting my bloody time. Don't tell me you can't discuss anything civilly after all these years! After all that bloody knowledge I've shoved between your ears. (*Pause*) Look here, I'm sorry. I wish you'd say something.

HELLALOOYA: You're working yourself up into a state.

STUBB: I'm trying to settle my mind, if you'd only bloody well help me.

HELLALOOYA: All right, then. I think it is a good idea. Sell out, square the debt. It's a logical solution.

(*Pause*)

STUBB: You don't really mean that. Do you? I can tell. You're only saying it to make me feel better.

HELLALOOYA: Please, sit down.

STUBB: I don't want to sit down. Admit it. You're only saying that to make me feel better. Admit it.

HELLALOOYA: You're working yourself up . . .

STUBB: You're bloody well working me up! Don't stand there with a house and twenty acres of fertile bloody African soil in the palm of your hand and tell me to sell it out to pay my debts and expect me to believe you relish the idea! (*Hellalooya takes up one of the newspapers*) I'm talking to you.

HELLALOOYA: You're talking to yourself and drawing your own conclusions.

STUBB: I'm trying to get an honest answer from you. (*Hellalooya reads the newspaper*) You're bloody annoying me, you know that, don't you? You know you're causing me serious mental anxiety.

(*Pause. Hellalooya looks to Stubb*)

HELLALOOYA: That is precisely what I'm trying to avoid.

STUBB: You don't really want me to sell, do you?

HELLALOOYA: No.

STUBB: Ha. I knew it. All you had to do was bloody well say so. (*Hellalooya reads*) Would you like to know what Evvie said? He said you were waiting for me to conk out so you could collect. Well it looks as though he was right, doesn't it? It looks as if I made a bit of bloody fool of myself in defending your integrity. Integrity. Ever heard the word? (*Pause*) I'd appreciate it if you'd permit me the courtesy of your attention. (*Hellalooya looks up at Stubb*) Are you? (*Pause*) I asked you a question. Are you?

HELLALOOYA: What?

STUBB: Waiting for me to conk out? Well? Answer me.

HELLALOOYA: No. I am not waiting for you to conk out.

STUBB: Do you want to know something? I don't bloody well believe you.

HELLALOOYA: I know.

(*Silence. Hellalooya reads. Stubb remains watching Hellalooya*)

STUBB: A lot of things are becoming plainly obvious. Do you know that? There's some writing on the wall. What the hell does it matter to you if I get sores or not? (*Hellalooya looks up*) I mean, come on, what bloody business is that of yours? What's going to kill me quicker, sores on the crotch or mental anxiety? I mean you know all the medical answers. You explained exactly how it works, how anxiety stimulates the heart, the heart races, pushes the blood through faster, how the rush of blood dislodges the fatty build up on the artery walls. Come on, you know it all so you bloody well tell me, what's going to conk me quicker?

HELLALOOYA: What?

STUBB: What? Waking up pantless and in a bloody fury. Or waking up dressed and mentally content, that's what. Well? You've been doing it to kill me, haven't you? (*Silence*) Not even a denial? (*Pause*) You want to kill me, but you don't want the responsibility. You want it to look as natural as all bloody hell, don't you? Don't you? (*Pause*) You're not even trying to help me. You're not even trying to pacify me. Why don't you try and pacify me? Calm me down. Why don't you try?

(*Silence. Hellalooya reads. Stubb takes the rifle. Hellalooya looks up*)

HELLALOOYA: What are you doing with that?

STUBB: I need it.

HELLALOOYA: What for?

STUBB: Because I'm going out.

HELLALOOYA: Where?

STUBB: For a walk. (*Pause*) Or is that off limits?

HELLALOOYA: The doctor said it was all right provided you did not overdo it.

STUBB: How considerate of you to tell me. Do you want to know where I'm going? (*Pause*) I'm going to Mwanza. (*Pause*) I'm going on one of my proverbial tramps, and I'm going to get there at about sunset which gives me about five and a half hours, and I'm going to walk in over that bloody hill, right down the main road, in through Sarrel's flyscreen bloody door, bang my fist down on his bar and do you know what I'm going to do? I am *not* going to wet my pants! I'm going to bang my fist down on his bloody bar and tell them all, all of them that you, sir, are a bloody black bastard!

(*Silence*)

HELLALOOYA: You'll kill yourself.

STUBB: Oh no I won't. Not by a bloody long shot. You'd like that, but I won't. I'll get there all right and the first thing I'm going to do is get that will from Johnson's safe, tear the bloody thing to shreds, then I'm going to put this property up for sale, collect, pay off and go back to England. That's precisely what I'm going to do. (*Pause*) Do you hear? Do you hear me?

HELLALOOYA: You had better sit down and rest now.

STUBB: Go to hell! (*Stubb moves to door. Hellalooya*

starts forward lowering the paper. Stubb points the rifle at Hellalooya, cocks it) Don't you try any physical hindrance stuff, old boy, don't try any of that! Don't try bloody coming after me, or you'll get one right between the bloody eyes.

(*Silence. Stubb exits exterior door. Hellalooya moves to the door. Looks out. Crosses to window as if following a moving figure. A long pause. Hellalooya sits in Stubb's chair. Hellalooya looks up, as Stubb did, but not as steeply. Hellalooya begins to lower his head and eyes as if watching something making a slow circular descent)*

The End

John Bowen

TREVOR

John Bowen

Born in 1924 in Calcutta, India, John Bowen was reared by "various relatives in various parts of England." He returned to India in 1940, served in the Indian Army during the war, and was demobilized in 1947. He obtained a place at Pembroke College, Oxford, where he studied modern history as an undergraduate; graduated and was awarded the Frere Exhibition in Indian Studies by the University; and from there went on to do postgraduate work at St. Anthony's College.

He was in the United States from the fall of 1952 to 1953, "partly teaching Freshman English at Ohio State University, partly hitch-hiking and partly on a scholarship to the Kenyon School of Letters at the University of Indiana." He returned to Oxford, promptly ran out of money, and took a job as assistant editor with a fortnightly magazine, *The Sketch*. To augment his income, he also worked at intervals in advertising, as an actor, and reviewed ballet for the British Broadcasting Corporation ("After a while I couldn't think of anything more to say").

Mr. Bowen has written six novels, of which four—*After the Rain, The Centre of the Green, The Birdcage* and *A World Elsewhere*—have been published in the United States.

His first play, *I Love You, Mrs. Patterson,* was produced at St. Martin's Theatre (London) in 1964. As the author recalls the event, "It was sort of Ibsenish, about marriage. It ran for five weeks—in a heat wave."

His second work for the stage, *After the Rain,* was decisively more impressive. A "very free adaptation" of his novel of the same title, the drama originally was presented in 1966 at the Hampstead Theatre Club, then transferred to the Duchess Theatre in the West End. It was highly praised by the press and the *Daily Express* cited it as "the most fascinating new play in London."

After the Rain opened on Broadway (with Alec McCowen repeating his London role) in the fall of 1967 and although it ran for only sixty-four performances, the New York first-night jurors hailed both author and play for "providing

theatregoers with the first solid food for thought of the season."
The drama garnered additional honors when Otis L. Guernsey,
Jr., editor of the theatre yearbook, selected it as one of the
"ten best plays of the New York theatre season, 1967–1968."
A French translation of *After the Rain* has been performed at
the Théâtre de l'Athénée, Paris, and a German one in the
Kammerspiele, Frankfurt.

Trevor and its companion piece, *The Coffee Lace,* com-
prise John Bowen's double bill, *Little Boxes,* which initially
opened in London on February 26, 1968. Its success was immediate and again Mr. Bowen was acclaimed by the critical
gentry. Harold Hobson wrote in the *London Sunday Times*
that, ". . . a major talent, disturbing, brooding and despite its
humour, essentially tragic, has come into the British theatre."
The critic for the British magazine, *Plays and Players,* described
Trevor as "a brilliant theatrical idea . . . a play that I found
extremely funny. In fact, Mr. Bowen seems to me to belong
with Peter Shaffer and Robert Bolt as one of the best dramatists
we've got writing within the inherited tradition of the well-
made play." Clive Barnes, covering the London presentation
for *The New York Times,* joined in the chorus of international
praise: "This is a remarkably funny and adroit work. In
Trevor, Bowen is still being provocative, but he has written a
farcical comedy that is as neat and as deft as you could wish."

The New York premiere of *Little Boxes* took place at
The New Theatre on December 3, 1969, and once again *Trevor*
(and its imported British star, Tony Tanner) was warmly
received by a majority of the critics. Mr. Barnes, at the helm
of the first-night press, confirmed his original impression by
declaring that *"Trevor* is a very funny and imaginative farce
. . . but beneath the farce Mr. Bowen has a deeper purpose . . .
illusion, its need and maintenance."

After completing *Little Boxes,* Mr. Bowen made a "pirat-
ical raid" into the texts of the various Medieval Mystery Plays,
selecting and adapting to create a work entitled *Fall and Redemption* which he himself directed at the London Academy

of Music and Dramatic Art and later at the Pitlochrie Festival Theatre. His latest play, *The Corsican Brothers,* was written specially for the new theatre at Greenwich (England) and is scheduled for a spring, 1970, opening.

Mr. Bowen also has written extensively for television and is a regular contributor to the *London Sunday Times,* the *Sunday Observer* and *The New York Times Book Review.*

When recently queried about plays of ideas, the author (who lives in the top flat of two attached houses, built in 1824, in South Kensington) observed, "Plays are concerned with action, ideas are expressed in action. You must bring people who have ideas and moral principles into conflict to have a play of ideas. But every *good* play *is* a play of ideas."

Characters:

JANE KEMPTON
SARAH LAWRENCE
TREVOR
MRS. LAWRENCE
MR. LAWRENCE
MRS. KEMPTON
MR. KEMPTON
MR. HUDSON

Scene:

The top floor flat (two rooms, kitchen and bathroom) shared by Jane and Sarah, two young upper-middle-class women in their late twenties, both earning a good salary.

The two lower floor rooms are divided by a passage that runs the full depth of the stage. There is a short winding staircase opening off the passage, that leads to a small kitchen which is at a higher level than the other rooms. A door at the far end of the passage opens to a well-furnished bathroom. Next to it, but opening to the right off the passage, is the door to the downstairs world.

The flat has been fairly recently decorated—the furniture, pictures and objects have been collected over the last three years, so that they express a unity of taste in a pleasant Sunday Color Magazine way. Books. Record player. Television. Indirect lighting. Central heating. Wall-to-wall carpets in downstairs rooms and hall. An intercom set in the wall of the hall by the door and an ordinary telephone on a hall table.

There is one rather odd aspect of the set which will not be immediately obvious, but will appear—what are normally a bedroom and living room have been hastily rearranged to look like two bed-sitters.

The time is the present. It is about 3:30 on a Saturday afternoon in February. Jane is lying on the studio couch in the room on the right, smoking a cigarette and read-

ing a book. A table is laid for tea: cups and saucers, knives, forks and spoons, milk jug, jam in a pottery dish, butter in a saucer, a Fullers cake.

The door to the outside is opened by a latchkey. Jane looks up and listens. Sarah brings Trevor into the hall. He is a young actor with traces of the North Country in his speech.

SARAH: Shall I take your coat?
TREVOR: What? . . . Yes . . . Thank you.
(*She hangs up his coat together with her own, which she removes without his help. While:*)
SARAH: Straight in. It's the door on the left.
(*Trevor goes into the room at the left. He looks around, admiring the room, and clearly a stranger to it. Having hung up the coats, Sarah follows, closing the door behind her*)
TREVOR: You've got a nice place here.
SARAH: I share it with another girl.
TREVOR: You've each got your own room?
SARAH: Yes, and we share the kitchen and bathroom.
TREVOR: Where is she?
SARAH: She's gone out.
(*Jane looks at her watch. Then she returns to reading*)
SARAH: Would you like a drink?
TREVOR: I'm not used to this.
SARAH: To what?
TREVOR: This . . . (*Gesture*) luxury.
SARAH: Oh, really!
TREVOR: And I'm not used to being taken home by girls, as a matter of fact.
SARAH: Who usually takes you home?
TREVOR: That's not what I meant. (*Pause*) Of course . . . my own place . . .

SARAH: Yes?

TREVOR: It's not much to take anyone back to.

SARAH: Why not?

TREVOR: I haven't got much money.

SARAH: Then why fritter it away, hanging around pubs?

TREVOR: You've got to do something.

SARAH: You could try work.

TREVOR: I told you; I'm an actor.

SARAH: Sorry. I forgot.

TREVOR: What do *you* do?

SARAH: I told you; I design fabrics.

TREVOR: That's right; you did. (*Pause*) Shall we . . . (*Indicates studio-couch*) I mean, do you want to sit down?

SARAH: (*Sits in a chair*) Thank you.

(*Trevor hovers, uncertain whether he is expected to share the chair with her*)

TREVOR: Shall I sit down with you?

SARAH: No.

(*Pause. Jane looks up, looks at her watch again, half gets up, decides against it, and returns to reading*)

TREVOR: You're a funny girl.

SARAH: Why?

TREVOR: I mean, you picked *me* up. Standing there in your plastic mac, rubbing yourself up against me.

SARAH: I was not rubbing—

TREVOR: Asking me to come home with you.

SARAH: For a drink.

TREVOR: I thought you wanted to make all the running. Well, I didn't mind. Only now it looks as if I've got to do it. I'm not very good at that, as a matter of fact, because I'm a bit shy. I've got no instinct for it. I never know when it's time to put my hand on your leg—I mean, what the right moment is. Every girl I've ever been with has had to—sort of let me know —you know, tactfully—they move tactfully. I always have to know it's all right before I can go on to the next step.

SARAH: (*Rises*) I'll get you that drink.

TREVOR: Don't bother. I'm not much good if I've had too much to drink, as a matter of fact.

SARAH: (*Goes to drinks cupboard*) There's vodka and tonic.

TREVOR: (*Sits in the chair she's left*) Thank you.

(*Jane looks at her watch again, gets up, opens her door cautiously, goes into the hall, and on up to the kitchen. From the cupboard, she takes a bowl and a packet of Scone Mix. She lights the oven. A buttered tin tray is already on the kitchen table. She starts to make scones. Meanwhile, Sarah has given Trevor his drink—he thanks her—and goes to sit on the studio-couch, leaving Trevor in the chair. Jane makes some slight noise in the kitchen. Trevor hears it*)

TREVOR: What was that?

SARAH: What?

TREVOR: I thought I heard something.

SARAH: It's an old house. It makes noises.

TREVOR: Oh.

SARAH: Built by Gianino Pisco in 1824. You'll find it in *The A to Z of Historic London* if you're interested. Under P.

TREVOR: Ah.

(*Pause*)

SARAH: } Do you—
TREVOR: } You aren't— (*Both stop*)

SARAH: I'm sorry.

TREVOR: *You* aren't having a drink.

SARAH: No. I had more than I wanted in the pub.

(*Pause. He puts down his drink. There is another noise from the kitchen. He looks up, but Sarah seems to have noticed nothing. He gets up, and goes towards her*)

SARAH: Don't *touch* me!

TREVOR: What?

SARAH: I don't want you to touch me.

TREVOR: I'm sorry.

SARAH: No, it's my fault. I'm sorry, Trevor. I'm very nervous.

TREVOR: My name's not Trevor.

SARAH: Never mind.

TREVOR: Why did you think I was called Trevor?

SARAH: It doesn't matter.

TREVOR: Did you go to that pub to meet someone called Trevor? Have you made a mistake?

SARAH: I did, and I haven't.

TREVOR: What?

SARAH: I did go to that pub to meet someone called Trevor, and I haven't made a mistake.

TREVOR: I don't understand you.

SARAH: (*Notices his slight accent*) You're from the north, aren't you? You're what they call a new wave actor.

TREVOR: Yes. There's a lot of us. That's why I'm not in work.

SARAH: Please sit down. Finish your drink. I'm sorry I snapped at you.

(*Trevor goes back to his chair. Jane puts the scones into the oven. Then she looks at her watch again, and comes back into the hall. While:*)

TREVOR: I wish I knew what you're talking about.

(*Jane hesitates, then enters the room stage left*)

JANE: Well?

SARAH: Trevor, this is Jane.

JANE: Have you told him?

SARAH: Not yet.

JANE: It's three forty-five. I've just put the scones in.

TREVOR: Er . . . (*He crosses his legs*)

JANE: There's only half an hour.

SARAH: How long do they take? The scones?

JANE: Don't worry about it. I'll see to it.

SARAH: Is there anything you want me to do?

JANE: No. I did it all while you were out.

(*Trevor crosses his legs the other way. They look at him, considering how to start. Jane begins*)

JANE: Trevor—

TREVOR: I'm sorry. I told your friend. My name's not Trevor.

JANE: Yes, it is.

TREVOR: She made a mistake.

SARAH: (*To Jane*) He was on his own. He's an out-of-work actor. He needs money. I'm sorry about the accent, but a lot of people have accents now, you know they do.

JANE: The accent doesn't matter. If they take against him, they'll be all the more pleased when I break it off.

TREVOR: Look . . . (*Recrosses his legs uncomfortably*)

JANE: Don't worry. We're just going to explain.

TREVOR: Then, if you wouldn't mind . . .

SARAH: Yes?

TREVOR: I mean, if it's going to take a bit of time . . .

JANE: (*Looks at watch*) It can't take much.

TREVOR: I had a lot of beer in that pub, and . . .

SARAH: It's at the end of the hall.

TREVOR: (*Gets up*) Thank you. (*He leaves the room and goes up the hall into the bathroom*)

JANE: You took your time.

SARAH: It wasn't easy.

JANE: All you had to do was go up to someone and . . .

SARAH: You can't just approach a man like that. I had to stand there for hours, rubbing myself up against him.

JANE: Rubbing yourself up!

SARAH: Metaphorically. Then when we got back, he thought . . .

JANE: I know what he thought.

SARAH: Well, he was bound to. I had to discourage him.

(*Pause*)

JANE: Love, I'm sorry. I am sorry, love. I was here . . . reading . . . wondering.

SARAH: I know. I could feel you wondering all the way

from the pub. Wonder and jealousy. They were very thick on the stairs when we came in.

JANE: Jealous! Of him?

SARAH: You'd be jealous of the *Manchester Guardian* if it was delivered every day.

JANE: I'll tell him. I'll just put it to him. He can only say, No.

SARAH: I wish we didn't have to.

JANE: We do have to.

SARAH: Couldn't we say Trevor had a business conference or something?

JANE: Script conference. My Trevor writes for television: do try to remember. *Your* Trevor's in ICI.

SARAH: Sorry. Couldn't we say he had a script conference and couldn't get here? Then I'd ring up from a phone box and pretend to be him. (*Jane gives her a look*) Well, they wouldn't hear my end of the conversation.

(*The WC is flushed in the bathroom. Trevor appears, and comes down the hall, while:*)

SARAH: We'll have to do that anyway if he refuses.

(*Trevor returns*)

TREVOR: Who uses Arpège? I took some. I like using other people's things. It's a kind of kleptomania. I thought I might brush my teeth with your toothbrush, but I don't really know you well enough, do I?

SARAH: I can smell the Arpège. It's very strong.

TREVOR: That's the trouble. When it belongs to somebody else, I always put too much on.

JANE: Trevor . . .

TREVOR: I told you . . .

JANE: That's the first thing. You've got to get used to answering to the name.

TREVOR: Why?

JANE: Just listen. You're not very well off, are you?

TREVOR: No.

JANE: And you're an actor. (*To Sarah*) That's a bonus,

Sarah, getting an actor. It's worth the extra time. (*To Trevor*) We want you to act.

TREVOR: What in?

JANE: Just for this afternoon. My parents are coming to tea. They live in Paignton, and I hardly ever see them, but once a year they make a family tour—a weekend in Maidenhead with my married sister, during which they visit me, then up to Buxton to my brother . . .

SARAH: He's a mining engineer. You might have met him.

TREVOR: I'm from Bolton.

SARAH: It's all the north, isn't it?

JANE: Then back home. They'll be here in (*Looks at her watch*) fifteen minutes. They must think you're my fiancé.

TREVOR: Where is your fiancé?

JANE: I haven't got a fiancé. But I'm twenty-seven. My parents think I should have one.

TREVOR: (*To Sarah*) But why did *you* . . .

SARAH: I picked you up because Jane's a friend of mine. She had to get things ready here. Finding you was the best way to help her.

TREVOR: (*To Jane*) But twenty-seven's nothing. People get engaged at any age.

JANE: That's what I tell my parents. But my mother is rather a bossy woman, Trevor. She doesn't want me to become a dried-up spinster, and she does want to see some positive evidence of my intention to avoid that. (*Pause*) But don't worry. I shall certainly break it off. It won't come to anything.

SARAH: We thought if you played up your accent a bit, and took milk first in tea, and dribbled your scones, Jane's mother might break it off herself.

TREVOR: But why couldn't you get one of your own friends to do it?

JANE: We'll pay you five pounds for the afternoon. Do you agree?

(*Pause*)

TREVOR: I see.

JANE: What do you see?

TREVOR: If this is a bed-sitter, where's the dressing table?

JANE: In the other room.

TREVOR: The bedroom?

(*Pause*)

JANE: Yes. (*To Sarah*) He's quick, isn't he? It must come from working in the theatre.

TREVOR: (*To Sarah*) And *your* mother?

SARAH: My mother's the President of the local Liberal Party, and she runs the Welfare Clinic, and she does part-time teaching of retarded children. She doesn't care if I get married or not, but she says she'd like me to be sexually fulfilled. Consequently *my* Trevor is a married man who works for Shell.

JANE: ICI.

SARAH: ICI. (*To Trevor*) But you don't have to bother about *my* Trevor.

TREVOR: What a pity!

SARAH: Do you need work that badly?

TREVOR: I didn't mean that. I meant . . . What a pity! I'm sorry.

JANE: We don't need your pity. Will you take the job? (*The doorbell rings. She looks at her watch.*) They're early. Quickly—Will you do it?

TREVOR: Yes.

JANE: (*Going*) Sarah, fill him in.

(*She goes to answer the door by the doorphone. Sarah hastily briefs Trevor*)

SARAH: You're Trevor Hudson. You live in Chelsea—quite near here—in Paultons Square—a flat. Christ, I can't remember the number. Never mind; they won't ask. You're a staff-writer for the BBC: that's why you never get your name in the *Radio Times*. You do research and linking bits for programs about animals and the Com-

JANE: (*Conversation not really heard*) Mother? . . . What? . . . I can't hear . . . Oh! . . . Yes . . . (*Thinks*) I'm sorry; the door buzzer isn't working. She'll

mon Market. You're writing a have to come
novel. It takes you ages because you down.
can never think of the right words.
You had some poems published
when you were at the university.

TREVOR: Which?

SARAH: Any you like.

TREVOR: Oxford, then. I did *Charley's Aunt* at Southport
two years ago.

(*Jane returns, appalled*)

JANE: It's *your* parents.

SARAH: What?

JANE: It's your parents. They wanted to surprise you.
I told them the buzzer wasn't working. You'll have to go
down and let them in.

SARAH: Jesus! (*Going quickly*) Fill him in. (*She runs
into the hall, and out through the door*)

JANE: Trevor works for ICI. He's married.

TREVOR: What about the scones? Shouldn't we take them
out of the oven?

JANE: (*Looks at her watch*) Oh God! God! Come on!

(*They go quickly upstairs to the kitchen to get the scones
out of the oven, while:*)

JANE: Trevor has two children. Twins. They were an
accident. He doesn't like them much.

TREVOR: What's his name?

JANE: Hudson.

TREVOR: But that's . . .

JANE: They're both called Hudson. Both Trevors. Hers
and mine.

TREVOR: Convenient.

JANE: It's the landlord's name.

TREVOR: Trevor?

JANE: Hudson. Trevor, do listen! Trevor's an economist.
He . . .

TREVOR: What's the landlord's first name?

JANE: How do *I* know? Landlords don't have first

names. Put the scones in that basket and cover them with a napkin. I'd better make some more.

TREVOR: He's an economist?

JANE: Very brilliant and young. He was married at eighteen. That's where the twins came from. It was a shotgun wedding in the chapel of Dulwich College. He and Sarah met at the National Gallery one lunch-time. He picked her up in front of a Study of Small Children Being Mobbed by Apes.

TREVOR: He did?

JANE: No. *I* did.

(*Door from outside opens. Sarah heard. Both react*)

SARAH: Go straight in.

(*Mr. and Mrs. Lawrence, both in their late fifties, enter. Sarah follows*)

SARAH: I'll take your coat, mother. It's the room on the left.

TREVOR: There they are.

JANE: You'd better take the scones down.

MRS. LAWRENCE: I thought you said Trevor was here.

SARAH: He is.

(*Mrs. Lawrence goes into Sarah's room*)

MRS. LAWRENCE: No, he isn't.

TREVOR: Hey!

JANE: Yes?

TREVOR: What do I do when *your* parents come?

JANE: I'll have to tell them Trevor had a script conference.

TREVOR: I could drop in for a drink later.

JANE: *You* could?

TREVOR: Trevor could.

MRS. LAWRENCE: He's not here, Sarah.

(*Sarah joins her in the room, leaving Mr. Lawrence to hang up his coat, take his scarf off, etc.*)

SARAH: Well, he should be. (*Calls from the door*) Trevor!

TREVOR: (*Calls*) I'm in the kitchen, making some scones.

(*He comes downstairs, carrying the scones in a basket, with a napkin over them. In the kitchen, Jane puts the kettle on and lays a tray for tea. Trevor stops to speak to Mr. Lawrence*)

TREVOR: How do you do?

MR. LAWRENCE: Very well, thank you.

TREVOR: Stock Market's recovering, I see.

MR. LAWRENCE: What?

TREVOR: Stocks and shares. They're very buoyant.

MR. LAWRENCE: Oh . . . Good.

TREVOR: You have to keep a sharp eye on the state of the market in my job. I'll take these in. (*He goes into Sarah's room with the scones.*)

(*Mr. Lawrence has begun to get the full aroma of the Arpège. He gazes after Trevor, and sniffs the air, surprised*)

TREVOR: Scones. Eat them while they're hot.

SARAH: Mother, this is Trevor.

TREVOR: How do you do? Your husband and I have just been discussing stocks and shares.

MRS. LAWRENCE: I'm so glad to meet you, Trevor. I've heard a lot about you. (*To Sarah*) Sarah dear, you're wearing a very heavy perfume. I didn't notice it when we came in.

TREVOR: No, it's me. I put too much on. (*Sudden thought*) Oh my Gawd, I forgot the kettle. (*He goes swiftly out again, passing Mr. Lawrence at the door of the room, and on up the stairs into the kitchen. Mr. and Mrs. Lawrence look after him, and then at each other*)

MRS. LAWRENCE: That's Trevor?

SARAH: I told you so, mother.

MRS. LAWRENCE: My dear, I hope you haven't made a mistake.

SARAH: Don't be ridiculous.

MR. LAWRENCE: What was that about stocks and shares?

SARAH: He takes an interest in them.

(*Trevor has reached the kitchen and sees the kettle already on*)

TREVOR: Oh, you've done it. What about cups and saucers?

JANE: There's the tray. How's it going?

TREVOR: Early to say. I'm concentrating on making a good impression. No cake?

JANE: There's a cake in the other room. You'd better cut it in half.

(*Trevor gathers up the tray*)

TREVOR: I'll come back when it whistles.

JANE: No. Let Sarah do it.

TREVOR: Oh, I don't — (*Realizes Jane wants reassurance*) Righty-ho. (*Ready to go downstairs*) I'd start making those extra scones if I were you.

(*Jane takes a packet of scone mix from the cupboard, and begins on the scones*)

MRS. LAWRENCE: Now we *are* here, we can take you and Trevor out for the evening. Your father's brought his Barclaycard.

SARAH: But Trevor's married. He has a family in Blackheath.

MRS. LAWRENCE: Then what's he doing here, baking scones?

SARAH: He comes round on Saturday afternoons sometimes.

MRS. LAWRENCE: Don't be silly, Sarah. If you only had the afternoon, you'd spend it in bed, not up to your elbows in dough.

MR. LAWRENCE: Steady on, Hetty.

SARAH: As a matter of fact, we . . .

MRS. LAWRENCE: Don't say you've been. That bed's not even rumpled.

MR. LAWRENCE: Hetty!

MRS. LAWRENCE: I've no time for prudery about sex, Harold. You ought to know that, if anyone does.

MR. LAWRENCE: I do, dear; I do.

(*Trevor comes in*)

MRS. LAWRENCE: Trevor, my husband and I thought you

and Sarah might like to come out with us this evening. There
was a Hungarian film in the Sunday papers.

TREVOR: (*Begins to set the table*) Hungarian?

SARAH: (*Helps*) I'll help you.

MRS. LAWRENCE: We hardly ever see Hungarian films in
Bury St. Edmunds. If one has to come to London, one oughtn't
to waste the trip. (*To Sarah*) I've already taken your father
round the Victoria and Albert Museum.

MR. LAWRENCE: I'll sit down for a bit if I may, and take
my shoes off.

MRS. LAWRENCE: We'll see the six o'clock show and have
dinner afterwards. Then we'll be able to catch the 10:45 home.
Harold, what did you do with the *Good Food Guide?* We'd
better find somewhere to eat between King's Cross and the
Curzon Cinema.

TREVOR: That'll be lovely.

SARAH: But Kathy's expecting you. (*Slight emphasis*) At
home.

TREVOR: Who? . . . Oh, Kathy. Yes, that's right; Kathy's
expecting me. I've got a wife and family. (*To Mr. Lawrence*)
Twins. But I don't like them very much. If it hadn't been for
them, I wouldn't be married. It's hard to forgive a thing like
that.

SARAH: You're not trying, are you?

TREVOR: I'd better get the cake. (*To Mrs. Lawrence*)
We're only having half a cake because Jane's expecting *her*
parents.

(*Bell rings. Jane hears it, and begins to come downstairs,
leaving the scones on the baking tray*)

TREVOR: That's them now. (*He meets Jane in the hall*)
Getting the cake.

JANE: I haven't had time to put the scones in.

(*He goes on into the room stage right. Jane answers the
door phone. Overlapping:*)

MRS. LAWRENCE: Jane?   JANE: Mother? . . . Do
That's the girl . . . ?   come up. Push the door when

SARAH: The girl I share   it buzzes.
with.

MR. LAWRENCE: (*Has his shoes off*) That's better. That's
much better.

(*Jane pushes the buzzer that lets people in downstairs.
Trevor fusses with cutting the cake in half and looking
for another plate to put his half on. He finds one under a
plant*)

MRS. LAWRENCE: How do you get on with her? You never
say.

SARAH: Oh, very well. We don't really see much of each
other. She has her friends, and I have mine. She's engaged, as
a matter of fact.

(*Jane has the door open and is looking down the stairs.
Kettle whistles in the kitchen*)

TREVOR: (*Shouts*) Sarah, can you go?

SARAH: I won't be a moment, mother. (*She goes into
the hall*)

(*Jane turns to her for a moment. Sarah takes Jane's hand
and squeezes it, then goes quickly up into the kitchen*)

MRS. LAWRENCE: There's something wrong with that
young man.

MR. LAWRENCE: Lots of men wear scent nowadays.

MRS. LAWRENCE: If one's going to be somebody's mistress,
it's not up to *him* to bake the scones. It's not the basis of a
satisfactory relationship. I think we'd better find out a little
more about him.

(*Jane has turned to look after Sarah. Consequently her
attention is off the door through which Mrs. Kempton,
a woman in her late fifties, now comes sailing*)

MRS. KEMPTON: Jane, dear!

JANE: Hullo, mother.

(*Mrs. Kempton folds Jane in her arms, as Trevor comes
out of the room stage right with half a cake on the plant-
plate. Mrs. Kempton drops Jane and advances to him*)

MRS. KEMPTON: And you're Trevor.

TREVOR: Yes.

JANE: No! (*Moves behind her mother to sign to Trevor*)

TREVOR: Eh?

(*Mrs. Kempton sniffs, and turns to Jane*)

MRS. KEMPTON: Jane, you're wearing too much perfume.

TREVOR: No, it's me.

MRS. KEMPTON: I beg your pardon.

TREVOR: I went a bit mad with the Arpège. Nerves, I expect. Knowing I was going to meet you.

JANE: Mother, you've made a mistake.

MRS. KEMPTON: No, no, Jane dear, it's quite all right. (*To Trevor*) I understand.

JANE: No, you don't.

MRS. KEMPTON: Trevor wished to make a good impression on his fiancée's parents and accidentally put on too much after-shave lotion. That's not hard to understand. (*As Mr. Kempton, a man in his late fifties, appears, exhausted by the stairs*) Harold, this is Trevor. (*To Trevor*) My husband takes longer to come upstairs than I because he likes to have a little rest on every landing.

TREVOR: How do you do, Mr. . . . er . . .

MR. KEMPTON: How do! She ought to have a lift. You tell her. (*To Jane*) You ought to have a lift, Janey. Get one put in.

JANE: Mother, this isn't Trevor.

MRS. KEMPTON: What?

JANE: This isn't Trevor.

MRS. KEMPTON: (*Turns to Trevor*) But . . .

TREVOR: Well . . . maybe I'm not.

MRS. KEMPTON: Then why did you say you were?

(*Sarah comes downstairs from the kitchen with the teapot*)

SARAH: Trevor . . . (*Stops dead as they all look at her. Pause*)

MRS. KEMPTON: I don't know what's got into you, Jane.

SARAH: I'm so sorry. I interrupted.

MRS. KEMPTON: (*To Trevor*) Are you Trevor or are you not?

TREVOR: Sort of yes and no, in a manner of speaking.

JANE: Mother . . .

MRS. KEMPTON: Just a minute, Jane. (*To Sarah*) You're the girl my daughter shares the flat with. How do you do?

SARAH: Yes, I am. How do you do?

MRS. KEMPTON: Sarah Lawrence.

SARAH: Yes. You're Mrs. Kempton.

MRS. KEMPTON: Exactly. (*Indicates Mr. Kempton*) My husband.

MR. KEMPTON: How do you do?

MRS. KEMPTON: I know your name, Miss Lawrence. Little else. Jane writes very little about you.

SARAH: I'm sorry.

MRS. KEMPTON: Don't apologize. You have your own life to lead; that's as it should be. Sharing a flat is a matter of convenience. I don't approve of close friendships between young women.

TREVOR: I'll just take the cake in.

MRS. KEMPTON: (*To Sarah*) You know Mr. Hudson, of course?

SARAH: Trevor? Yes.

MRS. KEMPTON: Thank you. (*To Trevor*) Take the cake in, Trevor, by all means. I shall join you in a moment. Jane dear, no doubt you wish to show me where to wash my hands. Harold, follow Trevor.

JANE: (*Indicates the door*) In here, mother.

TREVOR: (*Gives Sarah the cake*) For you.

(*Sarah forestalls surprise in Mrs. Kempton*)

SARAH: My parents have come to tea unexpectedly. Trevor thought I ought to have half the cake.

MRS. KEMPTON: Ah! . . . I am glad my daughter bought one large enough.

JANE: This *way*, mother.

(*Mrs. Kempton and Jane go into bathroom. Sarah and Trevor look at Mr. Kempton*)

SARAH: Will you be coming in to say hullo to my parents?

TREVOR: I think I'd better, don't you?

SARAH: I'm sure you'd better.

TREVOR: (*To Mr. Kempton*) Sarah's father's very interested in writing for television. We don't often get the chance to talk.

MR. KEMPTON: Which is Jane's room?

TREVOR: (*Points*) That one.

MR. KEMPTON: I'll just take my shoes off. We've been to see Queen Mary's dolls. My wife likes to keep active.

(*He goes into Jane's room, sits, and takes his shoes off*)

SARAH: What happened?

TREVOR: She thought I was Jane's Trevor.

SARAH: So I gather. And Jane?

TREVOR: Wanted *you* to have me.

SARAH: Yes . . . Blast! I mucked it up.

TREVOR: Now you've both got me.

SARAH: But hardly both at once.

TREVOR: It's just like *The Corsican Brothers* I must say. I've always wanted to play twins. I'd better come in with you for a bit, and then get back to the others.

SARAH: (*Giving it*) Take the cake.

(*Sarah opens the door and enters her own room. Trevor following. As she sees him, Mrs. Lawrence says:*)

MRS. LAWRENCE: Trevor . . .

(*And at the same time the bathroom door opens and Mrs. Kempton comes out, and says*)

MRS. KEMPTON: Trevor . . .

(*A frozen moment. Then the phone rings*)

TREVOR: (*Gives Sarah the cake quickly*) I think it's for me. (*He answers the phone*) Hullo? . . . What? . . . This is Trevor Hudson speaking. Yes, it's I.

(*Signs to Jane who closes the door. Gives a conciliatory*

smile to Mrs. Kempton. Then, unseen by her, but seen by the audience if possible, cuts himself off from the caller at the other end, while continuing to speak)

TREVOR: No, you tell Huw Wheldon I can't do it for that. He'll have to get Jonathan Miller . . . No, I'm sorry. Not a penny under two thousand . . . That's right. You tell him. *(He puts down the phone, and his smile to Mrs. Kempton is much more confident)* I'm so sorry. Do forgive me. It's really not at all important, but my agent gets distraught if he doesn't know where to find me. Do please go in. Jane, did you put the kettle on?

JANE: No.

TREVOR: I'll do it. *(Opens the door for Mrs. Kempton)* With you in a moment. I just want to whip up some scones to supplement the cake.

MRS. KEMPTON: Whip?

TREVOR: Only a manner of speaking. Nothing kinky.

(Mrs. Kempton enters the room, giving another sniff at the reek of Trevor's Arpège. Mr. Kempton looks up at her)

MR. KEMPTON: I thought I'd take my shoes off.

MRS. KEMPTON: There's something odd about that young man.

MR. KEMPTON: Oh, I don't know. Lots of men wear scent nowadays. I thought it was rather attractive.

MRS. KEMPTON: That will do, Harold.

MR. KEMPTON: He's a writer, isn't he? Bound to be artistic.

MRS. KEMPTON: I don't want Jane getting into the newspapers. I think we'd better find out a little more about him. *(Looks around)* Why isn't there a wardrobe in here?

(Trevor has been leaning against the wall of the hall with his eyes closed, recovering, watched by Jane)

JANE: Who was on the phone?

TREVOR: I don't know. Someone with asthma.

JANE: What?

TREVOR: Heavy breathing.

JANE: Oh . . . him.

TREVOR: You know him?

JANE: All the women in this district know him. He's called the Chelsea Breather. I usually put the phone down.

TREVOR: Well, let him breathe a bit next time. You owe him something. He saved my life. (*Moves*) I'll get the scones in. That should give me a few minutes with Sarah's parents while they're baking. (*As he goes*) I hope you noticed that two thousand quid's my minimum fee for scripts.

JANE: Yes. As far as my parents know, that's how much you make in a year.

TREVOR: (*Going*) Ah! . . . Well, you can't win them all. (*Jane goes in to her parents. Trevor goes to the kitchen and puts scones in the oven. He looks round for something to serve them on, and finds a plate and napkin. Meanwhile Sarah has been pouring tea for the Lawrences, handing scones, jam, butter, etc.*)

MRS. LAWRENCE: Where's Trevor?

SARAH: He had a phone call. Business.

MRS. LAWRENCE: He's gone?

SARAH: No. He'll be in in a minute.

MR. KEMPTON: Where's Trevor?

MRS. KEMPTON: He had a phone call. Something about two thousand pounds.

MR. KEMPTON: Good God!

MRS. KEMPTON: He refused it.

MR. LAWRENCE: (*Biting*) He makes a good scone.

SARAH: He enjoys cooking.

MRS. LAWRENCE: (*Looks at Mr. Lawrence*) I suppose he doesn't get the opportunity at home.

SARAH: No, his wife does it all.

MRS. LAWRENCE: Is that why he comes here?

SARAH: No, he comes to see me. As you know.

MRS. KEMPTON: I suppose men's after-shaving lotion is designed to linger nowadays.

JANE: Why do you say that?

MRS. KEMPTON: If Trevor shaved this morning, it's still rather strong.

JANE: It's not after-shave; it's scent. It belongs to Sarah. Trevor found it in the bathroom and put some on just before you arrived.

MRS. KEMPTON: Did he?

JANE: He told you; he was nervous.

MRS. KEMPTON: It's all right, dear; I said I understood. (*Looks around*) There's something odd about this room. I'll put my finger on it in a minute.

(*Trevor puts the scones in the oven and comes downstairs to join the Lawrences, going quietly past the Kemptons' door*)

TREVOR: (*Makes an entrance*) Everybody happy?

MRS. LAWRENCE: What was your phone call?

TREVOR: Oh . . . financial matters.

MRS. LAWRENCE: On Saturday afternoon?

TREVOR: Well, you know how it is.

MRS. LAWRENCE: No, I don't.

MR. LAWRENCE: I don't either.

SARAH: Trevor does a lot of free-lance work in his spare time.

TREVOR: That's right. I've got a wife and family to support.

SARAH: He's a consultant.

TREVOR: Yes.

SARAH: Firms consult him.

TREVOR: Always at it.

SARAH: He advises them.

TREVOR: They pay for my advice.

MRS. LAWRENCE: He must be very brilliant.

TREVOR: Yes, I am.

MRS. LAWRENCE: Tell me, Trevor, what exactly do you do at ICI?

(*Pause*)

TREVOR: I'm glad you asked that question.

(*With the Kemptons:*)

MRS. KEMPTON: Jane dear, how much do you really know about Trevor?

JANE: I've told you. He's a scriptwriter. He's . . .

MRS. KEMPTON: We know what he does for a living; that's not the point.

JANE: What is the point?

MRS. KEMPTON: How well do you really know him?

MR. KEMPTON: Your mother's afraid he might be a nancy boy.

JANE: What?

MR. KEMPTON: Homosexual. You know the sort of thing. Exposing himself in public lavatories.

JANE: Why?

MR. KEMPTON: Just because he wears scent and likes cooking. I told her everybody wears scent these days. She said she didn't want you getting into the papers.

JANE: (*To Mrs. Kempton*) You don't approve of my fiancé, mother?

MRS. KEMPTON: I never said that. I just don't want you to rush into things and be sorry afterwards.

JANE: But you told me I ought to get married.

MRS. KEMPTON: To the right man. Yes.

JANE: I wish you'd make your mind up. Last time, you said that at my age I couldn't afford to be choosy.

(*Pause*)

MRS. KEMPTON: He's a long time with the scones, dear. Do you think you ought to go and . . .

JANE: . . . see what he's up to? Don't worry, mother. He's hardly likely to be exposing himself in the kitchen.

TREVOR: And that's it really.

MRS. LAWRENCE: It doesn't seem very clear to me.

SARAH: Of course it is, mother. It's quite clear.

MRS. LAWRENCE: But *do* large commercial corporations work like that?

TREVOR: Of course they do. If you watched television as much as I do, you'd know they do.

MRS. KEMPTON: (*Gets up*) He shouldn't be doing the cooking. It's not a man's job. I'll help him.

JANE: No.

MRS. KEMPTON: It will give us the chance for a little talk. (*Opens the door*) Trevor . . .

JANE: Mother, I said no. (*At the door*) I won't have you making Trevor nervous.

MRS. KEMPTON: Really, Jane, what . . .

JANE: Trevor gets nervous very easily. I'll go.

(*She goes into the hall, closing the door firmly behind her*)

MRS. KEMPTON: (*Sitting*) I don't like this, Harold. I don't care for it at all.

MRS. LAWRENCE: Was that someone calling?

SARAH: No, I don't think so.

MRS. LAWRENCE: Somebody wanted Trevor. I heard them distinctly.

SARAH: Jane's parents are here. I told you.

MRS. LAWRENCE: But what should they want with Trevor?

TREVOR: I give them advice sometimes. On financial matters.

(*Jane has gone upstairs to the kitchen, looked for Trevor and seen he isn't there. She comes downstairs into the hall, and hovers outside the bathroom door*)

JANE: Trevor?

MRS. LAWRENCE: There!

SARAH: That was Jane.

MRS. LAWRENCE: But why should Jane . . .

SARAH: Mother, don't be so suspicious of everything.

MRS. LAWRENCE: Suspicious? I don't know what you mean. What is there to be suspicious about?

TREVOR: (*To Sarah*) Don't you have a cat called Trevor?

SARAH: (*Angry*) No.

TREVOR: Just trying to be helpful.

(Jane still undecided, looks at door of Sarah's room, then smells the scones burning in the kitchen)

JANE: Oh Christ! The scones!

MRS. KEMPTON: What are they talking about up there? They're a very long time.

MR. KEMPTON: Dammit, they're engaged.

MRS. KEMPTON: He's supposed to be meeting us, not gossiping with Jane in the kitchen. Besides, I don't want Jane talking about me to that young man.

MR. KEMPTON: She's obviously done that already. That's why he put on all that scent.

(Jane has shot upstairs to the kitchen and taken the scones out of the oven. She puts them on the plate Trevor has left out, and covers them with a napkin. While:)

TREVOR: I suppose I ought to say Hullo to Jane's parents. I mean, they might be a bit hurt if I ignored them.

SARAH: They're very fond of Trevor.

MRS. LAWRENCE: I thought you said you saw very little of Jane.

SARAH: I don't see much of her. Trevor just happens to get on with her parents. He collects people.

TREVOR: I'm terribly good with older women. *(Going)* Do excuse me. I shan't be a moment.

(He crosses the hall, opens the door, and goes in to Mr. and Mrs. Kempton, just missing Jane as she comes downstairs with the scones on a plate)

TREVOR: I'm so sorry. The scones won't be a moment.

MRS. KEMPTON: But where's Jane?

TREVOR: Jane?

MRS. KEMPTON: She went to fetch you.

TREVOR: Did she? That's right, she did. *(To Mrs. Kempton)* Jane went to fetch me.

MRS. KEMPTON: Then where is she?

TREVOR: She hasn't come back yet.

(Jane hesitates, then knocks at Sarah's door, and goes in. She is surprised not to see Trevor)

JANE: Er . . . (*Pause. All look at her*) I . . . er . . .

MRS. LAWRENCE: Are you looking for my daughter's lover?

MR. LAWRENCE: Hetty!

JANE: No . . . No . . . I . . . (*Scones*) I just brought you these.

MRS. LAWRENCE: But we have scones already.

JANE: These are hot.

MRS. KEMPTON: And where are the scones?

TREVOR: Scones?

MRS. KEMPTON: You went to "whip them up."

TREVOR: (*At the door*) That's right. They're ready. I'll get them.

MRS. KEMPTON: Can't Jane bring them?

TREVOR: Oh, she'll need a bit of help. My scones are terribly heavy.

(*He goes quickly into the hall and up into the kitchen, sees Jane isn't there, goes to take the scones out of the oven and finds they're gone*)

JANE: Well . . . I'd better get back.

SARAH: Thank you for the scones.

JANE: That's quite all right.

MR. LAWRENCE: (*Eating one*) They're very good.

MRS. LAWRENCE: I have a great deal of difficulty keeping my husband away from starchy foods.

JANE: (*Going*) I'm so glad to have met you, Mrs. Lawrence.

MRS. LAWRENCE: You will find Trevor with your parents. He is giving them advice on financial matters.

(*Jane is out and crosses the hall. Trevor has looked for scone mix, found none, and is haphazardly mixing flour, milk and eggs in the mixing bowl. Jane is surprised not to find Trevor with her parents*)

MRS. KEMPTON: And where is Trevor?

JANE: Trevor?

MR. KEMPTON: He went to help you.

JANE: Oh . . . Trevor. He's making scones.

MRS. KEMPTON: Again!

JANE: The first lot didn't take.

(*The phone rings. Jane and Sarah both respond to it as a welcome diversion*)

JANE: I'll go.

SARAH: I'll go.

(*Both go into the hall, where Trevor is already on his way down to answer the phone. Pause. They look at each other. Both shut the doors to their rooms behind them. Phone still ringing. Trevor picks it up, and holds it a moment*)

TREVOR: Just letting him breathe. (*Puts down phone*)

SARAH: I can't keep it up.

TREVOR: *You* can't?

SARAH: We should never have started. It's ridiculous. Like a farce.

JANE: We can't tell them.

SARAH: I'm sick of it. I'm sick of deceit.

JANE: Love, we've started the deception. We have to go on. If they find out now . . .

TREVOR: That's right. If you hadn't invented *me,* you could just be two friends sharing a flat.

SARAH: Well, we've got to do something.

JANE: What?

TREVOR: If you could just get rid of one set of parents, we could manage.

JANE: How?

TREVOR: Unless you'd rather get rid of me. I don't mind suicide in a good cause. I've often thought of it.

(*Doors to both rooms are opened simultaneously. Mrs. Kempton and Mrs. Lawrence have grown impatient*)

MRS. KEMPTON: ⎫
MRS. LAWRENCE: ⎬ Who was . . .

MRS. KEMPTON: I beg your pardon.

MRS. LAWRENCE: Not at all. (*To Sarah*) Who was it, dear?

TREVOR: Wrong number. (*Looks from one to another*) Ah well, back to the kitchen.

MRS. KEMPTON: (*As he goes*) Why?

SARAH: (*Quickly*) Oh mother, I don't think you know Jane's mother. Mrs. Kempton . . . this is my mother.

MRS. KEMPTON: How do you do?

MRS. LAWRENCE: I'm so glad to meet you. (*To Sarah*) Sarah, why did Trevor . . .

JANE: And *we* haven't really been introduced, have we? I brought you some scones just now, but we never really met.

SARAH: Mother, this is Jane.

MRS. LAWRENCE: How do you do? I was just telling my daughter, she never mentions you. Though apparently Trevor . . .

JANE: We lead rather separate lives, I'm afraid.

MRS. KEMPTON: I'm sure Mrs. Lawrence understands that, Jane.

MRS. LAWRENCE: Sarah tells me your daughter's engaged to be married.

MRS. KEMPTON: (*Looks towards kitchen*) Yes, we . . .

SARAH: (*Jumps in almost hysterically*) And Mr. Kempton, mother. You haven't met Mr. Kempton.

MRS. KEMPTON: Trevor . . .

SARAH: (*Waving through door*) Hullo, Mr. Kempton! Hullo! This is my mother.

MR. KEMPTON: What? . . . What? . . .

SARAH: (*To Mrs. Kempton*) It's so nice to have met you. (*Pulling Mrs. Lawrence back into her own room*) Come along, mother. Mustn't let the scones get cold.

MRS. LAWRENCE: (*As she goes*) Will Trevor be long?

MRS. KEMPTON: Is that girl right in the head?

JANE: Of course she is.

MRS. KEMPTON: There's no of course about it.

JANE: She's having . . . rather a difficult love affair at the moment. It makes her nervous.

MRS. KEMPTON: What did that woman mean?

JANE: What woman?

MRS. KEMPTON: "Will Trevor be long?"

JANE: Sarah's mother is not "that woman," mother. Her name is Mrs. Lawrence.

MRS. KEMPTON: What did she mean: "Will Trevor be long?"

JANE: You must have misheard her.

MRS. KEMPTON: Nonsense. I hope she understands that Trevor . . .

JANE: He advises her husband on scripts. It's a free-lance thing he does.

MRS. KEMPTON: But she didn't know you. She had to be introduced to you.

JANE: She knows Trevor. I . . . (*Inventing*) I met Trevor through Sarah.

MRS. KEMPTON: Indeed!

JANE: She gave a party, and of course she had to ask me. Trevor was one of the guests.

MRS. KEMPTON: But you told me you met Trevor at the National Gallery in front of a picture . . .

JANE: (*Outburst*) Mother, for God's sake will you stop questioning everything I say?

(*Pause*)

MRS. KEMPTON: I don't know what's got into you today. (*She goes back into Jane's room. Jane is left in the hall. She would like to join Sarah, looks at the door to that room, takes a step, but of course she can't go in. At this point, Trevor, in the kitchen, drops the mixing bowl and says, "Blast!" Since his arrival there, he has looked doubtfully at his mixture, lit the oven, and kept himself unobtrusively occupied in scone preparation until this moment. Jane hears him, is undecided whether to go up, but decides against, and follows her mother. Trevor picks the bowl off the floor and attempts to roll out the mixture which has got very sticky. While:*)

SARAH: I'm sorry. I really can't bear Jane's mother.

MRS. LAWRENCE: But . . .

SARAH: I don't want to talk about it. If you can't bear someone you can't.

MR. LAWRENCE: Where's Trevor?

SARAH: In the kitchen. Making . . .

MRS. LAWRENCE: (*Holds up two brimming plates of scones*) Scones?

SARAH: I don't know what he's making.

MRS. LAWRENCE: Harold, go and find out.

SARAH: No. Leave Trevor alone.

MRS. LAWRENCE: Run along, Harold.

SARAH: Why?

MRS. LAWRENCE: Because I want to talk to you privately, dear.

(*Pause*)

MR. LAWRENCE: (*To Sarah*) Back soon. (*Goes*)

SARAH: Father, you've forgotten your shoes.

MR. LAWRENCE: (*In hall*) Can't get them on. My feet have swollen.

(*As Mr. Lawrence gets into hall, the phone rings*)

SARAH: I'll go.

MRS. LAWRENCE: (*Calls*) Answer it, Harold, will you?

(*She closes the door firmly. Mr. Lawrence answers the phone*)

MR. LAWRENCE: Hullo? . . . Hullo?

MRS. KEMPTON: Harold dear, why don't you have a word with Trevor?

MR. KEMPTON: Eh?

JANE: What about?

MR. LAWRENCE: Hullo? . . . Hullo? . . .

MRS. KEMPTON: If you intend to marry Trevor, dear, then naturally your father ought to get to know him. In the kitchen, Harold.

MR. KEMPTON: Oh . . . All right.

MR. LAWRENCE: Speak up. What do you want? This is (*Looking*)—one of those number things. Used to be Free-mantle, but they changed it.

JANE: Why does father have to go? Trevor'll be back in a moment.

MRS. KEMPTON: Because I want to have a little talk with you.

JANE: Why . . . ?

MRS. KEMPTON: (*Straight over her*) And I don't want your father to be embarrassed.

MR. LAWRENCE: Hullo?

MR. KEMPTON: (*To Jane*) Back soon, Janie. (*Going*)

JANE: Father, you've forgotten your shoes.

MR. KEMPTON: Never mind. (*Closes the door behind him*)

MR. LAWRENCE: Hullo? . . . (*Puts the phone down. Sees Mr. Kempton*) Nobody there.

MR. KEMPTON: Wrong number?

MR. LAWRENCE: Don't know. He didn't say.

MR. KEMPTON: How do you know there was anybody there at all?

MR. LAWRENCE: Asthma.

(*Trevor puts the new tray of scones in the oven, and comes downstairs. Seeing the fathers, he tries to back away but is spotted*)

MR. KEMPTON: There you are, young man. I was just coming to have a word with you.

MR. LAWRENCE: So was I.

MR. KEMPTON: Were you? Why?

TREVOR: *Were* you? Ah, you were. Yes, of course you were. You both were. But you won't both want to have a word with me at the same time, will you? No, you won't.

MR. KEMPTON: My wife says we've got to get to know each other.

MR. LAWRENCE: (*Puzzled*) But you do know each other.

TREVOR: Better. We should know each other better. We all should. Everyone should.

MR. LAWRENCE: Trevor gives you advice.

MR. KEMPTON: No, that's what he gives you.

MR. LAWRENCE: He gives you advice about . . .

TREVOR: I give everyone advice. It's a fault. Can't mind my own business. Mr. Kempton, Mr. Lawrence. Mr. Lawrence, Mr. Kempton.

MR. KEMPTON: ⎫
MR. LAWRENCE: ⎭ *(Together)* How do you do?

TREVOR: *(To Mr. Kempton)* I expect you'd like to go to the loo, wouldn't you?

MR. KEMPTON: No, I wouldn't.

TREVOR: Your wife went. It's nice in there.

MR. KEMPTON: No, I don't think so, thanks.

MR. LAWRENCE: Wait a minute. There's something I don't understand.

TREVOR: Never miss an opportunity, because you don't know when you'll get another chance. Royalty do it. They're always doing it. And President de Gaulle and everybody.

MR. KEMPTON: No, thanks.

TREVOR: You could be out walking. Any minute you'd pass a fountain. Or a mountain stream. Trickle, trickle! Imagine it.

MR. KEMPTON: I said no thank you.

TREVOR: They've got blue bleach in the cistern. It colors the bowl when you flush. You pull the chain and the water goes zzzzzz.

MR. LAWRENCE: My wife wanted me to find out what you were doing in the kitchen.

TREVOR: Making scones.

MR. LAWRENCE: Again? Bit obsessional isn't it?

(The phone rings)

MR. KEMPTON: *(To Trevor)* That for you?

TREVOR: No. Why?

MR. KEMPTON: Thought it might be another of your . . .

TREVOR: No. It isn't.

MR. LAWRENCE: Probably that fellow with asthma.

TREVOR: The Chelsea Breather. (*To Mr. Kempton*) It's someone who breathes.

MR. KEMPTON: I'll take it, then. (*Picks the phone up*) Hullo? (*Listens then nods to the others*) Now look here, breather . . .

MR. LAWRENCE: My wife says you've got to understand these people.

MR. KEMPTON: They need a shock. A sharp shock. (*Into the phone*) Breather, you need a shock.

MR. LAWRENCE: They did some experiments at the Howard League. Got a lot of them in a group, breathing at each other. Found they preferred that to using the phone.

MR. KEMPTON: (*Into the phone*) You run along and find some other breathers. We've had enough of you here. We . . . Hah! (*To the others*) Hung up. (*Phone down*) We shan't hear from him again. What was that about scones? (*To Mr. Lawrence*) He's always making scones, this fellow, but you never see any.

MR. LAWRENCE: Never *see* any?

(*Phone rings*)

MR. KEMPTON: I'll leave it off. (*Does so*)

TREVOR: (*To Mr. Kempton*) Look, sir, whatever you wanted to chat about, it's probably a bit personal, isn't it? So (*Indicating the door*) if Mr. Lawrence wouldn't mind . . .

MR. LAWRENCE: Oh, I can't go back in there.

(*Smoke has begun to emerge from the oven door*)

TREVOR: Ah! . . . (*Turns to Mr. Kempton*) Er . . .

MR. KEMPTON: Nor can I.

TREVOR: Oh.

MR. LAWRENCE: My wife sent me out of the room. I can't go back.

MR. KEMPTON: So did mine. Wanted to have a heart-to-heart with Jane.

MR. LAWRENCE: Mine wanted to have a heart-to-heart with Sarah.

TREVOR: What about? (*Quick second thoughts*) Wait! Don't tell me.

MR. KEMPTON: Can you smell anything burning?

(*Trevor sniffs. Then he returns to the kitchen, the other two following. Thick smoke from oven. He opens it, looks inside, then closes the door again and turns the oven off*)

TREVOR: You have to watch them.

MR. KEMPTON: No scones, eh?

MR. LAWRENCE: You could have some of ours. We've got lots.

TREVOR: There's some brandy in the cupboard.

MR. KEMPTON: Ah. Wonder which of the girls it belongs to.

MR. LAWRENCE: Sarah wouldn't mind.

MR. KEMPTON: Or Jane.

TREVOR: Let's have some. (*Getting the bottle*) Where do they keep the glasses?

MR. KEMPTON: If you don't know, who does?

TREVOR: How true! Of course, they're downstairs, aren't they in the . . . in Sarah's . . . Jane's . . .

MR. LAWRENCE: What?

TREVOR: In the chiffonier.

MR. KEMPTON: (*Finds them in the kitchen cupboard*) Here you are.

TREVOR: Oh, *those* glasses. (*Filling them*) You don't mind it neat. (*Toasting*) Cheers.

(*All drink*)

TREVOR: I needed that.

MR. KEMPTON: Must be a bit of a strain.

TREVOR: You don't know how much.

MR. LAWRENCE: Meeting the parents.

TREVOR: Exactly.

MR. KEMPTON: Silly business. Unnecessary.

TREVOR: Yes.

MR. KEMPTON: What young people do nowadays; it's nothing to do with their parents.

TREVOR: No.

MR. LAWRENCE: You can't get Sarah's mother to see that, though.

MR. KEMPTON: Or Jane's.

MR. LAWRENCE: If two people want to live together . . .

MR. KEMPTON: Oh, I don't know about living together.

MR. LAWRENCE: (*To Trevor*) Anyway, you're not living together.

MR. KEMPTON: No, he's not.

TREVOR: No, I'm not.

MR. LAWRENCE: But the point is, if you did want to, you'd do it. Please yourselves.

MR. KEMPTON: (*To Trevor*) Would you?

MR. LAWRENCE: Your love life is your own affair. Nothing to do with your parents. (*To Mr. Kempton*) Our generation should stay out of it.

MR. KEMPTON: (*To Trevor*) But you're not going to live together?

TREVOR: No, I'm not.

MR. KEMPTON: Jane's not that kind of girl. I'm sure she's not.

TREVOR: (*Pouring*) Let's have another drink.

MR. LAWRENCE: Jane?

MR. KEMPTON: My daughter.

MR. LAWRENCE: Oh, Jane! Well, Jane would move out, I assume.

MR. KEMPTON: Why?

MR. LAWRENCE: Well, you weren't thinking . . .

TREVOR: No, he wasn't.

MR. KEMPTON: What?

TREVOR: You weren't thinking.

MR. LAWRENCE: No, I didn't imagine Jane would stay here if you were living together. Even my wife isn't that broad-minded.

MR. KEMPTON: She wouldn't want to stay here. No room, for one thing.

MR. LAWRENCE: Exactly.

MR. KEMPTON: I don't understand this. (*To Trevor*) You're not going to live together.

MR. LAWRENCE: I don't see why *you're* so bothered, Kempton.

TREVOR: Cheers.

MR. KEMPTON: } Cheers.
MR. LAWRENCE:

MR. LAWRENCE: Funny.

TREVOR: What is?

MR. LAWRENCE: My wife thought you might be queer.

TREVOR: Queer?

MR. LAWRENCE: You know . . . homosexual. That kind of thing.

MR. KEMPTON: A nance. So did my wife.

TREVOR: Oh, I don't think people say "nance" nowadays, do they?

MR. LAWRENCE: I told her everyone wears scent in 1969.

MR. KEMPTON: I don't. Never have.

TREVOR: Don't you?

MR. KEMPTON: I wouldn't mind, though. I like scent. I respond to it.

TREVOR: (*Shifts a little away uneasily*) Do you?

MR. LAWRENCE: I've never been attracted to scent. Smell, yes. Not scent. Sweat. I've always found sweat attractive.

TREVOR: (*Wipes his hands nervously*) Let me fill your glass.

MR. KEMPTON: My wife wears Yardley's Lavender. It's not the same.

MR. LAWRENCE: My wife hardly sweats at all.

MR. KEMPTON: Funny my wife thought you were a nance.

TREVOR: Hilarious.

MR. KEMPTON: Cheers.

(*All drink*)

MR. LAWRENCE: Of course she used to sweat when she was younger. We went to Antibes for our honeymoon and she sweated like a horse. Now she buys one of those roll-on deodorants.

(*Conversational focus shifts downstairs. The men continue to drink in the kitchen*)

SARAH: This is ridiculous. I won't have this conversation.

MRS. LAWRENCE: He's not at all suitable.

SARAH: Suitability's got nothing to do with it. I'm not marrying him. You wanted me to be fulfilled. Well, I am fulfilled. Trevor fulfills me every Saturday afternoon, and now you're complaining.

MRS. LAWRENCE: A man like that couldn't fulfill anyone.

SARAH: What do you want? A blow-by-blow account?

MRS. LAWRENCE: Sarah!

SARAH: That shocks you, doesn't it? But you're supposed to be unshockable, mother; you're the one that understands people. All my life you've told me to understand people, and now I'm understanding you.

MRS. LAWRENCE: What's that supposed to mean?

SARAH: Try working it out. Why you've nagged at me to find a lover, and why you don't like it now I've found one.

TREVOR: If your feet have swollen, you could put them in the fridge.

MR. LAWRENCE: Cheers.

TREVOR:
MR. KEMPTON: } Cheers.

MRS. LAWRENCE: I don't want you to be unhappy.

SARAH: Don't you?

MRS. KEMPTON: I don't want you to be unhappy, Jane. A man like that . . .

JANE: Like that?

MRS. KEMPTON: You know what I mean.

JANE: No. Tell me.

MRS. KEMPTON: I don't say Trevor's . . . effeminate.

JANE: Then?

MRS. KEMPTON: He's clearly unstable. He's not stable, dear. Not the sort of man you could rely on.

JANE: What if I'll settle for someone who'll rely on *me?*

MRS. KEMPTON: Don't make debating points.

JANE: Damn you, mother. I've had enough.

MRS. KEMPTON: What?

SARAH: I've had enough.

JANE: You come here, meet someone—

SARAH: —for the first time. You don't really know—

JANE: —a single bloody thing about him—

SARAH: —and in fifteen minutes—

JANE: —you've written him off.

SARAH: You tell me you're concerned about my future.

JANE: You don't give a damn for anyone but yourself.

SARAH: Just because Trevor wears scent—

JANE: —and bakes scones—

MRS. KEMPTON: Jane! Please!

MRS. LAWRENCE: Sarah!

SARAH: Oh, you're so broad-minded, mother, so understanding—

JANE: Narrow-minded! Intolerant!

MRS. LAWRENCE: But, Sarah, if you love him—

MRS. KEMPTON: —if you really love him that's a different matter.

MRS. LAWRENCE: If you're sure you love him.

(*Pause*)

SARAH: What?

JANE: Oh . . .

MR. KEMPTON: I'll tell my wife, "You've got it all wrong," I'll say.

MR. LAWRENCE: Yes, *I'll* say that. (*To Trevor*) Don't you worry. I'll have a word with her.

MR. KEMPTON: "He's not in the least queer. He's just a very obliging fellow."

MR. LAWRENCE: Cheers.

MR. KEMPTON: ⎫
TREVOR: ⎭ Cheers.

JANE: I'm sorry. I got carried away.

SARAH: I got carried away, mother. I didn't mean to hurt you.

MRS. LAWRENCE: No, no, dear. I've no right to interfere.

SARAH: I was cruel. I didn't mean . . .

MRS. LAWRENCE: You did, dear.

SARAH: No.

MRS. LAWRENCE: And you were right. I look at myself and what do I see? Prurient curiosity. And jealousy afterwards. I'm ashamed, Sarah.

MRS. KEMPTON: I've been a bossy woman all my life. Of course, your father encourages it.

JANE: But, mother . . .

MRS. LAWRENCE: Hearing you defend Trevor, "Lord, lord!" I thought, "I've had the impertinence to talk to this girl about fulfillment!"

SARAH: But I didn't mean to defend him. I just lost my temper.

MRS. KEMPTON: You wouldn't be my daughter if you didn't pick someone unsuitable to marry.

JANE: But, mother, if he *is* unsuitable . . .

MRS. LAWRENCE: Your father used to be a very passionate man.

MR. LAWRENCE: I think she'd been reading the BO advertisements.

MRS. LAWRENCE: I forgot who spoke to me about it.

MR. LAWRENCE: I couldn't very well tell her, "I *like* BO."

MR. KEMPTON: Cheers.

MR. LAWRENCE:
TREVOR: } Cheers.

JANE: I'm trying to say, you may be right.

SARAH: I have had . . . doubts about Trevor.

JANE: If you really think I should give him up . . .

MRS. KEMPTON: No, dear, no.

MRS. LAWRENCE: No, Sarah. It's your own life.

SARAH: Perhaps if I didn't see him for a while . . .

JANE: If we tried a separation until I feel clearer in my mind.

SARAH: I could talk to him. If he really loves me . . .

JANE: —he'd want me to be certain of what I feel; I'm sure of that.

MRS. LAWRENCE: Perhaps later . . .

SARAH: No, I'll do it now.

MRS. LAWRENCE: He's still in the kitchen with your father.

MRS. KEMPTON: Your father's talking to him in the kitchen.

JANE: Yes, that's right. (*Going*) I'll send daddy down.

SARAH: (*Going*) I shan't be long. I think it's better if he leaves straight away.

MRS. LAWRENCE: Oh, my dear, if you're sure.

SARAH: I am.

JANE: I shan't bring Trevor back. He's bound to be a bit upset.

MRS. KEMPTON: My brave girl!

(*Both girls go into the hall, closing doors behind them. Both mothers sigh exhausted sighs. Pause*)

MR. LAWRENCE: Cheers.

MR. KEMPTON: Cheers.

TREVOR: (*Stands*) Excuse me.

JANE: I've promised to give him up.

SARAH: So have I.

JANE: I said I'd talk to him and he'd leave right away.

SARAH: Have you got the five pounds?

JANE: In my bag.

SARAH: Oh, love! Love!

(*They kiss, as Trevor comes downstairs*)

JANE: Trevor . . .

TREVOR: I don't feel well.

SARAH: No!

TREVOR: I had a lot of beer in the pub. And then vodka.

And I've been drinking brandy with your fathers. I feel very strange.

JANE: Get him into the bathroom. (*As they do so*) You'll be all right, Trevor. You'll be all right.

TREVOR: (*Last words*) I'm not Trevor.

(*Upstairs the two fathers sip brandy*)

MR. LAWRENCE: Think he's all right?

MR. KEMPTON: My wife doesn't care for him.

MR. LAWRENCE: Looked a bit shaky, I thought.

MR. KEMPTON: Oh . . . that. Probably not used to it.

MR. LAWRENCE: Used to what?

MR. KEMPTON: Drinking brandy in the afternoon. Got out of the habit.

(*The door to downstairs is opened with a latch-key. It is the landlord, Mr. Hudson, a man in his late fifties. He enters, looks round, sees the phone is off the hook and replaces it censoriously. He looks about him, then crouches to peer through the keyhole of the door right*)

MR. KEMPTON: Tell you a devil for the brandy. Old Johnny Chinaman.

MR. LAWRENCE: Johnny?

MR. KEMPTON: Manner of speaking. Old Johnny Chink.

MR. LAWRENCE: Ah!

MR. KEMPTON: Used to see a lot of those fellows during the war. Chiang Kai-shek's fellows. Devils for brandy. They'd knock it back by the tumblerful. "Banzai," they'd say . . .

MR. LAWRENCE: (*Pouring*) Couldn't have been "Banzai."

MR. KEMPTON: By George, you're right there. What *did* they say. I wonder? Neat brandy. Tigers for it. (*Raising his glass*) Banzai.

MR. LAWRENCE: Cheers.

MR. KEMPTON: No, no, old boy. It was something Chinese. Something colloquial. You'd learn it off a record nowadays, but in my time we actually had to meet these fellows.

(*Hudson has been puzzled by what he's seen through the keyhole of Jane's room. He has left that door, looked*)

*about him, and tried the door of Sarah's room. Nobody
there but an old woman on her own. Equally puzzling.
Now there is a gurgle from Trevor in the bathroom*)

JANE: (*Heard*) Get his head under water.

(*Hudson goes to the bathroom door and peers through*)

MR. LAWRENCE: I suppose he is all right. Trevor.

MR. KEMPTON: (*Stands*) I'll go and see. I could do with
a leak. Too much talk about fountains. (*He descends the
stairs and sees Hudson*) Ah, bit of a queue, is there?

HUDSON: (*Startled*) What?

MR. KEMPTON: Bit of a queue. (*Notices the phone*)
That's funny. Thought I left it off. (*Takes it off again*) I hope
he won't be long in there. At my age, the old kidneys . . .

HUDSON: You shouldn't leave the telephone off the hook.

MR. KEMPTON: Why not?

HUDSON: (*Replaces it*) The Post Office don't like it.

MR. KEMPTON: You're from the Post Office, are you?

HUDSON: Er . . .

MR. KEMPTON: Thought I hadn't seen you before.
(*Towards the bathroom*) Tell you what; let's bang on the
door. He might have passed out.

HUDSON: Who?

MR. KEMPTON: I had to climb over a lavatory door once
in Dehra Dun. Been knocking it back a bit with a friend of
mine. Brother officer, you know. In he went, locked the door,
never came out. Couldn't let him down, so over the top I
went. It was pretty to see him lying there, curled around the
bowl.

HUDSON: *Who* may have passed out?

MR. KEMPTON: But it was rather difficult to explain to
the brigadier, when we both came out together.

HUDSON: *Who* . . .

MR. KEMPTON: You wouldn't know him. Lumley—
Mahratha Light Infantry. Oh—in there? My daughter's fiancé.

(*Mrs. Kempton opens the door to Jane's room, and looks
out*)

MRS. KEMPTON: Harold, to whom are you talking?

MR. KEMPTON: Fellow from the Post Office come in for a bit of a leak.

MRS. KEMPTON: From the *Post Office!* In here?

MR. KEMPTON: (*To Hudson*) By George, that's true. Just because you're in the government service, that doesn't give you the right to barge into a private flat every time you want to . . .

HUDSON: I am not . . .

MR. KEMPTON: Bloody Trades Unions throwing their weight around again. Dammit, you've got pillar boxes for that sort of thing.

MRS. KEMPTON: Why should a man from the Post Office . . .

MR. KEMPTON: I'd left the phone off the hook. (*To Hudson*) Had to. One of those breathers kept ringing up. Dring! Dring! Couldn't hear yourself speak. He'll ring again in a minute.

HUDSON: No, he won't.

MRS. KEMPTON: How did he get in?

(*Mrs. Lawrence opens the door of Sarah's room, and looks out*)

MRS. LAWRENCE: Harold!

MR. KEMPTON: Yes? (*Comes to her*) How do you do? I'm Jane's father; I don't think we've met. And this is a man from the Post Office come in for a . . .

MRS. KEMPTON: That will do, Harold.

MR. KEMPTON: (*Goes on into Sarah's room*) You don't mind if I sit down? Not much point in standing around when you're not even first in the queue. (*Sits*)

MRS. LAWRENCE: I was calling my husband.

MR. KEMPTON: (*Gets up*). Ah! (*Crosses to the door. Calls*) Lawrence, your wife wants you.

(*He returns to his seat. Mr. Lawrence hears the call and stands*)

MR. LAWRENCE: What?

MRS. KEMPTON: (*To Mrs. Lawrence*) I have been trying to discover how this man gained entry to the flat. (*To Hudson*) If you're from the Post Office, why aren't you in uniform?

HUDSON: I'm not from the Post Office.

MRS. LAWRENCE: A burglar? (*To Mrs. Kempton*) Is he a burglar?

HUDSON: I'm the landlord.

MR. KEMPTON: (*Makes a discovery*) I say! Lots of scones *here!*

HUDSON: I came to put the phone back on the hook.

(*Mr. Lawrence descends the stairs from the kitchen*)

MRS. LAWRENCE: Harold, where is Trevor?

MR. LAWRENCE: Kempton went to find out. (*Passing Hudson*) How do you do? (*Sees Mr. Kempton*) Kempton, where's Trevor?

MR. KEMPTON: Still in there. Probably passed out.

MR. LAWRENCE: (*Joins him in the room*) You've found the scones, I see.

MR. KEMPTON: (*Passing them*) Have one.

MR. LAWRENCE: Not allowed. Tea?

MR. KEMPTON: God, no.

MR. LAWRENCE: Ah! You haven't . . . ?

MR. KEMPTON: Not yet. I told you. He's still in there.

MRS. LAWRENCE: (*From the door*) Harold, this man says he's the landlord.

MR. KEMPTON: How did he get in, then?

MRS. LAWRENCE: (*To Hudson*) How did you . . .

HUDSON: (*Crosses her and comes into the room. Indignant to Mr. Kempton*) I have a key. I let myself in. I have the right to do so. (*Looks round*) And now I shall go.

(*Mrs. Kempton joins Mrs. Lawrence, so that they bar his way back into the hall*)

MRS. KEMPTON: There's no proof of that.

MR. KEMPTON: That's right. He could be a damned

thief, come sneaking in here, pretending he wants to use the loo. (*Stands*) Come here, sneak thief; I'm going to search your pockets.

MRS. LAWRENCE: He said he wanted to put the phone back on the hook.

MR. KEMPTON: How did he know the phone was off the hook?

(*Pause. Hudson now uneasy. Mrs. Lawrence and Mrs. Kempton come into the room, so that he is surrounded*)

MRS. KEMPTON: Well, my man?

MRS. LAWRENCE: How did you know the phone was . . .

MR. LAWRENCE: It *was* off, though.

MR. KEMPTON: What?

MR. LAWRENCE: I mean, he is right. The phone was off the hook.

MRS. LAWRENCE: But how could he know that?

(*Pause*)

HUDSON: I have . . . ways of knowing.

MR. LAWRENCE: What ways?

HUDSON: Mind your own business.

(*Pause*)

MR. KEMPTON: By George, you're not the landlord at all; you're that breather. You've been ringing up and breathing at us, and when I took the phone off the hook, you couldn't bear it.

HUDSON: I'm the landlord. I have the keys. It's natural for me to be here.

MR. KEMPTON: You stole them, you breather.

HUDSON: No.

MR. LAWRENCE: I suppose he could be both.

MRS. LAWRENCE: What, Harold?

MR. LAWRENCE: Landlord and breather. He could be both.

(*Pause. Mrs. Kempton closes the door of the room*)

MRS. KEMPTON: Do you mean that a man who breathes at women on the telephone has the key to my daughter's flat?

(*Bathroom door opens. Trevor, Sarah and Jane come into the hall cautiously*)

SARAH: It's all right. There's nobody here.

HUDSON: But I never use it.

TREVOR: Shouldn't I say goodbye to *anyone?*

JANE: No.

MRS. KEMPTON: Never use it? Of course you use it. You're using it now.

JANE: Just go. Quietly. We'll explain.

TREVOR: It's so impolite. Both of me just creeping off like this.

HUDSON: Only because the telephone was off the hook.

SARAH: Goodbye, Trevor.

JANE: Good*bye,* Trevor.

TREVOR: Wait a sec. I forgot something.

(*He returns to the bathroom*)

HUDSON: You can ask your daughters. I never come here.

(*Trevor flushes the* WC.)

MR. KEMPTON: By George, he's out. (*Quickly to the door*) Excuse me.

HUDSON: But . . .

MR. KEMPTON: No, old boy. You've forfeited your turn. (*Opens the door*) Jane, there's a breather in here, says he's your landlord. (*Passing Trevor*) There you are, Trevor. Feeling better?

TREVOR: Much better.

MR. KEMPTON: You took your time.

TREVOR: Sorry.

(*Mr. Kempton into the bathroom, closing the door*)

SARAH: Trevor! Go!

MRS. LAWRENCE: (*Looks through the open door*) Sarah dear, just come in for a moment, will you please? Oh, is Trevor going? Just a minute. I'll have a word with him.

SARAH: Mother, I've already had a word with him.

TREVOR: Yes, she has, and I quite understand. Goodbye, Mrs. Lawrence. Goodbye, Sarah. Goodbye, Jane. (*He has the front door open*)

MRS. KEMPTON: (*Calls*) Is that Trevor?

TREVOR: (*Calls*) Goodbye, Mrs. Kempton.

MRS. KEMPTON: (*Comes into hall*) I'll have a word with him before he goes. (*To Jane*) Go on in, Jane dear; I just want a word with Trevor.

MRS. LAWRENCE: Run along, Sarah.

SARAH: Mother, you *don't* want a word with him.

MRS. LAWRENCE: Just to show there are no hard feelings, dear.

(*Jane and Sarah look at each other, and at Trevor. Then they go into Sarah's room. Hudson regards them piteously*)

HUDSON: There's been a mistake.

SARAH: Yes.

(*Mrs. Kempton closes the door*)

MRS. KEMPTON: Now, Trevor . . .

TREVOR: Please, please! I know what you both want to say.

MRS. LAWRENCE: All *I* wanted to tell you . . .

TREVOR: No need to put it into words.

MRS. KEMPTON: There are no hard feelings.

TREVOR: Just say goodbye. Believe me, I do understand. It's better.

MRS. LAWRENCE: (*To Mrs. Kempton*) No hard feelings?

MRS. KEMPTON: None.

MRS. LAWRENCE: But I have no hard feelings for Trevor. I'm the one with no hard feelings.

MRS. KEMPTON: Why should *you* have no hard feelings?

TREVOR: Surely if neither of you has any hard feelings, there's no need to go on about it.

MRS. LAWRENCE: Because Sarah is going to give him up.

MRS. KEMPTON: No, no, my dear, Jane is going to give him up.

MRS. LAWRENCE: Sarah's going to give the affair time to cool.

MRS. KEMPTON: Jane wants to be certain what she feels for him.

TREVOR: Mrs. Lawrence . . .

MRS. KEMPTON: Trevor is Jane's fiancé, Mrs. Lawrence.

TREVOR: Mrs. Kempton . . .

MRS. LAWRENCE: Trevor is Sarah's lover, Mrs. Kempton. (*Pause*)

TREVOR: Anyway, if they're both going to give me up, there's no harm done, is there?

(WC *flushed. Mr. Kempton comes out of the bathroom*)

MRS. KEMPTON: Harold, take Trevor into Miss Lawrence's room.

MR. KEMPTON: *Take* him?

(*Trevor looks from Mr. Kempton to the women, then closes the door*)

TREVOR: I'll come quietly.

(*He follows Mr. Kempton into Sarah's room*)

SARAH: They know?

TREVOR: Yes.

MR. LAWRENCE: Hello, Trevor. We've caught your breather.

HUDSON: I do not breathe. I have a right to telephone my own tenants.

MR. KEMPTON: I don't understand this.

(*Mrs. Kempton and Mrs. Lawrence follow them in, closing the door*)

MRS. KEMPTON: Now.

HUDSON: I am not obliged to explain to you. All my tenants are single women. I have a duty . . .

MRS. KEMPTON: What is this person talking about?

HUDSON: I do not breathe at women.

MRS. LAWRENCE: No time for that now. Well, Sarah?

MRS. KEMPTON: Well, Jane?

MR. LAWRENCE: What's up?

MR. KEMPTON: Don't ask me.

SARAH: Mother's found out that Trevor's Jane's fiancé as well as my lover.

MR. LAWRENCE: What?

MR. KEMPTON: Steady on.

SARAH: He's single as well as married, and he works for the BBC as well as Shell.

JANE: ICI.

MRS. KEMPTON: Mr. Hudson . . .

HUDSON: My name's Hudson.

TREVOR: Not Trevor?

HUDSON: Wallace.

MRS. KEMPTON: I'm waiting for an explanation.

JANE: We put him up to it.

MRS. LAWRENCE: Why?

JANE: You wanted Sarah to have a lover. (*To Mrs. Kempton*) You wanted me to be engaged. You both went on about it. We invented Trevor. Both of him. Then you wanted to meet him. Well, you only come up to London one day a year; it didn't seem too difficult. We couldn't know Sarah's parents would arrive on the same day.

MRS. KEMPTON: But why?

HUDSON: You've moved the furniture. That wardrobe belongs in the bedroom.

MR. LAWRENCE: I thought you said you never used your key.

MRS. KEMPTON: The bedroom?

SARAH: We don't have two bed-sitters. We have a bedroom and a living-room. The two couches push together.

TREVOR: Sarah, love, enough's enough.

SARAH: No, I'm sick of it. I'm sick of deception.

JANE: Sarah!

SARAH: I told you. I'm sick of deception (*To Mrs. Lawrence*) Jane and I live together, mother.

MRS. LAWRENCE: Yes, dear. You share a flat.

SARAH: We *live* together. There isn't any Trevor. There's just Jane and me.

MRS. KEMPTON: Yes, my dear; you told us. It was a stupid deception, but I'm sure your mother won't hold it against you.

SARAH: Jane, *tell* them.

JANE: Sarah means . . .

MRS. KEMPTON: We know what she means, dear. You and Sarah share a flat.

SARAH: Yes.

MRS. KEMPTON: Naturally you're friends . . .

SARAH: Yes, we are friends.

MRS. KEMPTON: (*Riding on*) It would be very inconvenient if you weren't. And since you're both a little shy. (*To Mrs. Lawrence*) Jane's always been shy.

MRS. LAWRENCE: And Sarah. Ridiculous. Pathologically.

MRS. KEMPTON: Naturally you're embarrassed that you've neither of you found a young man yet.

SARAH: Yet!

MRS. KEMPTON: I blame myself. (*To Mrs. Lawrence*) I push Jane too much; I know I do. I had to push her when she was a girl, or she'd never have done anything.

MRS. LAWRENCE: They're a more puritanical generation now. We were very frank about sex in the thirties. Perhaps I'm too outspoken. I brought Sarah up on D. H. Lawrence.

MRS. KEMPTON: Did you?

MRS. LAWRENCE: So she invents a lover. Then she's ashamed.

MRS. KEMPTON: (*To Jane*) You chose to play a joke on us, my dear. Not in very good taste, but perhaps we deserved it.

SARAH: Daddy . . . Mr. Kempton . . . do you believe this?

MR. KEMPTON: (*Fiddling with shoes*) I can't get these shoes on.

MR. LAWRENCE: They're mine.

MR. KEMPTON: Oh, is that it?

(*He gives the shoes to Mr. Lawrence who puts them on*)

MRS. KEMPTON: I don't know whose particular friend Trevor happens to be.

SARAH: Nobody's. I picked him up in a pub.

MRS. LAWRENCE: There! You do go out and meet people.

SARAH: We never go out.

MRS. KEMPTON: Anyway, now you have met Trevor, I'm sure you'll get to know each other better.

TREVOR: My name's not Trevor.

MRS. LAWRENCE: You must bring him down to Bury St. Edmunds, Sarah.

MRS. KEMPTON: Jane, you must bring him to Torquay. (*To Mr. Kempton*) Harold!

(*Mr. Kempton gets up*)

SARAH: (*To Jane*) They're going. They won't listen.

MR. KEMPTON: (*Kisses Jane awkwardly*) Bye, Janey . . . Er . . .

JANE: Yes?

(*Mr. Kempton looks at his wife, then decides against what he was going to say*)

MR. KEMPTON: I'll just get my shoes.

(*He goes into Jane's room, and puts them on*)

MRS. KEMPTON: Will you get the coats, Jane?

SARAH: You don't want to know, then?

MRS. KEMPTON: Goodbye, Sarah my dear. I'm so glad to have met you at last. (*To Mrs. Lawrence*) Goodbye, Mrs. Lawrence. (*To Mr. Lawrence*) Goodbye.

(*She and Jane go out into the hall, and Jane gets the coats. Mr. Kempton joins them*)

SARAH: Mother, you've been open-minded all your life. You've boasted of it. Your mind was so open, I used to fall in.

JANE: Here are your coats.

(*Mrs. Kempton kisses her. Jane entirely unresponding*)

MRS. KEMPTON: Goodbye, my dear. You know we always enjoy seeing you.

MR. KEMPTON: Bye, Janey.

JANE: Goodbye, daddy.

(*Mrs. Kempton opens the front door*)

MRS. KEMPTON. You're such a silent sulky little thing when you're upset. (*She goes, her husband following*)

JANE: Goodbye, mother. (*She remains, gazing after them, then closes the door, while*)

SARAH: I was cruel to you just now, do you remember, when we were arguing about Trevor? I was nervous and hating everything and I lost my temper. I mocked you for being unshockable and always understanding people. I said you ought to understand yourself for a start. And you took it, mother. You shamed me by seeing what I saw, and accepting it. Now accept me.

MRS. LAWRENCE: You overdramatize, dear. (*To Jane, who returns*) Doesn't she overdramatize, Jane?

SARAH: Do you remember that Easter I didn't come home? Jane didn't go home either. We'd just met—picked each other up in the National Gallery.

MRS. LAWRENCE: You met in the National Gallery?

TREVOR: In front of a picture of small children . . .

SARAH: We went away together that Easter, to a cottage near Cirencester. It was down a long muddy path. We took Jane's haversack, full of healthfood bread and salami and tins of stuffed vine leaves and a pheasant in jelly, and we bought eggs and cream from the farm. We'd lie in bed very late, and one of us would wash up while the other chopped wood for the fire, and we'd go for long walks in the afternoons. It was warm spring weather. We walked through wild anemones and celandines, through primroses and bluebells and wild garlic. We hunted for fossils in the quarry. At night, we'd pile the fire high with wood and sit in front of it, playing bezique and eating chocolates.

MRS. LAWRENCE: We must get our coats.

SARAH: I'm trying to explain something to you, mother. I'm trying to get you to feel something.

MRS. LAWRENCE: Sarah dear, you don't need to explain to me about friendship. It's very rare. (*To Jane*) Real friends are very rare, and much to be prized. (*To Mr. Lawrence*) Harold!

MR. LAWRENCE: (*Stands*) Off now, are we?

SARAH: I wasn't talking about friendship, mother. I was talking about love. We made love.

MRS. LAWRENCE: Goodbye, Jane. I'm so happy to have met you. (*Into the hall*) Goodbye, Trevor.

MR. LAWRENCE: (*Following*) Bye, Trevor . . . Jane . . .

TREVOR: Goodbye.

(*Sarah follows her parents into the hall, as they get their coats*)

MRS. LAWRENCE: If you do want to bring Trevor down for a weekend, dear, we've plenty of room.

SARAH: Mother, if you're going to understand people, you'd better begin with what they do in bed.

MRS. LAWRENCE: (*Going*) Sarah, Sarah, *how* you exaggerate!

MR. LAWRENCE: (*Going*) I like Trevor, you know. And your mother's quite come round to him.

(*They have gone. Sarah returns to the others*)

SARAH: Oh . . . .

(*Here follows the most extreme obscenity that the Lord Chamberlain will permit a British actress to say on the stage in the late nineteen sixties: whatever the word is, she says it several times*)

TREVOR: What did you expect?

(*Sarah sits in the armchair*)

JANE: Shut up, Trevor.

HUDSON: If I understand you . . .

JANE: Yes?

HUDSON: There will be no question of . . . young men.

JANE: What?

HUDSON: In the flat. Visiting. (*Looks at Trevor*) Well, they may visit. From time to time. But . . .

JANE: We have few visitors and no young men. You understand correctly.

HUDSON: Ah! I let all my properties to single women, you see. I like to feel . . . in a fatherly relationship. One can do very little to discourage young men, but I dislike them visiting.

TREVOR: What *can* you do?

HUDSON: If there are too many, I don't renew the lease.

JANE: We shall be model tenants in that respect.

HUDSON: Thank you. You won't object if I . . . ring up from time to time? I shan't speak, of course.

JANE: We'll know who it is.

HUDSON: I'll say farewell then. Miss Kempton . . . Miss Lawrence . . . Mr. . . . .

TREVOR: Goodbye.

HUDSON: (*Going*) I'll show myself out.

TREVOR: (*As he goes*) You know your way.

(*Hudson goes. Pause*)

TREVOR: It's just us, then. (*Pause.*) Not my most successful performance, I'm afraid.

JANE: It wasn't your fault.

TREVOR: They do know, you know.

JANE: Yes.

TREVOR: It's just that they don't want to put it into words.

JANE: No.

TREVOR: You can't blame them.

JANE: I don't.

TREVOR: Sarah does.

JANE: Yes.

(*Pause*)

TREVOR: I don't suppose you'll be taking me down to Bury St Edmunds. Or Torquay.

JANE: No.

TREVOR: Thank you for the five pounds.

JANE: You earned it.

TREVOR: No, really, I enjoyed . . . Well, I did enjoy it actually. (*Pause*) Shall I see you around? (*Pause*) If you were going out for a drink or anything. I'm often in that pub when I'm not working.

SARAH: We don't go out, Trevor. We hardly ever go out. (*Pause*)

TREVOR: My name's not Trevor. (*He goes into the hall, and out by the front door*)

(*They listen to it close. Jane sits on the arm of Sarah's chair, and puts a hand round Sarah's shoulders. Lights fade leaving a single box of hard, white light, then all front lights fade, leaving them backlit. They are sitting very still. Hold it*)

The curtain falls

Adrienne Kennedy

FUNNYHOUSE
OF A NEGRO

Adrienne Kennedy

When *Cities in Bezique,* described as "two journeys of the mind in the form of theatre pieces," was presented at the New York Shakespeare Festival's Public Theatre in 1969, the director of the evening, Gerald Freedman, thoughtfully provided a program note about the gifted young author: "Adrienne Kennedy is a poet of the theatre. She does not deal in story, character and event as a playwright. She deals in image, metaphor, essence and layers of consciousness." On that same occasion, Richard Watts, Jr. wrote in the *New York Post,* "Adrienne Kennedy is a remarkable writer who may well possess a touch of genius . . . what is certain is that she can weave a spell of phantasmagoric intensity and delve into the hidden recesses of a tormented mind with the rarest sort of somber dramatic imagination."

In *Funnyhouse of a Negro,* as with much of her work, Miss Kennedy is concerned with the problems of identity and self-knowledge and her writing is pervaded by powerful imagery and an intense desire to unite a self fragmented by opposing forces. Originally produced in 1964 at the East End Theatre, New York, the play, in its newly polished form, appears in an anthology for the first time in *The Best Short Plays 1970.*

Adrienne Kennedy was born in Pittsburgh, Pennsylvania, in 1931, and grew up in Cleveland, Ohio. She attended Ohio State University but found the social structure there so opposed to Negroes that she did little academic work and started writing at twenty. Her plays include: *The Owl Answers; A Lesson in Dead Language; A Rat's Mass; A Beast's Story;* and *Funnyhouse of a Negro* for which she received a 1964 Off-Broadway "Obie" Award. Additionally, she has written two novels, as well as stories and poems.

In His Own Write, Miss Kennedy's stage adaptation (in collaboration with John Lennon and Victor Spinetti) of Lennon's book was presented by Britain's National Theatre Company at The Old Vic, London, in 1968.

A recent recipient of a Rockefeller Foundation grant and an award from the New England Theatre Conference, Miss

Kennedy acknowledges Edward Albee as a major influence in her career. In 1962, she joined his playwriting workshop at Circle in the Square where she received, and continues to receive, much encouragement from him.

Author's Note

The play takes place in Sarah's room; all the scenes are segments of Sarah's mental processes as she sits in this room in the West Nineties, in New York City, mental processes that lead to her suicide by hanging.

Characters:

SARAH, *the Negro*
QUEEN VICTORIA, *one of herselves*
DUCHESS OF HAPSBURG, *one of herselves*
PATRICE LUMUMBA, *one of herselves*
JESUS, *one of herselves*
THE MOTHER
LANDLADY, *the funnyhouse lady*
RAYMOND, *the funnyhouse man*

Beginning:

Before the closed curtain A Woman dressed in a white nightgown walks across the stage carrying before her a bald head. She moves as one in a trance and is mumbling something inaudible to herself. She appears faceless, wearing a yellow whitish mask over her face with no apparent eyes. Her hair is wild, straight and black and falls to her waist. As she moves holding her hands before her she gives the effect of one in a dream. She crosses the stage from right to left. Before she has barely vanished, the curtain opens. It is a white satin curtain of a cheap material and a ghastly white, a material that brings to mind the interior of a cheap casket. Parts of it are frayed and look as if it has been gnawed by rats.

The Scene:

Two Women are sitting in what appears to be a Queen's Chamber. It is set in the middle of the stage in a strong white light while the rest of the stage is in unnatural blackness. The quality of the white light is unreal and

ugly. The Queen's Chamber consists of a dark monu-
mental bed resembling an ebony tomb, a low, dark chan-
delier with candles and wine colored walls. Flying about
are great black ravens. Queen Victoria is standing before
her bed holding a small mirror in her hand. On the white
pillow of her bed is a dark, indistinguishable object. The
Duchess of Hapsburg is standing at the foot of the bed.
Her back is to us as is the Queen's. Throughout the entire
scene, they do not move. Both Women are dressed in royal
gowns of white, a white similar to the white of the cur-
tain, the material cheap satin. Their headpieces are white
and of a net that falls over their faces. From beneath both
their headpieces spring a headful of wild kinky hair. Al-
though in this scene we do not see their faces, I will
describe them now. They look exactly alike and will
wear masks or be made up to appear a whitish yellow.
It is an alabaster face, the skin drawn tightly over the
high cheekbones, great dark eyes that seem gouged out
of the head, a high forehead, a full red mouth and a
head of frizzy hair. If the characters do not wear a mask
then the faces must be highly powdered and possess a
hard expressionless quality and a stillness as in the face of
death.
    We hear knocking.

VICTORIA: (*Listening*) It is my father. He is arriving
again for the night.
(*The Duchess makes no reply*)
VICTORIA: He comes through the jungle to find me. He
never tires of his journey.
DUCHESS: How dare he enter the castle, he who is the
darkest of them all, the darkest one. My mother looked like a
white woman, hair as straight as any white woman's. And at
least I am yellow, but he is black, the blackest one of them all.

I hoped he was dead. Yet he still comes through the jungle to find me.

(*The knocking is louder*)

VICTORIA: (*Looking at herself in the mirror*) He never tires of the journey, does he, Duchess?

DUCHESS: How dare he enter the castle of Queen Victoria Regina, Monarch of England. It is because of him that my mother died! The wild black beast put his hands on her. She died.

VICTORIA: Why does he keep returning? He keeps returning forever, coming back ever and keeps coming back forever. He is my father.

DUCHESS: He is a black Negro.

VICTORIA: He is my father. I am tied to the black Negro. He came when I was a child in the south, before I was born he haunted my conception, diseased my birth.

DUCHESS: Killed my mother.

VICTORIA: My mother was the light. She was the lightest one. She looked like a white woman.

DUCHESS: We are tied to him, unless of course, he should die.

VICTORIA: But he is dead.

DUCHESS: And he keeps returning.

(*The intensity of the knocking increases. The lights go out in the Queen's Chamber. The woman in the white nightgown, carrying the bald head, reappears. This time we hear her speak*)

MOTHER: Black man, black man, I never should have let a black man put his hands on me. The wild black beast raped me and now my skull is shining.

(*She disappears. The light focuses on a single white square wall that is suspended and stands apart at the left of the stage. Sarah, the Negro, steps slowly through the wall, stands still before it. On first glance she might be a young person, but at a closer look, the impression of an*

ancient character is given. The most noticeable aspect of
her looks is her wild kinky hair, part of which is missing
and which she carries in her hand. With the other hand,
she clutches a hangman's rope. She is dressed in black)

SARAH: Part of the time I live with Raymond, part of
the time with God, Maximilian and Albert Saxe-Coburg. I
live in my room. It is a small room on the top floor of a brownstone in the West Nineties in New York, a room filled with
my dark old volumes, a narrow bed and on the wall old photographs of castles and monarchs of England. It is also Victoria's
chamber. Queen Victoria Regina's. Partly because it is con-
sumed by a gigantic plaster statue of Queen Victoria who is my
idol and partly for other reasons; three steps that I contrived
out of boards lead to the statue which I have placed opposite
the door as I enter the room. It is a sitting figure, a replica of
one in London, and a thing of astonishing whiteness. I found
it in a dusty shop on Morningside Heights. Raymond says it
is a thing of terror, possessing the quality of nightmares, suggesting large and probable deaths. And of course he is right.
When I am the Duchess of Hapsburg I sit opposite Victoria
in my headpiece and we talk. The other time I wear the dress
of a student, dark clothes and dark stockings. Victoria always
wants me to tell her of whiteness. She wants me to tell her of a
royal world where everything and everyone is white and there
are no unfortunate black ones. For as we of royal blood know,
black is evil and has been from the beginning. Even before my
mother's hair started to fall out. Before she was raped by a
wild black beast. Black was evil.

. . . As for myself I long to become even a more pallid Negro
than I am now; pallid like Negroes on the covers of American
Negro magazines; soulless, educated and irreligious. I want to
possess no moral value, particularly value as to my being. I
want not to be. I ask nothing except anonymity.

. . . I am an English major, as my mother was when she
went to school in Atlanta. My father majored in social work.
I am graduated from a city college and have occasional work in

libraries, but mostly spend my days preoccupied with the placement and geometric position of words on paper. I write poetry
filling white page after white page with imitations of Edith
Sitwell. It is my dream to live in rooms with European antiques
and my Queen Victoria, photographs of Roman ruins, walls of
books, a piano, oriental carpets and to eat my meals on a white
glass table. I will visit my friends' apartments which will con-
tain books, photographs of Roman ruins, pianos and oriental
carpets. My friends will be white.

. . . I need them as an embankment to keep me from reflecting too much upon the fact that I am a Negro. For, like all
educated Negroes—out of life and death essential—I find it
necessary to maintain a stark fortress against recognition of
myself. My white friends like myself will be shrewd, intellectual and anxious for death. Anyone's death. I will mistrust
them, as I do myself, waver in their opinion of me, as I waver in
the opinion of myself. But if I had not wavered in my opinion
of myself, then my hair would never have fallen out. And if
my hair hadn't fallen out, I wouldn't have bludgeoned my
father's head with an ebony mask.

. . . In appearance I am good looking in a boring way; no
glaring Negroid features, medium nose, medium mouth and
pale yellow skin. My one defect is that I have a head of frizzy
hair, unmistakably Negro kinky hair; and it is indistinguishable.
I would like to lie and say I love Raymond. But I do not. He
is a poet and is Jewish. He is very interested in Negroes.

(*As Sarah continues, the following characters—Queen
Victoria, Duchess of Hapsburg, Jesus, Patrice Lumumba
—come through the wall, disappearing off into varying
directions in the darkened night of the stage.*

*Jesus is a hunchback, yellow-skinned dwarf, dressed in
white rags and sandals.*

*Patrice Lumumba is a black man. His head appears to
be split in two with blood and tissue in eyes. He carries
an ebony mask*)

SARAH: The rooms are my rooms; a Hapsburg chamber,

a chamber in a Victorian castle, the hotel where I killed my father, the jungle. These are the places myselves exist in. I know no places. That is I cannot believe in places. To believe in places is to know hope and to know the emotion of hope is to know beauty. It links us across a horizon and connects us to the world. I find there are no places only my *funnyhouse*. Streets are rooms, cities are rooms, eternal rooms. I try to create a space for myselves in cities—New York, the midwest, a southern town—but it becomes a lie. I try to give myselves a logical relationship but that too is a lie. For relationships was one of my last religions. I clung loyally to the lie of relationships, again and again seeking to establish a connection between my characters. Jesus is Victoria's son. Mother loved my father before her hair fell out. A loving relationship exists between myself and Queen Victoria, a love between myself and Jesus but they are lies.

(*A white light focuses upon a suspended stairway at the right side of the stage. At the foot of the stairway stands the Landlady. She is a tall, thin, white woman dressed in a black hat with red and appears to be talking to someone in a suggested open doorway in a corridor of a rooming house. She laughs like a mad character in a funnyhouse throughout her speech*)

LANDLADY: (*Who is looking up the stairway*) Ever since her father hung himself in a Harlem hotel when Patrice Lumumba was murdered she hides herself in her room. Each night she repeats, "He keeps returning. How dare he enter the castle walls, he who is the darkest of them all, the darkest one. My mother looked like a white woman, hair as straight as any white woman's. And I am yellow but he, he is black, the blackest one of them all. I hoped he was dead. Yet he still comes through the jungle."

I tell her, "Sarah, honey, the man hung himself. It's not your blame." But, no, she stares at me: "No, Mrs. Conrad, he did not hang himself, that is only the way they understand it, they do, but the truth is that I bludgeoned his head with an ebony skull that he carries about with him. Wherever he goes, he carries out black masks and heads."

She's suffering so till her hair has fallen out. But then she did always hide herself in that room with the walls of books and her statue. I always did know she thought she was somebody else, a Queen or something, somebody else.

Blackout

Scene:

Funnyman's place.

This must be suggested as being above Sarah's room and is etched in with a prop of blinds and a bed. Behind the blinds are mirrors and when the blinds are opened and closed by Raymond this is revealed. Raymond turns out to be the funnyman of the funnyhouse. He is tall, white and ghostly thin and dressed in a black shirt and black trousers in attire suggesting an artist. Throughout his dialogue he laughs. The Duchess of Hapsburg is partially disrobed and their attitudes imply physical intimacy—he is standing and she is sitting before him clinging to his leg. During the scene Raymond keeps opening and closing the blinds. His face has black sores on it and he is wearing a black hat. Throughout the scene he strikes her as in affection when he speaks to her.

DUCHESS: (*Carrying a red paper bag*) My father is arriving and what am I to do?

(*Raymond walks about, opening the blinds and laughing*)

FUNNYMAN: He is arriving from Africa, is he not?

DUCHESS: Yes, yes, he is arriving from Africa.

FUNNYMAN: I always knew your father was African.

DUCHESS: He is an African who lives in the jungle. He is an African who has always lived in the jungle. Yes, he is a nigger who is an African who is a missionary teacher and is now dedicating his life to the erection of a Christian mission in the middle of the jungle. He is a black man.

FUNNYMAN: He is a black man who shot himself when they murdered Patrice Lumumba.

DUCHESS: (*Goes on wildly*) Yes, my father is a black man who went to Africa years ago as a missionary teacher, got mixed up in politics, was revealed and is now devoting his foolish life to the erection of a Christian misson in the middle of the jungle in one of those newly freed countries. Hide me! (*Clinging to his knees*) Hide me here so the nigger will not find me.

FUNNYMAN: (*Laughing*) Your father is in the jungle dedicating his life to the erection of a Christian mission.

DUCHESS: Hide me here so the jungle will not find me. Hide me.

FUNNYMAN: Isn't it cruel of you?

DUCHESS: Hide me from the jungle.

FUNNYMAN: Isn't it cruel?

DUCHESS: No, no.

FUNNYMAN: Isn't it cruel of you?

DUCHESS: No.

(*She screams and opens her red paper bag and draws from it her fallen hair. It is a great mass of dark wild hair. She holds it up to him. He appears not to understand. He stares at it*)

DUCHESS: It is my hair. (*He continues to stare at her*) When I awakened this morning it had fallen out, not all of it but a mass from the crown of my head that lay on the center of my pillow. I arose and in the greyish winter morning light of my room I stood staring at my hair, dazed by my sleeplessness, still shaken by nightmares of my mother. Was it true, yes, it was my hair. In the mirror I saw that, although my hair remained on both sides, clearly on the crown and at my temples my scalp was bare.

(*She removes her black crown and shows him the top of her head*)

FUNNYMAN: (*Staring at her*) Why would your hair fall out? Is it because you are cruel? How could a black father haunt you so?

DUCHESS: He haunted my very conception. He was a wild black beast who raped my mother.

FUNNYMAN: (*Laughing*) He is a black Negro.

DUCHESS: Ever since I can remember he's been in a nigger pose of agony. He is the wilderness. He speaks niggerly groveling about wanting to touch me with his black hand.

FUNNYMAN: How tormented and cruel you are.

DUCHESS: (*Not comprehending*) Yes, yes, the man's dark, very dark skinned. He is the darkest, my father is the darkest, my mother is the lightest. I am between. But my father is the darkest. My father is a nigger who drives me to misery. Any time spent with him evolves itself into suffering. He is a black man and the wilderness.

FUNNYMAN: How tormented and cruel you are.

DUCHESS: He is a nigger.

FUNNYMAN: And your mother, where is she?

DUCHESS: She is in the asylum. In the asylum, bald. Her father was a white man. And she is in the asylum.

(*He takes her in his arms. She responds wildly*)

Blackout

(*The knocking is heard. As it continues, a figure appears in the darkness, a large dark faceless man carrying a mask in his hand*)

MAN: It begins with the disaster of my hair. I awaken. My hair has fallen out, not all of it, but a mass from the crown of my head that lies on the center of my white pillow. I arise and in the greyish winter morning light of my room I stand staring at my hair, dazed by sleeplessness, still shaken by night-mares of my mother. Is it true? Yes. It is my hair. In the mirror I see that although my hair remains on both sides, clearly on the crown and at my temples my scalp is bare. And in the sleep I had been visited by my bald crazy mother who comes to me crying, calling me to her bedside. She lies on the bed watching the strands of her own hair fall out. Her hair fell out after she married and she spent her days lying on the bed watching the strands fall from her scalp, covering the bedspread until she was bald and admitted to the hospital. Black man, black man, my mother says I never should have let a black man put his hands on me. She comes to me, her bald skull shining. Black diseases, Sarah, she says. Black diseases! I run. She follows me, her bald skull shining. That is the beginning.

(*The Mother crosses briefly before him carrying her bald head*)

Blackout

Scene:

Queen's Chamber.

Queen Victoria acts out the following scene in panto-mime: she awakens and discovers her hair has fallen. It is on her pillow. She rises and stands at the side of the bed with her back toward us staring at hair. Her hair is in a small pile on the bed and in a small pile on the floor. Sev-eral other small piles of hair are scattered about her and her white gown is covered with fallen out hair.

The Duchess of Hapsburg enters the room, comes around, standing behind the Queen, and they stare at the hair. Victoria picks up a mirror. The Duchess then picks up a mirror and looks at her own hair. She opens the red paper bag that she is carrying and takes out her hair, attempting to place it back on her head (for unlike Vic-toria, she does not wear her headpiece now).

Blackout

(*The unidentified man returns out of the darkness and speaks. He carries the mask*)

MAN: I am a nigger of two generations. I am Patrice Lumumba. I am a nigger of two generations. I am the black shadow that haunted my mother's conception. I belong to the generation born at the turn of the century and the generation born before the depression. At present I reside in New York City in a brownstone in the West Nineties. I am an English major at a city college. My nigger father majored in social work, so did my mother. I am a student and have occasional work in libraries. But mostly I spent my vile days preoccupied with the placement and geometric position of words on paper. I write poetry filling white page after white page with imitations of Sitwell. It is my vile dream to live in rooms with European antiques and my statue of Queen Victoria, photographs of Roman ruins, walls of books, a piano and oriental carpets and to eat my meals on a white glass table. It is also my nigger dream for my friends to eat their meals on white glass tables and to live in rooms with European antiques, photographs of Roman ruins, pianos and oriental carpets. My friends will be white. I need them as an embankment to keep me from reflecting too much upon the fact that I am Patrice Lumumba who haunted my mother's conception. They are necessary for me to maintain recognition against myself. My white friends, like myself, will be shrewd intellectuals and anxious for death. *Anyone's* death! I will despise them as I do myself. For if I did not despise myself then my hair would not have fallen and if my hair had not fallen then I would not have bludgeoned my father's face with the ebony mask.

(*A light remains on him. Before him, a bald head is dropped on a wire; someone screams*)

SARAH: I always dreamed of a day when my mother

would smile at me. My father . . . his mother wanted him to be Christ. From the beginning in the lamp of their dark room she said, "I want you to be Jesus, to walk in Genesis and save the race. You must return to Africa, find revelation in the midst of golden savannas, nim and white frankopenny trees, white stallions roaming under a blue sky. You must walk with a white dove and heal the race, heal the misery, take us off the cross." She stared at him anguished in the kerosene light . . . at dawn he watched her rise, kill a hen for him to eat at breakfast, then go to work down at the big house till dusk, till she died. His father told him the race was no damn good. He hated his father and adored his mother. His mother didn't want him to marry my mother and sent a dead chicken to the wedding. "I *don't* want you marrying that child," she wrote, "she's not good enough for you. I want you to go to Africa." When they first married they lived in New York. Then they went to Africa where my mother fell out of love with my father. She didn't want him to save the black race and spent her days combing her hair. She would not let him touch her in their wedding bed and called him *black*. He is black of skin with dark eyes and a great dark square brow. Then in Africa he started to drink and came home drunk one night and raped my mother. The child from the union is me. I clung to my mother. Long after she went to the asylum I wove long dreams of her beauty, her straight hair and fair skin and grey eyes, so identical to mine. How it anguished him. I turned from him, nailing him on the cross, he said, dragging him through grass and nailing him on a cross until he bled. He pleaded with me to help him find Genesis, search for Genesis in the midst of golden savannas, nim and white frankopenny trees and white stallions roaming under a blue sky, help him search for the white doves. He wanted the black man to make a pure statement; he wanted the black man to rise from colonialism. But I sat in the room with my mother, sat by her bedside and helped her comb her straight black hair and wove long dreams of her beauty. She had long since begun to curse the place and spoke of herself trapped in *blackness*. She preferred the company of night owls. Only at night did she rise, walking in the garden among the trees with the owls. When I spoke to her she saw I was a black man's child and she preferred speaking to owls. Nights my father came from his school in the village struggling to embrace me. But I fled and hid under my mother's bed while she screamed of remorse. Her hair was falling badly and after a while we had to return to this country.

. . . He tried to hang himself once. After my mother went to the asylum he had hallucinations: his mother threw a dead chicken at him, his father laughed and said the race was no damn good, my mother appeared in her nightgown screaming she had trapped herself in blackness. No white doves flew. He had left Africa and was again in New York. He lived in Harlem and no white doves flew. "Sarah, Sarah," he would say to me, "the soldiers are coming and they are placing a cross high on a tree and are dragging me through the grass and nailing me upon the cross. My blood is gushing. I wanted to live in Genesis in the midst of golden savannas, nim and white franko-penny trees and white stallions roaming under a blue sky. I wanted to walk with a white dove. I wanted to be a Christian. Now I am Judas. I betrayed my mother. I sent your mother to the asylum. I created a yellow child who hates me." And he tried to hang himself in a Harlem hotel.

(A bald head is dropped on a string. We hear laughing)

Blackout

Scene:

> *The Duchess of Hapsburg's place which is a chandeliered ballroom with snow falling, a black and white marble floor; a bench decorated with white flowers. All of this should be made of obviously fake materials as they would be in a funnyhouse. The Duchess of Hapsburg is wearing*

her white dress and the white headpiece with her kinky hair springing out from under it.

Jesus enters the room which is at first dark, then suddenly brilliant. He starts to cry out at the Duchess, who is seated on the bench under the chandelier. He pulls his own hair from the red paper bag holding it up for the Duchess to see.

JESUS: My hair.
(*The Duchess does not speak; Jesus again screams*)
JESUS: My hair! (*He holds the hair up, waiting for a reaction from the Duchess*)
DUCHESS: (*Oblivious*) I have something I must show you. (*She goes quickly to shutters and darkens the room, returns, standing before Jesus. She then slowly removes her headpiece and from under it takes a mass of her hair*)
DUCHESS: When I awakened I found it fallen out, not all of it but a mass that lay on my white pillow. I could see, although my hair hung down at the sides, clearly on my white scalp it was missing.
(*Her baldness is identical to Jesus's*)

Blackout

The lights come back up. They are both sitting on the bench examining each other's hair, running it through their fingers, then slowly the Duchess disappears behind the shutters and returns with a long red comb. She sits on the bench next to Jesus and starts to comb her remaining hair over her baldness. This is done slowly. Jesus then takes the comb and proceeds to do the same to the Duchess of Hapsburg's hair. After they finish, they place the Duchess's headpiece back on and we can see the strands of their hair falling to the floor. Jesus then lies down across the bench while the Duchess paces back and forth. The knocking does not cease.

They speak in unison as the Duchess walks about and Jesus lies on the bench in the falling snow, staring at the ceiling.

DUCHESS AND JESUS: (*Their hair is falling more now; they are both hideous*) My father isn't going to let us alone. (*Knocking*) Our father isn't going to let us alone. Our father is the darkest of us all. My mother was the fairest, I am in between, but my father is the darkest of them all. He is a black man. Our father is the darkest of them all. He is a black man. My father is a dead man.

(*They suddenly look up at each other and scream. The lights focus on their heads and we see that they are totally bald. The knocking continues. The lights go to the staircase and the Landlady*)

LANDLADY: He wrote to her saying he loved her and asked her forgiveness. He begged her to take him off the cross. He had dreamed she would stop them from tormenting him, the one with the chicken and his cursing father. Her mother's hair fell out, the race's hair fell out because he left Africa, he said. He had tried to save them. She must embrace him. He said his existence depended on her embrace. He wrote her from Africa where he is creating his Christian center in the jungle and that is why he came here. I know that he wanted her to return there with him and not desert the race. He came to see her once before he tried to hang himself, appearing in the corridor of my apartment. I had let him in. I found him sitting on a bench in the hallway. He put out his hand to her, tried to take her in his arms, crying out, "Forgiveness, Sarah, is it that you never will forgive me for being black? Sarah, I know you were a child of torment. But forgiveness!" That was before his breakdown. Then, he wrote her and repeated that his mother hoped he would be Christ but he failed. He had married her mother because he could not resist the light. Yet, his mother from the beginning in the kerosene lamp of their dark rooms in Georgia said, "I want you to be Jesus, to walk in Genesis and save the race, return to Africa, find revelation in the black." He went away.

. . . But Easter morning, she got to feeling badly and went into Harlem to see him; the streets were filled with vendors selling lilacs. He had checked out of that hotel. When she arrived back at my brownstone he was here, dressed badly, rather drunk; I had let him in again. He sat on a bench in the dark hallway, put out his hand to her, trying to take her in his arms, crying out, "Forgiveness, Sarah. Forgiveness for my being black, Sarah. I *know* you are a child of torment. I know on dark winter afternoons you sit alone weaving stories of your mother's beauty. But Sarah, answer me, don't turn away, Sarah. *Forgive my blackness!*" She would not answer. He put out his hand to her. She ran past him on the stairs, left him there with his hand out to me, repeating his past, saying his mother hoped he would be Christ. From the beginning in the kerosene lamp of their dark rooms, she said, "Wally, I want you to be Jesus, to walk in Genesis and save the race. You must return to Africa, Wally, find revelation in the midst of golden savannas, nim and white frankopenny trees and white stallions roaming under a blue sky. Wally, you must find the white dove and heal the pain of the race, heal the misery of the black man, Wally, take us off the cross, Wally!" In the kerosene light she stared at me anguished from her old Negro face—but she ran past him leaving him. And now he is dead, she says, now he is *dead*. He left Africa and now Patrice Lumumba is dead.

>   (*Jesus is still in the Duchess of Hapsburg's place. Apparently he has fallen asleep and is just awakening and sits there as if in a trance. He rises, terrified, and speaks*)
>   JESUS: Through my apocalypses and my raging sermons I have tried so to escape him, through God Almighty I have tried to escape being black! (*He then appears to rouse himself from his thoughts and calls*) Duchess, Duchess.

(He looks about for her; there is no answer. He walks slowly back into the semi-darkness and there we see that she is hanging from the chandelier; her bald head suddenly drops to the floor and she falls upon Jesus. He screams)

JESUS: I am going to Africa and kill this black man named Patrice Lumumba. *Why?* Because all my life I believed my Holy Father to be God, but now I know that my father is a black man! I have no fear for whatever I do, I will do in the name of God, I will do in the name of Albert Saxe-Coburg, in the name of Victoria, Queen Victoria Regina, the monarch of England, I will!

Blackout

Scene:

In the jungle, red sun, flying things, wild black grass. The effect of the jungle is that unlike the other scenes, it covers the entire stage. The jungle has overgrown the chambers and all other places with a violence and a dark brightness, a grim yellowness. Jesus is the first to appear in the center of the jungle.

JESUS: I always believed my father to be God!
(Suddenly they all appear in various parts of the jungle —Patrice Lumumba, Queen Victoria, Duchess of Hapsburg—wandering about, speaking at once. Their speeches are mixed and repeated by one another)
"He never tires of the journey, he who is the darkest one, the darkest one of them all. My mother looked like a white woman, hair as straight as any white woman's. I am yellow but he is black, the darkest one of us all. How I hoped he was dead, yet he never tires of the journey. It was because of him that my mother died, because she let a black man put his hands on her.

Why does he keep returning? He keeps returning forever, keeps returning and returning and he is my father. He is a black Negro."

"They told me my Father was God but my father is *black!* He is my father. I am tied to a black Negro. He returned when I lived in the south back in the twenties, when I was a child, he returned. Before I was born at the turn of the century, he haunted my conception, diseased my birth, killed my mother. He killed the light. My mother was the lightest one. I am bound to him unless, of course, he should die."

"But he is dead."

"And he keeps returning. Then he is not dead."

"Then he is not dead."

"Yet, he is dead, but dead he comes knocking at my door."

(*This is repeated several times, finally reaching a loud pitch, with all rushing about. They stop and stand perfectly still. All speaking tensely at various times in a chant*)

"I see him! The black ugly thing is sitting in his hallway, surrounded by his ebony masks, surrounded by the blackness of himself. My mother comes into the room. He is there with his hand out to me, grovelling, saying, 'Forgiveness, Sarah, is it that you will never forgive me for being black?'"

"Forgiveness, Sarah, I know you are a nigger of torment."

"*Why?* Christ would not rape anyone."

"You will never forgive me for being black."

"Wild beast! Why did you rape my mother? Black beast, Christ would not rape anyone!"

"He is in grief from that black anguished face of his. Then at once, the room will grow bright and my mother will come toward me smiling while I stand before his face and bludgeon him with an ebony head!"

"*Forgiveness, Sarah, I know you are a nigger of torment . . .*"

(*Silence. Then they suddenly begin to laugh and shout victoriously. They continue for some minutes, running about laughing and shouting*)

Blackout

Scene:

> *Another wall drops. There is a white plaster statue of Queen Victoria which represents Sarah's room in the brownstone. The room has suggestions of dusty volumes of books and old yellowed walls and appears near the staircase, highly lit and small. The main prop is the statue but a bed could be suggested. The figure of Queen Victoria is a sitting figure, one of astonishing repulsive whiteness.*
>
> *We hear the knocking. The lights come on quickly. Sarah is hanging by the hangman's rope in her room.*
>
> *The lights come up on the laughing Landlady. And at the same time remain on the hanging figure of Sarah.*

LANDLADY: The poor bitch has hung herself!

(*Raymond appears from his room at the commotion*)

LANDLADY: The poor bitch has hung herself . . .

RAYMOND: (*Observing her hanging figure*) She was a funny little liar.

LANDLADY: Her father hung himself in a Harlem hotel when Patrice Lumumba died.

RAYMOND: Her father never hung himself in a Harlem hotel when Patrice Lumumba was murdered. I know the man! He is a doctor, married to a white whore. He lives in the city in rooms with European antiques, photographs of Roman ruins, walls of books and oriental carpets. Her father is a nigger who eats his meals on a white glass table.

End

William Saroyan
THE NEW PLAY

William Saroyan

William Saroyan, one of the Twentieth Century's most eminent (and influential) American authors, was born of Armenian parentage in Fresno, California, on August 31, 1908. He began working as a newsboy at eight, became a telegraph boy at thirteen; at fifteen he left public school and pruned vines alongside Japanese and Mexican laborers in his uncle's vineyards in Northern California.

Largely self-educated, the avant-courier of mid-century drama and the irrepressible *enfant terrible* of the literary milieu, he was determined to write at an early age: "I began to send stuff to magazines soon after I paid thirteen dollars for an Underwood typewriter in Fresno in 1921 when I was just thirteen. . . ." As personal curriculum, he digested most of the works of the great writers during his moments away from his menial chores. At the age of seventeen, he settled in San Francisco where he began to write in earnest. According to legend, the youthful author wrote a story a day in an unheated room, bundled up in woolens; the floor around him littered with discarded or torn sheets of manuscript.

When his first short story, *The Daring Young Man on the Flying Trapeze,* was published in Whit Burnett's *Story* magazine in 1934, it created something of a sensation among the literati. That same year, the story was issued in book form and from then on, his success was assured.

Two of Mr. Saroyan's prime characteristics as a writer have continued undiminishingly through the years: his intense love affair with life and his remarkably prolific output. The author of almost fifty books and plays, he has declared, "I wrote in a hurry for many reasons, the best of which was the simplest and I think the truest: I was impatient to reach the best in me, and I knew there was no short cut, I had to work to reach it." And reach it he did with several major novels (*The Human Comedy; My Name is Aram; Boys and Girls Together*), scores of short stories (some of which have become modern "classics"), essays, poems, and above all, his plays.

William Saroyan met with almost instant success in the

theatre. After making a striking debut as a dramatist with *My Heart's in the Highlands* (1939), he scored doubly with *The Time of Your Life,* the first play ever to win both the New York Drama Critics Circle Award and the Pulitzer Prize, 1939–40. (Saroyan rejected the Pulitzer Prize, nonetheless the award stood.) According to the author, the much-lauded comedy-drama was written in six days and as he later told a newspaper interviewer, "After all, the stuff in the play has been gathering ever since I was old enough to see and feel life. This isn't a 'play' in the accepted sense of the word. I think there isn't enough 'play' in plays. Something ought to be done about it, and that's what I'm trying to do. You might just as well call plays 'mechanical,' because that's what most of them have become."

The Time of Your Life was anything but "mechanical." It fostered a new style of drama, one that undeniably has influenced many of our latter-day avant-gardists. At its 1939 Broadway premiere, *The New York Times'* drama critic, Brooks Atkinson, hailed the play as "something worth cherishing—a prose poem in ragtime with a humorous and lovable point of view." Critic Richard Watts, Jr., in his columnar paean, wrote, "Mr. Saroyan's new play is a delight and joy. A sort of cosmic vaudeville show, formless, plotless and shamelessly rambling, it is a helter-skelter mixture of humor, sentimentalism, philosophy and melodrama, and one of the most enchanting theatrical works imaginable." Precisely thirty years later, The Repertory Theatre of Lincoln Center opened its season with an enormously successful revival of the play. In covering the 1969 presentation for *Variety,* Hobe Morrison termed it "an enjoyable, satisfying and astonishingly timely play now. *The Time of Your Life* is a provocative item in American theatre history and, it's good to see, still a vastly entertaining show."

Since 1939, Mr. Saroyan's dramatic works have been performed on stages in every conceivable corner of the world. To list some in non-chronological order: *The Beautiful People; My Heart's in the Highlands; Love's Old Sweet Song; Across the Board On Tomorrow Morning; Hello Out There; Sweeney*

*in the Trees; Get Away Old Man; Jim Dandy; The Violin
Messiah; Once Around the Block; Talking to You;* and *The
Cave Dwellers.*

No stranger to direction, Mr. Saroyan also has staged a
number of his own plays including: *The Time of Your Life*
(with co-director Eddie Dowling; Booth Theatre, New York,
1939); *The Beautiful People* (Lyceum Theatre, New York,
1941); *Across the Board On Tomorrow Morning* (Belasco
Theatre, New York, 1942); and *Sam, the Highest Jumper of
Them All* (Theatre Royal, Stratford, England, 1960).

Versatile as well as prolific, he also wrote the scenario for
a popular ballet, *The Great American Goof,* initially presented
in 1940 by the Ballet Theatre and, in 1943, won Hollywood's
Academy Award for his original screenplay, *The Human
Comedy.*

Recently, Mr. Saroyan published two collections of his
works: *I Used to Believe I Had Forever Now I'm Not So Sure*
(fifty-two short pieces written over a period of thirty-four years);
and a volume of *The Dogs, or The Paris Comedy, and Two
Other Plays: Chris Sick, or Happy New Year Anyway; and
Making Money, Nineteen Other Very Short Plays.* In June, 1970,
came *Days of Life and Death and Escape to the Moon,* "a very
personal journal" that records the author's thoughts on an assortment of subjects.

Two segments from Mr. Saroyan's *Anybody and Any-
body Else,* an evening of theatre comprised of thirty-one separate
episodes, appeared in *The Best Short Plays 1968—Dentist and
Patient/Husband and Wife.* The publication of *The New Play*
in this annual marks its first appearance anywhere in print.

In self-imposed exile from the Broadway scene that initially brought him international renown as a dramatist, Mr.
Saroyan now divides his time between Fresno, San Francisco
and Paris. In a recent letter to this editor, he related, "I quit
Broadway during the three years I was a private in the Army.
I chose to stay quit, for a lot of reasons. In the meantime, I
tend to write one new play a year, and quite a few short plays,

and fresh variations of the central idea of the theatre in general: *Anybody and Anybody Else* gives a hint of this.

"Yes, I am writing a new play and a new novel, although the novel might not strictly speaking be the right word—a book. I find doing two at the same time makes for variety—the play refreshes the other, and vice versa."

An ardent disciple (as well as an acclaimed master) of the modern short play, Mr. Saroyan concludes, "The short story has flourished with incredible variety and freshness and successful experiment—it is an easy form to read. Well, I think the short play can be made just as effective and popular as the short story. *All* writers have written in the short play form, some unintentionally of course. When it *is* intentional, the writer is simply thinking in terms of the theatre in one or another of its contemporary forms. And he is thinking of people acting out character parts in front of an audience."

Characters:

THE WRITER
THE SECRETARY
THE COCKTAIL PARTY MAN FOLGER
THE COCKTAIL PARTY WOMAN DINAH
THE MAN WHO LOOKS LIKE ABE LINCOLN IN THE MOVIES
THE PROFESSOR OF EVERYTHING

Scene: A stage.

Scene One

A plain Secretary brings the Writer a cup of coffee. He takes a sip. She lights his cigarette. He takes a puff, inhales deeply, holds the smoke in a long time, then lets it out.

SECRETARY: We were at work on The New Play.

WRITER: We were?

SECRETARY: Yes. We had come to where you were bored, and would not go on.

WRITER: When was *that?*

SECRETARY: Yesterday afternoon at half past two. You went to sleep. Shall we proceed?

WRITER: Well, first, let's think about it a minute.

SECRETARY: Yes, sir.

WRITER: Suppose I *do* write The New Play? Act One—flawless. Act Two—more flawless than Act One. Act Three—so flawless that half the people in the theatre *die.* They don't applaud. They just die. (*He reflects*)

SECRETARY: Yes, sir.

WRITER: Is *that* what I want to do? Kill the people? Coffee and cigarettes in the morning for me, ideas all day long, money and fame? So much fame that it *bores* me. Fame *past* people—fame among little birds, animals, weeds, because I *am* a writer. (*Pause*) Is that what I want to do? Kill the people?

SECRETARY: Oh, no, sir! Not *you!*

WRITER: (*Quickly*) Just a minute. They can't live *forever.* Why *shouldn't* I kill them—with laughter? The other writers are killing them with lies, aren't they? Take the books one by one and look at them. All lies!

SECRETARY: Surely not—Shakespeare.

WRITER: Worst of all. Everybody rants and raves. And then somebody runs and somebody stabs somebody.

SECRETARY: Mr. Panafran, I came to work yesterday morning, and I'm sure it's going to take a day or two to get acquainted, but I'm afraid I can't stay on if you're the kind of writer who considers everybody else in the world dishonest. My father, Mr. Panafran . . .

WRITER: My name is *not* Panafran.

SECRETARY: Franapan . . .

WRITER: It's not Franapan, either.

SECRETARY: My father—was a gentleman.

WRITER: No doubt, and I'm a writer. Now, what the devil do you think you're doing to the *morning?* Here I am, ready to decide how to kill the people, and you've gone to work and half-stopped me from being wonderful, haven't you?

SECRETARY: (*Professionally*) No, sir. I *am* writing everything down.

WRITER: Thank you. Let's just let *me* be the lunatic around here. Let's just let *you* be a good secretary. Got that?

SECRETARY: Yes, sir.

WRITER: (*Smiles, steps forward*) As a matter of fact, I don't *work* with a secretary. (*He notices the Secretary writing quickly*) Oh, no, that wasn't for *you.*

SECRETARY: I'm sorry, sir, I've written it all down. After all, I *am* a secretary and a very good one.

WRITER: Well, I'm glad, but I don't *have* a secretary.

SECRETARY: I'm writing it all down, Mr. Panafran.

WRITER: Go ahead, write it. I never had a secretary in my life.

SECRETARY: A secretary keeps *all* of a writer's ideas. She doesn't let him throw them away.

WRITER: I don't *have* any ideas.

SECRETARY: Oh, *yes,* you do.

WRITER: None at all.

SECRETARY: What's all this in the book, then?

WRITER: Morning. Coffee and cigarettes. If only I could be pompous. Existentialism. Do you know what that is?

SECRETARY: Yes, sir.

WRITER: The devil you do.

SECRETARY: It's a philosophy.

WRITER: Just like that! What was it *before* somebody said existentialism?

SECRETARY: Well, I'm sure you can't say anything against —food inspection!

WRITER: I can't say anything against *morning,* that's all.

SECRETARY: What can you say against afternoon?

WRITER: It's not the *same* as morning.

SECRETARY: Evening?

WRITER: By evening you're confused.

SECRETARY: Night?

WRITER: At night it's *all* lost. You've got to wait until morning again.

SECRETARY: Shall we go back to The New Play?

WRITER: I *wrote* it. I produced it. I directed it. It was *all* very exciting. It bored me. I throw away in ten minutes greater plays than the ones that win the prizes. I've thrown this one away, too.

SECRETARY: Shall we begin again, then?

WRITER: Well, it's still morning, if that's what you mean.

SECRETARY: Mr. Panafran, for six years I worked for Jerry, and Jerry always said a movie is only as good as its villain.

WRITER: What else did he say?

SECRETARY: He said a money-making movie must have a girl who, no matter how much clothes she wears, looks naked.

WRITER: Did he say anything about how a *naked* girl should look?

SECRETARY: No, he didn't, but my six years with Jerry were the happiest of my life because I knew I was contributing something.

WRITER: Why aren't you working for him now, then?

SECRETARY: (*Softly*) Jerry died.

WRITER: The only decent thing he ever did, most likely.

SECRETARY: (*Outraged*) Mr. Panafran, if you're going to make fun of everybody I hold dear, I don't have to keep this job. I can't imagine what kind of a writer you are, anyway. In your opinion everybody's an idiot. The fact that my father was a gentleman makes no difference. You haven't the slightest respect for story construction, plot atmosphere, or character development. I was told at the employment agency that the job was with a writer, and having had six years with Jerry, I felt I was qualified, but I don't think you want a secretary, Mr. Panafran, I think you want a—jezebel.

WRITER: I never had a secretary in my life. (*Pause*) What *killed* Jerry?

SECRETARY: Heart attack. He was only thirty-three, poor boy.

WRITER: And he always said a movie is only as good as its villain?

SECRETARY: Yes.

WRITER: What a pompous bore!

SECRETARY: He's *dead,* Mr. Panafran. You can't speak that way of the dead.

WRITER: Why? Did he change when he died? He wasn't dead when he kept saying a movie is only as good as its villain, was he? He was alive *then,* if that's what you want to call it, wasn't he?

SECRETARY: Don't you dare imply that Jerry wasn't alive when he was alive. He *was*. He was the most alive young man that ever lived. You don't want a secretary, you want a . . .

WRITER: No, I don't. (*Smiles*) That's all for today.

SECRETARY: But you haven't even gotten *started!*

WRITER: It's all right.

SECRETARY: You haven't even got a villain. You've *got* to have a villain.

WRITER: Not me.

SECRETARY: Well, I'll type out these crazy remarks, then. (*He goes in one direction. She goes in the other*)

Scene Two

The writer is stretched out on a plain black sofa in the middle of the stage. The secretary is seated on a plain chair at the head of the sofa, notebook and pencil ready.

SECRETARY: (*To herself*) I should have married Jerry. Instead, *he's* dead, and I work for a writer who sleeps. If I had been his wife, Jerry wouldn't have died.

WRITER: What would he have done?

SECRETARY: I thought you were asleep.

WRITER: I was. If you had married him, what would he have done?

SECRETARY: He would have lived.

WRITER: Where?

SECRETARY: Office and home. (*Pause*) I'm ready if you are. (*She waits a moment, then looks at his face closely*) Fast asleep again. Jerry *never* slept. Jerry created. He created and created. Stories, plots, characters, heroes, villains, themes, suspense, excitement . . .

WRITER: (*Jumps off the sofa*) Write this down. I've waited forty-eight years for this. I knew I'd get it if I waited long enough.

SECRETARY: (*Following him around*) Yes, sir.

WRITER: (*Softly*) And.

SECRETARY: (*Writes*) And.

WRITER: At last! (*He lies down on the sofa again*)

SECRETARY: And *what*? (*Pause*) Fast asleep again. He waited forty-eight years for *And*. I don't believe he's a writer at all. Perhaps he's a bank robber. (*Pause*) No. They're all so sleepless. At least they were in Jerry's movies. And courteous, too, many of them. (*She looks at the Writer*) Perhaps he's the brains of an underworld gang that deals in counterfeit money. (*Pause*) I should have married Jerry.

WRITER: And.

SECRETARY: I should have had a son.

WRITER: And.

SECRETARY: A daughter.

WRITER: And.

SECRETARY: A personal maid.

WRITER: And.

SECRETARY: A gardener.

WRITER: And.

SECRETARY: Everything! (*Pause*) I never know when he's awake or asleep. I can't tell the difference, almost. When he jumps up I always think he's awake, but he isn't, he's still asleep, with his eyes wide open. (*Louder, directly to the Writer*) And *everything!* (*Pause*) God knows where he is now. Jerry was always awake, and I always knew what he was thinking. Success. *More* success. If he hadn't died he would now be thirty-six years old. If I had married him the year before he died, our son would now be three years old. Oh, what a handsome boy. Lost forever. There will never be another Jerry.

WRITER: How fortunate for us.

SECRETARY: Don't you dare speak that way of the dead! (*No answer*)

SECRETARY: Oh, wake up, please.

WRITER: What for?

SECRETARY: It's half past two in the afternoon—time to work.

WRITER: This *is* my work.

SECRETARY: Your work is to write.

WRITER: I *am* writing.

SECRETARY: (*Comically shrill*) It's got no plot!

WRITER: You refer, I presume, to Jerry's life.

SECRETARY: I refer to your play.

(*No answer. She looks at his face intently again*)

SECRETARY: Gone again. You never know when he's likely to arrive, or liable to go. I must ask the employment agency to send me to a mystery writer. *They're* dependable. Somebody kills somebody. It could be any one of six or seven people. Now it seems it's this one, now it seems it's that. I'm comfortable near a mystery. Not like here, where I never know whether I'm going or coming. (*She looks at him intently and with impatience*) Oh, wake up, please. (*Pause*) Well, then, if you won't wake up, I think the least you can do is tell me about your childhood. I'm sure you were desperately unhappy.

WRITER: Happy.

SECRETARY: *You?*

WRITER: All the time.

SECRETARY: (*Mocking*) I'll *bet* you were.

WRITER: I *was.*

SECRETARY: *Prove* it.

WRITER: I'm happy *now*. What *better* proof is there?

SECRETARY: Well, I'm *not* happy now. As I child I was *bitterly* unhappy. My father was a gentleman, but my mother wasn't a lady. She humiliated my father. She humiliated *me.* I was terribly ashamed of her. (*Pause*) May I stretch out on the sofa, too?

WRITER: Of course not.

SECRETARY: I can speak more freely if I'm stretched out.

WRITER: It's not necessary to speak more freely.

SECRETARY: It might do me good. I've always wanted to tell somebody about my mother, but I haven't had anybody to speak to freely.

WRITER: Keep it that way. I'm rather fond of your mother, and I'd rather she weren't belittled.

SECRETARY: Oh, please wake up, and let's get to work. At this rate, you'll never get the play written.

(*No answer. She looks at his face intently again*)

SECRETARY: One word. All afternoon. *And*. Great writer!

WRITER: Slob.

SECRETARY: Well, I'll say one thing, awake or asleep, you don't leave yourself out of your unkind thoughts for the human race.

WRITER: I *am* the human race.

SECRETARY: (*Quickly and comically*) You are *not*!

WRITER: Am.

SECRETARY: Aren't.

WRITER: Who is, then?

SECRETARY: The multitudes.

WRITER: Where'd you get that from?

SECRETARY: Everybody knows the millions and millions of people all over the world, far away, are the human race. (*Again no answer*) Asleep again. This is the lonesomest job I've ever had.

WRITER: There's no profession like it.

SECRETARY: He's fast asleep, of course.

WRITER: You bet your sweet life he is.

SECRETARY: Well, I've got *And* written down, but what good is it?

WRITER: (*Gets up, yawns, steps forward, smiles*) The government is dirty.

SECRETARY: I refuse to write that down.

WRITER: I am speaking of the government of ancient Greece.

SECRETARY: You are *not* speaking of the government of ancient Greece.

WRITER: Rome?

SECRETARY: Not Rome, either.

WRITER: Sicily?

SECRETARY: No.

WRITER: Venice?

SECRETARY: No.

WRITER: Carthage? Corsica? Macedonia?

SECRETARY: No, *none* of them.

WRITER: Oh. In that case, the government *isn't* dirty.

SECRETARY: What government?

WRITER: The government of ancient Greece of course.

SECRETARY: But a moment ago you said the government of ancient Greece *was* dirty.

WRITER: That was a moment ago. The past is past, isn't it?

SECRETARY: Is the government going to be the villain, then?

WRITER: What villain?

SECRETARY: In the play?

WRITER: There is no play. That's the end of today's work.

SECRETARY: The *end* of it? It didn't *start*. You were asleep.

WRITER: Even so.

(*He goes. She goes*)

Scene Three

The Writer has gotten out of his old clothes into rather neat ones. He is standing at a mobile bar-table, pouring gin into a large jar with ice cubes in it.

A Man named Folger arrives; the Writer hands him a drink.

FOLGER: I was thinking on my way here of the variety. (*He sips his drink*) Thank you. Very good.

(*A smiling, handsomely-dressed Woman of middle-years named Dinah comes to the table, receives a drink*)

FOLGER: Dinah, you're smiling about something. What is it?

DINAH: I haven't the faintest idea. Surely nothing new. (*She sips, as the Writer watches. She sips again and again*)

DINAH: Perfect, and, if I may, I believe I would like to cry. (*She smiles bigger than ever*) Comfort me, dear Mr. Folger.

FOLGER: If you persist in smiling, I shall only continue to distrust you.

DINAH: Comfort me. (*She smiles*)

FOLGER: What's your sorrow?

DINAH: It's untellable. (*She smiles*)

WRITER: (*Steps forward*) You've listened to us before. We can speak of anything. Listen. (*He turns to Dinah and Folger who are speaking, unheard. He calls out in a strong voice*) Apricots.

FOLGER: The tree is slender, with slender branches.

DINAH: A green soft leaf that stays cool even on the hottest day.

FOLGER: I especially like the freckles on the apricot itself.

DINAH: Yes. They're like freckles on a faceless cheek. New, smooth, tender, and the color of the sun.

FOLGER: Not at all, the color of the sun is orange.

DINAH: How absurd.

WRITER: (*Calls out again*) Pennies.

DINAH: I saw a most astonishing play night before last. There they were, intoxicated with a theory of meaning when suddenly . . .

FOLGER: You needn't tell me. I was there, too.

(*The Writer listens closely, watching*)

DINAH: I have always found the theory of meaning attractive only to children, but of course I mean only the very littlest of them.

FOLGER: My two small sons were quite good at knowing what they meant.

DINAH: What *did* they mean?

FOLGER: Why, nothing, of course, but while they were little they seemed to *believe* they meant a great deal, perhaps everything.

WRITER: No, no—*pennies.*

DINAH: The point of the play for me, whatever it may have been for you, dear Fred, was the unexpected behavior of the statesman from—oh, where *was* he from?

FOLGER: Gibraltar.

DINAH: Yes. When he was asked the metric weight of Gibraltar by the statesman from—now, where was *he* from?

FOLGER: Mesopotamia.

DINAH: Yes. And the man from Gibraltar misunderstood the question, believed he was being heckled, and began to bellow like a bull.

FOLGER: I was *there,* dear lady.

DINAH: I haven't said you weren't.

FOLGER: By which I mean the play bored me.

DINAH: You didn't go to be *amused,* I trust.

FOLGER: I went, to sleep. And wasn't permitted to.

DINAH: Whereupon the man from Iceland . . .

FOLGER: Gibraltar.

DINAH: I speak *now* of the man from Iceland.

FOLGER: I had no idea there *was* a man from Iceland.

DINAH: There *was.* Whereupon this man—performed I may say by a friend of my youngest daughter, and quite badly, too—I've asked her not to see him again . . .

WRITER: *Pennies.*

DINAH: . . . brought a handful of small coins out of his pocket, opened his hand, and held it out to the man bellowing like a bull. But this gentle Icelandic gesture of sympathy was *also* misunderstood by the bull—you know who I mean.

FOLGER: I haven't the faintest idea. I didn't like the play.

DINAH: Why must you imagine you *might* have? Who, then, in a rage, removed one of the small coins out of the hand of the man from Iceland, held it up for all to see, put it in his mouth and *swallowed* it. The bull did, I mean.

FOLGER: I don't remember that, and in any case I see nothing especially useful in your having brought it up.

DINAH: I am speaking of a number of people in a play,

but apparently *you* are thinking of another kind of people, perhaps people like ourselves, who do *not* do, or say, fanciful things.

FOLGER: I am drinking. I am thinking of no one, certainly not ourselves.

WRITER: (*To the audience*) The coin the man swallowed may have been a penny, but the fact remains that we can speak of anything. (*He turns back to Dinah and Folger*)

DINAH: The man from Gibraltar was a scoundrel of course, but I *like* them. I simply can't stand the righteous in plays. They're certainly difficult enough *out* of them.

WRITER: (*Returns to Dinah and Folger, fills their glasses*) Have you wept? Has he comforted you?

DINAH: (*Sips*) I've cried my eyes out, and he most certainly *hasn't* comforted me. I know of no one more heartless, and I love him for it.

FOLGER: You are much too attractive for *me* to understand. I have considerable difficulty with *plain* women. Pray, *when* did you weep?

DINAH: Oh, poor silly, I arrived in tears and I've been blubbering ever since. Every time we meet I become increasingly aware of the depth and enormity of your wisdom from the steadfast manner in which you hold out for arithmetic or nothing.

FOLGER: I am drinking, and the working of numbers is no part of it.

(*The Writer pours more gin into the glass jar. The Man who looks like Abe Lincoln in the movies comes in, his hands clasped behind him, his head bent down in thought. The Writer studies him doubtfully. Abe looks up, nods to Dinah, glances at Folger, takes the offered glass*)

WRITER: We were speaking of the winter flight of birds. (*He sips, to encourage Abe to sip, but Abe doesn't*)

DINAH: I was saying how clever I think it is of them to go so swiftly—directly to where they go. (*She sips, but Abe doesn't*) Excepting perhaps *owls*, which tend to *stay*, and for that, I suppose, are considered wise. (*She glances quickly for help, smiling enormously at the awkwardness*)

FOLGER: As a matter of fact, we were *not* speaking of the winter flight of birds. We were drinking. (*He sips*)

(*Abe nods, sips, and Dinah sighs with relief*)

DINAH: (*Of Folger*) His brilliance appalls me. He knows *so much* for a man who knows nothing. Absolutely nothing. (*She turns quickly to Abe, smiles, nods. Abe nods in return*)

ABE: Madam. At one time it fell to my lot to consider the right of right, which put me to walking. Barefoot, late at night, in a strange, spacious place, almost forgotten. As I walked, it further fell to my lot to consider the right of *wrong,* and the night wore on, the feet grew cold, and somebody thought, perhaps myself rather than another, although I cannot ever be sure, "There is no end." And so I went to my bed and knew I was dead.

DINAH: (*Sweetly, courteously*) Your life is so interesting. Please don't stop.

ABE: Not *my* life. I *am* rehearsing from a play I hope will some day be written. My name is Bob, although for years I've been called Abe. Not a writer myself, I must hope some day to meet one.

WRITER: Look no further.

ABE: Have I the honor of speaking to a Lincoln writer?

WRITER: The pleasure, I hope, of speaking to a *writer,* presently disengaged from the awful intensity of it, happily come upon evening and friends, but alas, *not* a Lincoln writer.

ABE: I seek a Lincoln writer.

WRITER: You will surely find him. In the meantime, you were rehearsing. You had come to, "There is no end." Quite a place for pause.

ABE: I spoke as Abe, not as actor. How shall I speak now?

DINAH: (*Cheerfully, sweetly*) As Abe *or* actor. It's surely six of one and half a dozen of another.

FOLGER: (*Quickly*) Six of one, half a dozen of another? I must remember that. A state of *sameness,* differently put.

DINAH: Mister Folger is devoted to numbers.

FOLGER: Actually I despise them, but they persist in my thoughts. I am counting everything.

ABE: I worked in a theatre in a small town somewhere once, and on the same bill was a man who called himself The Mathematical Marvel.

FOLGER: Was he *cheerful?*

ABE: No, but he *was* swift.

FOLGER: It's not the same.

ABE: And he had an excellent sense of timing.

FOLGER: As a matter of fact, it's impossible *not* to count everything. How many worlds are there?

ABE: One.

FOLGER: (*To Abe*) Wrong.

WRITER: (*Begins to pour for everybody*) Right or wrong, it's nice to speak about it in the evening. (*To Abe*) I must say I was quite impressed by the manner in which you delivered the speech about the barefoot walking. (*To Dinah*) Surely by now your sorrows have lost a little of their edge. (*To Folger, pouring*) Of course you must count everything.

FOLGER: And *dis*count nothing.

DINAH: Oh, how *glib.*

FOLGER: I wish to drink and be humbly stupid.

DINAH: Alas, for you, then, poor Fred. Even your wishes are ambitious and pompous. *Be* stupid like the rest of us, neither humbly nor proudly so. Stupidly stupid, as it were, and therefore charmingly so, however unintentionally. It is evening and cool at last. The apricots are on the trees. The freckles are on the apricots.

FOLGER: I thank you for your swift, soothing speech. Speak on.

DINAH: I would rather listen to Honest Abe.

ABE: I am a teller of jokes, they say.

DINAH: Oh, then, tell one, please.

ABE: As a boy in Illinois I came one day upon a pig stuck in the mud, and a little old woman of the hills who asked me to get the pig out of the mud for her.

DINAH: And *did* you?

WRITER: (*Steps forward*) Even in the evening, even in the time of friends and idle talk, art will not rest, and drunk with sorrow or joy or nothing at all, will nag a little more, say this, say that, and wait. And soon Friends One, Two and Three have had their fill of drink and talk and one another, and march off to where they were, to what they were *about*.

(*Dinah, Folger and Abe go. The Secretary comes in*)

WRITER: What are *you* doing here at this hour of the evening?

SECRETARY: I am here on *my own* time.

(*The writer pours a drink for her, holds it out*)

SECRETARY: I don't drink. I was at home with my mother who was dressing—that's *all* she does—and I said so. She in turn said I might take a hint from her, so I did.

WRITER: You dressed?

SECRETARY: Yes, and as Jerry's dead, and I *am* employed *here* . . .

WRITER: (*Mumbling*) I never had a secretary in my life.

SECRETARY: It seemed to me that you might just wish—

WRITER: (*Mumbling*) No such thing.

SECRETARY: And if that happened to be so, as it would have been if it were Jerry of a pleasant summer evening, then here suddenly I would be, waiting and ready. The New Play, Mr. Panafran, and I can only say it's part of my work.

WRITER: No thanks. The play's no good.

SECRETARY: Mr. Panafran, I wish you'd let the world judge your work.

WRITER: Is that from Jerry, too?

SECRETARY: *Of course*. All that I am today, I . . .

WRITER: Don't say it.

SECRETARY: Jerry said, "If fifty million people like my work, I owe it to them to give them more of it."

WRITER: What did he owe his mother, poor woman?

SECRETARY: He was kind to her. A telephone call on the first of every month. And a carbon copy of every one of his scenarios. Write your play, Mr. Panafran, and let the world judge it.

WRITER: Only *I* can judge what I write.

SECRETARY: I thought you were on your way to something quite exciting when you jumped up from the sofa this afternoon and asked me to write down *And*. It's right here in shorthand. *And*. Shall we go to work, then?

WRITER: I hope you won't mind, no.

(*He goes. She goes*)

Scene Four

The Professor of Everything has a pitch pipe for a singing lesson with the Writer.

PROFESSOR: Now, please. (*He blows pitch pipe, then demonstrates in a falsetto voice, on a rising scale*) Ah ha ha ha ha, ah ha ha ha ha, ah ha ha ha ha. Ready?

WRITER: (*Hung-over but courteous*) Not quite.

PROFESSOR: (*He blows pitch pipe again*) One, two, three —*now*. Ah ha ha ha ha?

(*The Writer does not join him. He stops, blows pitch pipe again*)

PROFESSOR: You must put your heart *into* it. Ah ha ha ha ha? Ready?

WRITER: What do you say we forget it for the time being?

PROFESSOR: Forget *singing*? Oh, no, we *must* sing! Ah ha ha ha ha? (*Blows pitch pipe quickly*) One, two, three—now.

WRITER: Listen, Professor . . .

PROFESSOR: No, no no, no no—ah ha ha ha ha?

WRITER: I'm not up to a lesson this morning.

PROFESSOR: But I am charging for one hour and I have worked only three minutes.

WRITER: That's O.K., Professor. Send me your bill and I'll send you a check.

PROFESSOR: I have been to Milano, you understand, and I have *memoirs* to write. Perhaps you would be kind enough to give me writing lessons in exchange for singing lessons.

WRITER: Yes, we might be able to do that, but not this morning.

PROFESSOR: But this is *Friday*—singing lesson day. A lesson every Friday, but not *once* have you *sung!*

WRITER: Professor, I don't really want to sing.

PROFESSOR: Oh, no, don't say that!

WRITER: It's just that when you came to the door six weeks ago and asked if I wanted to take singing lessons, three dollars an hour, I *was* impressed by your appearance . . .

PROFESSOR: A teacher of singing must present a good appearance at the front door.

WRITER: Yes, of course. And by the manner in which you held out the pitch pipe.

PROFESSOR: (*He holds it out dynamically*) Like *this*. It is the only way to do it.

WRITER: Yes, and being a writer, one who is interested in everybody—a *little* interested, at any rate—and always happy to have an excuse by which to postpone going to work, I accepted your offer.

PROFESSOR: And paid me in cash!—for which I thank you. Although from the first, you have not permitted me to give you one *full* lesson.

WRITER: Professor, the fact is *you* can't sing.

PROFESSOR: I am a *teacher*.

WRITER: And you can't *teach,* either. I know you need the work, and . . .

PROFESSOR: The money.

WRITER: Yes.

PROFESSOR: But I *have* been to Milano.

WRITER: Of course.

PROFESSOR: It is true that I did not *enter* the Opera House, but I *saw* it. (*Pause, then suddeny and shyly*) You do not have the cash this time?

WRITER: I spent all my cash last night.

PROFESSOR: Ah ha ha ha ha. What did you buy?

WRITER: Dinner for an actress.

PROFESSOR: Oh, they *must* eat! And *only* where the food is expensive. I know. I've *taught* acting.

WRITER: I can write a check of course.

PROFESSOR: No no. No need. I have . . . (*He examines contents of his pocket: nothing*)

WRITER: Well, *do* you have, Professor?

PROFESSOR: Today? No—I do not.

WRITER: Your other students, they will pay you something?

PROFESSOR: Today?

WRITER: Listen, Professor, if you don't *have* any other students, if you're hungry, go in there . . . (*He points*) . . . and get yourself some food.

(*The Professor goes, and soon a refrigerator door is heard to open. The Writer sits, writing a check. The refrigerator door is shut—he jumps. It is opened. He jumps. It is shut, and so on. The Professor returns eating a sandwich*)

PROFESSOR: (*Bites into sandwich*) If you do not feel well enough for a singing lesson, perhaps another lesson—spelling, conversation . . .

WRITER: I don't think so, Professor. (*Tears check out of the book, holds it out*) I'm sorry I've got no cash.

PROFESSOR: (*Takes another bite of the sandwich, accepts the check, looks at it*) Ten dollars? The lesson is *three* dollars.

WRITER: I'm paying a little in advance.

PROFESSOR: A lesson in Latin?

WRITER: I don't think so.

PROFESSOR: Painting?

WRITER: You teach painting, too?

PROFESSOR: Perhaps you have heard of Picasso.

WRITER: Yes, I have.

PROFESSOR: I have not only *heard* of Picasso, I have seen one of his paintings. In a magazine. In this kind of painting you want for the woman extra eyes, and for the man sorrow in the face.

WRITER: O.K., there's three dollars in the check for the painting lesson.

PROFESSOR: Composition?

WRITER: *Musical* composition?

PROFESSOR: Yes, of course. I teach only things of culture.

WRITER: O.K., Professor, I'll take a crack at that, too, then.

PROFESSOR: You have heard of Mozart?

WRITER: Yes, Professor, I've heard of Mozart.

PROFESSOR: I have heard this concerto for piano on the radio. In this kind of musical composition you need a man like Mozart, who has sadness, but sometimes also joy. Shershall forty-four, Longo thirty-three.

WRITER: I got it. There's three dollars in the check for that, too. Thank you very much, Professor.

PROFESSOR: Not yet. We have still left over one dollar.

WRITER: I don't think we need to bother about the dollar, Professor.

PROFESSOR: I have a suitable subject and lesson for a dollar, too—but *not* cultural.

WRITER: Well, O.K., if you say so.

PROFESSOR: You have seen a small boy flying a kite?

WRITER: Yes, I have.

PROFESSOR: To make a kite, then. You make a cross of two sticks. You put paper in front of the cross. You tie string around the cross. You paste paper around the string, and let the paste dry. Then more string in front, which you tie together where it crosses, and then you tie one end of a whole *ball* of string to the place where the string crosses, and you *fly* the kite.

WRITER: I got it.

PROFESSOR: But don't forget to tie on the tail, too.

WRITER: O.K. Thanks a lot, Professor.

PROFESSOR: I come again next Friday?

WRITER: Yes, I think so.

PROFESSOR: What subject shall we teach and learn?

WRITER: Oh, I leave that to you, Professor. I find that you teach one thing as well as another.

PROFESSOR: Thank you. I *try*.

WRITER: I don't really want any of the food in the kitchen, so on your way out, please help yourself.

PROFESSOR: Are you sure?

WRITER: All I want is the jar of instant coffee.

PROFESSOR: You are my best student. You learn very quickly.

(*The Professor goes. The Writer shakes his head, trying to clear it. Kitchen sounds are heard. The Professor returns with a small jar*)

PROFESSOR: What is *this?*

WRITER: Caviar.

PROFESSOR: I have never eaten caviar.

WRITER: There isn't very much in the jar, but there's enough for a *taste*.

PROFESSOR: You are sure you do not want it?

WRITER: No, Professor, I don't want it.

PROFESSOR: Thank you.

(*He goes. The refrigerator door is opened and shut several times again, and the Professor is heard "ah ha ha ha ha-ing" happily. The Secretary comes in, removes her coat, puts her handbag on the table, glances at the Writer, goes straight to the kitchen, comes back*)

SECRETARY: Who *is* that man out there?

WRITER: My teacher.

SECRETARY: He's taking everything out of the kitchen.

PROFESSOR: (*Returns with two big bags full of stuff*) I didn't take the instant coffee.

WRITER: Would you like a cup *now?*

PROFESSOR: Oh, no, it makes me nervous. Thank you. (*He bows to the Writer*) Good morning. (*The Writer nods. The Professor bows to the Secretary*) Good morning. (*The Secretary bows. The Professor goes*)

SECRETARY: Well, who *is* he, for heaven's sake?

WRITER: I've been taking singing lessons from him.

SECRETARY: *Singing?*

WRITER: Yes, singing.

SECRETARY: I can't understand what kind of a writer you are. (*Pause*) Well, I'd better get your coffee and cigarettes.

(*She hurries off. The Writer sits with his head in his hands a moment, then stands slowly, shakes his head three times quickly, pulls himself up to his full height, smiles and steps forward*)

WRITER: A writer is free to write *anything*. He is free to do so in any culture, any nation, and any time. He is free. He is very nearly the only man left who *is* free.

(*The Secretary returns with a cup of coffee and a package of cigarettes*)

SECRETARY: (*Swiftly*) Can't you at least give me time to get my book?

WRITER: (*Takes the cup of coffee*) Thank you. (*He takes a sip, half-enthusiastically*)

SECRETARY: (*With book and pencil*) Time to work, now.

WRITER: (*Smiles*) O.K.

SECRETARY: The New Play.

WRITER: O.K., The New Play.

SECRETARY: Are you still drunk?

WRITER: No doubt, but the morning's wearing away, and so I'll stretch out now and go back to sleep. (*He smiles, steps forward*)

SECRETARY: (*Stands quickly; angry*) But you haven't done any work!

(*The Writer goes. The Secretary stands, watching*)

Scene Five

*There is an enormous screen of a television set on the
stage. The Secretary is lying on the sofa. The Writer is
seated at the table behind the sofa. On the table is a deck
of cards. He takes a card off the top, looks at it, puts it
down.*

SECRETARY: My mother wasn't from the South, she was
from the North. All the same, she believed she was irresistible
to all men. My father wasn't from the East, he was from the
West, but in his old clothes he looked a little like a cowboy—
off his horse of course. He hardly ever spoke. My mother hardly
ever stopped. When she wasn't speaking at home, she was
speaking at one or another of the eleven or twelve clubs she
belonged to.

*(She stops. The Writer glances over at her, waits a mo-
ment. The Secretary blows her nose. The Writer gets
up, goes to the big television set, turns on a knob, there
are waves of light, and then Folger appears)*

FOLGER: Spend your money. Buy anything. Drive carefully. Watch out for cancer. Don't be afraid. Take out insurance.
Rent something. Get your hat blocked. Eat potatoes. Read books.
Marry somebody. Don't neglect your teeth. Vote for somebody.
Believe in something. Don't be ashamed to go mad. Go to
church. And now back to our story, *A Man and a Woman,*
brought to you by *Everything.*

*(Folger goes. Abe arrives, stands to one side. Dinah ar-
rives)*

DINAH: So then I said, "Well, why should *I* be the one?"
They said, "Because you're George's wife, and George's name
carries a lot of weight." I said, "Don't tell *me* how much weight
George's name carries. I happen to be an authority on the subject, and I say his name carries no more weight than anybody

else's." So then they said, "That's not so!" George, are you *listening* to me?

(*Abe nods*)

DINAH: So then I said, "Don't tell me what's so, and what isn't so. I *know*. Do it yourselves. I've done more than my share already, and *you* can begin to do a little for a change. Why should I be expected to do everything just because I happen to be married to George? If you really expect matters to improve, you simply must improve them yourselves."

(*Abe turns a little. He is holding a rolled newspaper. He tightens the paper*)

DINAH: So then they said, "It isn't as if we expected you to do anything that you haven't always *insisted* on doing." So I said, "Don't tell me what it isn't as if . . .

(*Abe whacks her on top of the head with the rolled newspaper. She goes right on talking*)

DINAH: I know better than you ever could what it isn't as if, and what it *is* as if, and I tell you it's as if you expect me to do everything, as always, and I want you to know once and for all I *won't*." So then nobody said anything, and finally I said, "All right, I'll do it again."

(*The Writer goes and stands very near the television set*)

DINAH: Well, then every one of them rushed up to embrace me, hypocrites that they are.

(*The Writer reaches for the knob. Dinah looks down at him*)

DINAH: Don't you dare turn me off! This is very important.

(*The Writer remains fixed but doesn't turn the dial. Dinah continues to speak*)

DINAH: I said, "If you are so sure that only I can do *all* of the work, then of course I *will* try my best to do it, although I will absolutely not tolerate chocolate frosting on *all* of the cakes any more. We've had enough of chocolate frosting.

(*Abe, standing behind Dinah winds up and is about to whack her again when he decides not to*)

DINAH: There are other kinds of frosting, and I think the sooner we agree to have them the better off we are going to be, and the better off . . . "

(*The Writer turns the knob of the television set, and the screen is instantly dark. He goes back to the table and sits down*)

SECRETARY: As a little girl my mother was terribly spoiled, and so there was always a very cruel streak in her— toward everybody, except any man who happened to be near by, and then she was all cooing sweetness and charm, although to me it was sickening, because it was really so pathetic and silly. She gloried in her figure inside her clothes, and she pitched her voice to what she believed was an exciting and irresistible pitch. She always said her laughter was like pretty little white birds suddenly taking to flight, and it disgusted my father.

WRITER: (*Gets up, goes forward*) Just in case she plans to talk forever, I'm going for a walk. (*He goes*)

SECRETARY: One day when my mother thought she was alone on the front porch, the postman came with two bills for my father, and my mother invited him to stop a moment. Well, my mother *wasn't* alone. I was just around the edge of the porch by the lilac tree, and I saw everything that happened. First, she insisted that he take off his postman's bag, and then she said it was silly for him to wear such a heavy coat on such a hot day, and then she wondered if he wouldn't like to go into the house for a little lemonade. *Well,* I ran around to the back of the house, to find a nice place to hide, and so I was there when they came in, and I'll never forget what happened.

Scene Six

The Writer is stirring a big jar full of gin and ice. There is a potted plant on one side of the stage: a good-looking little tree. On the other is a modern-style bird-cage with a

*couple of small birds in it. The Secretary comes in with
a tray of little things to eat, which she places on the table.
She leans over happily, kisses the Writer on the cheek,
and smiles.*

SECRETARY: Shall I bring in the children to say good
night, or would you rather put them to bed yourself?
WRITER: (*Aside*) What'd she say?
SECRETARY: (*Claps hands*) Wake up. (*The Writer looks
at her, a little befuddled*) They're watching *Annie Oakley* on
T.V., but it's almost over. Immediately afterwards they're to go
straight to bed. I don't like kids wandering around at a party.
All our friends let their kids do that, and you know it's no fun
at all for anybody, least of all the kids. They *like* to be rushed
to bed. I must say I wish you'd wake up. You're still thinking
about the play.
WRITER: Of course I am.
SECRETARY: Well, stop worrying about it. I'm sure it's
your best. Have a nice big drink, and then have another. Everybody else at every party gets drunk in no time at all. I've never
seen *you* drunk. Some of the best writing in the world was
done by men in their fifties. You'll feel much better just as soon
as our friends arrive. You need people a lot more than you
imagine. Everybody senses you feel he's an idiot. It's nothing
you *say*, necessarily. It's something everybody *feels,* though. I
know I do, and I know the children do, too. It's only the little
girl who doesn't. But then of course you really *do* make the
little girl feel grand—*all* the time. She really knows how much
you love *her*—how much more than you love anybody else in
the whole world. It's quite a compliment to a woman, and she
is a woman. Now, I hope you won't fly off the handle, I've
asked Jerry's brother to the party. He wants you to write a story
for a movie. He has an idea. What's wrong with letting him
tell you his idea? If you like it, fine. If not, fine. He wants to
talk business, pure and simple. He needs what you can write,
and you need money. You *will* be nice to him, won't you? I'm

not saying stop writing your *real* writing. I'm saying do a little for money, too. Try not to look scornful when you listen to him. Even if the idea is bad, try to see something in it that's good. Let him feel as if *he* were creating something. People like to feel they're a force behind the making of something good. I know he'll pay you well. Well, perhaps I'd better put the children to bed, after all.

(*She goes. The Writer smiles, steps forward*)

WRITER: The New Play—is this the end of the new play? (*He goes*)

The End

Joe Orton

THE RUFFIAN
ON THE STAIR

Joe Orton

The violent and untimely death of Joe Orton in 1967 left a singular void in the British theatre for as Ronald Bryden commented in *The Observer*, "Orton has established himself as a master-satirist of our national style of gilding the verbal fig-leaf." And although he never, during his lifetime, achieved popular success in the United States, *Variety* reported, "Orton was an important writer. His plays fall somewhere between the conventional and the absurd, delicately balancing rowdy humor and macabre social protest, graced by a sensitive ear for offbeat but often raucously funny dialogue."

Joe Orton was born in Leicester, England, in 1933. He left school at sixteen and two years later enrolled at the Royal Academy of Dramatic Art. His initial play to be staged, *Entertaining Mr. Sloane,* won the London Critics' *Variety* Award as the best play of 1964. It was presented at the Lyceum Theatre, New York, in 1965 and recently was made into a film with Beryl Reid, Harry Andrews, Peter McEnery and Alan Webb.

Loot, a macabre farce and the author's second staged work, brought him additional honors including the London *Evening Standard* Drama Award for the best play of 1966. It later was seen in New York at the Biltmore Theatre (1968).

In 1967, *The Ruffian on the Stair* and *The Erpingham Camp* were performed as a double bill at the Royal Court Theatre (London) under the title *Crimes of Passion*. The same tandem bill was presented on October 26, 1969 at the Off-Broadway Astor Place Theatre. In his coverage of the presentation for *The New York Times,* Clive Barnes characterized *The Ruffian on the Stair* as "possibly his (Orton's) most ambitious work . . . an impressive play. I expect to remember it."

Shortly before his death, Joe Orton completed a new farcical comedy, *What the Butler Saw,* which had its West End premiere in March, 1969 with a company headed by Sir Ralph Richardson and Coral Browne.

The Ruffian on the Stair is published for the first time in the United States in *The Best Short Plays 1970.*

Madam Life's a piece in bloom,
Death goes dogging everywhere:
She's the tenant of the room,
He's the ruffian on the stair.
                    W. E. HENLEY

Characters:

JOYCE
MIKE
WILSON

Scene One

A kitchen-living room with a bedroom alcove. Mike is shaving by the sink. Joyce enters from the bedroom carrying a tray with cups, saucers, egg cup, etc. She puts the tray on to the table.

JOYCE: Have you got an appointment today?

MIKE: Yes. I'm to be at King's Cross station at eleven. I'm meeting a man in the toilet. (*He puts away his shaving materials*)

JOYCE: You always go to such interesting places. Are you taking the van?

MIKE: (*Puts on a made-up bow tie*) No. It's still under repair.

(*Joyce takes the tray to the sink and puts the dishes into a bowl. She pours water on them*)

JOYCE: (*Putting on a pair of rubber gloves*) Where did you go yesterday?

MIKE: I went to Mickey Pierce's. I'd a message to deliver. I had a chat with a man who travels in electrically operated massage machines. He bought me a ham roll. It turns out he's on the run. He didn't say as much in so many words. (*He winks*) But I gathered.

JOYCE: A wanted man?

MIKE: I don't suppose his firm would pay the insurance if they realized his position.

JOYCE: No.

(*She begins to wash the dishes. Mike puts on his coat*)

JOYCE: You lead a more interesting life than I do.

MIKE: Hard, though.

JOYCE: Still, you've kept your looks.

MIKE: Yes. I'm a powerfully attractive figure. I can still cause a flutter in feminine hearts. (*He puts a flower into his buttonhole, and brushes his coat down*)

JOYCE: Have you seen the date?

MIKE: No.

JOYCE: It's our anniversary.

MIKE: As long as that, is it? How time flies.

JOYCE: Two years ago you came to my flat and persuaded me to give up the life I'd been leading.

MIKE: You're better off.

JOYCE: Nobody ever calls me Maddy now.

MIKE: (*Pause*) What?

JOYCE: Nobody calls me Madelein. I used that name for five years. Before that I was Sarah up North somewhere.

MIKE: (*Pause, he frowns*) Have you ever, since I met you, allowed another man to be intimate with you?

JOYCE: No!

MIKE: Good. I'd kill any man who messed with you. Oh, yes. I'd murder him.

(*Silence*)

JOYCE: (*Taking off her rubber gloves*) The papers were on form this morning.

MIKE: Were they? I'm glad people are still reading them.

JOYCE: I see where a man has appeared in court charged with locking his wife in a wardrobe. She tells of her night of terror. (*Pause*) What a way to celebrate your wedding anniversary.

(*Mike picks up his raincoat and folds it across his arm*)

MIKE: I'd do the same. I'd lock you up if you gave me cause for displeasure.

JOYCE: And, in the local paper, I saw there'd been an accident involving a tattooed man. He had a heart, a clenched fist and a rose all on one arm. And the name "Ronny" was on his body in two different places.

MIKE: Was that his name?

JOYCE: No. His name was Frank. A van ran him down. (*Silence*)

MIKE: I'm going now.

JOYCE: Are your boots clean?

MIKE: Yes.

JOYCE: Keep them clean. You may meet important people. You never know.

MIKE: Cheerio.

JOYCE: Give me a kiss. (*He kisses her cheek*) Do I have to remind you now? Two years ago you did it without thinking.

MIKE: I was young then. See you tonight.

(*He exits. Joyce goes into the bedroom, straightens the bed. She pushes Mike's pajamas under the pillow. The doorbell rings. She answers it. Wilson is standing outside*)

WILSON: (*Smiling*) I've come about the room.

JOYCE: I'm afraid there's been a mistake. I've nothing to do with allotting rooms. Make your inquiries elsewhere.

WILSON: I'm not colored. I was brought up in the Home Counties.

JOYCE: That doesn't ring a bell with me, I'm afraid.

WILSON: Is that the room?

JOYCE: That's my room.

WILSON: I couldn't share. What rent are you asking?

JOYCE: I'm not asking any.

WILSON: I don't want charity. I'd pay for my room.

JOYCE: You must've come to the wrong door. I'm sorry you've been troubled.

(*She tries to close the door, but Wilson blocks it with his foot*)

WILSON: Can I come in? I've walked all the way here.

(*Pause. He smiles*)

JOYCE: Just for a minute.

(*She lets him in and closes the door. He sits down*)

JOYCE: I'm so busy. I'm run off my feet today.

WILSON: How about a cup of tea? You usually make one about now.

(*Joyce nods. She goes to the sink but is pulled up sharp*)

JOYCE: How do you know?

WILSON: Oh, I pick up all sorts of useful information in my job.

JOYCE: What's that? (*She pours water from the kettle into the teapot*)

WILSON: I'm a gents' Hairdresser. Qualified. My dad has a business. Just a couple of chairs. I've clipped some notable heads in my time. Mostly professional men. Though we had an amateur street musician in a few weeks ago. We gave him satisfaction, I believe.

(*Joyce puts out two cups and pours his tea*)

WILSON: My brother was in the business too. Until he was involved in an accident. (*He puts sugar into his tea and milk*)

JOYCE: What happened?

WILSON: A van knocked him down.

JOYCE: (*Pours her own tea*) Was he tattooed?

WILSON: You've heard of him?

JOYCE: I've heard of his tattoos.

WILSON: They were unique. He had them done by a well-known artist. (*He takes a biscuit from the barrel*) His funeral was attended by some interesting people. He was a sportsman before his decease. He wore white shorts better than any man I've ever come in contact with. As a matter of fact, strictly off the record, I'm wearing a pair of his white shorts at this moment. They're inconvenient ... because ... (*He *blurts it out)* . . . there's no fly. *(Pause)* He wore them two days before he was killed.

(Joyce looks away in a brief spasm of embarrassment which quickly passes)

WILSON: I wasn't mentioned in the press. They didn't realize the important part I played in Frank's life. So I didn't get the coverage. I thought of revealing myself. But what's the good? *(Pause)* My brother's fiancée had her photo taken. Bawling her head off. She insisted we bury the engagement ring with him. It was just an idle, theatrical gesture. It's too much trouble now to put a bunch of flowers on the grave.

JOYCE: Perhaps the accident unhinged her mind.

WILSON: It *wasn't* an accident. *(He drinks his tea)* He was murdered.

JOYCE: You don't know that.

WILSON: Don't contradict me!

(Joyce stares in surprise)

JOYCE: *(Angry)* This is a private house. What do you mean by raising your voice? I'm not having perfect strangers talking to me like that.

(Wilson drinks his tea and eats a biscuit)

JOYCE: Drink that tea and clear off. I don't want to see you here again. My husband will be back soon.

WILSON: He's not your husband.

JOYCE: *(Furious)* How dare you! You've gone too far. Leave my room at once.

WILSON: You're not married. You want to watch yourself.

JOYCE: I've a good mind to call a policeman.

WILSON: You aren't on the phone.

JOYCE: I can knock on the floor.

WILSON: There's nobody downstairs.

JOYCE: I'll report you.

WILSON: *(Stands to his feet)* Come here.

JOYCE: *(Alarmed)* Keep away!

WILSON: *(Looks at her, cup in hand. He takes a sip of*

tea) Do you know I could murder you. Easy as that. (*He snaps his fingers*) That's how these assaults on lonely women are all committed. I could make a very nasty attack on you at this moment. If I was so inclined.

JOYCE: (*With a note of hysteria*) Don't come any nearer.

WILSON: Is your "husband" passionate with you?

JOYCE: (*Draws in a sharp breath*) I'm reporting you. Using filthy language.

WILSON: If I were to assault you would he avenge it?

JOYCE: Yes.

WILSON: Where does he keep his gun?

JOYCE: He hasn't got a gun.

WILSON: I have it on good authority that he keeps it loaded. (*He takes a step towards her. She backs away*) Where is it?

JOYCE: In the drawer. Over there.

(*Wilson goes to the drawer. He puts down his cup, opens the drawer and takes out a revolver. He checks that it is loaded, puts it back into the drawer and closes the drawer. Then he walks back to the table with the cup in his hand and drinks the last of his tea, placing the cup back on to the saucer*)

WILSON: (*Smiling*) Thanks for the tea.

JOYCE: (*Stares, puzzled*) Are you going?

WILSON: The room's not available, is it? I expect you think I'm Jewish or something. (*Pause*) Have you got a couple of bob to spare? I can't walk all the way back.

(*Joyce opens her handbag*)

JOYCE: (*Giving him money*) Here's half-a-crown. Don't let me see you round here again.

(*Wilson goes off. Joyce takes a bottle of pills from her handbag and swallows several*)

Scene Two

Later. The remains of an evening meal are on the table. Mike is smoking a small cigar. Joyce is reading a book. She has a pair of glasses on.

MIKE: I went to the King's Cross toilet like I told you. I met my contact. He was a man with bad feet. He looked as though life had treated him rough. He hadn't much to live for. I gave him the message from the . . . er . . . (*Pause*) The message was delivered. I went outside on to the platform. It was cold. I saw an old girl hardly able to breathe. Had something wrong with her. Hardly able to breathe. Her face was blue. (*Pause*) Are you listening, Joycie?

JOYCE: (*Taking off her glasses, and putting her book down*) Yes. (*Pause*) I've had a busy day.

MIKE: Are you tired?

JOYCE: A bit.

MIKE: Have a busy day, did you?

JOYCE: (*Sharply*) Yes. Why don't you listen? You never listen to anyone but yourself.

MIKE: I do.

JOYCE: You never listen to me.

MIKE: You never say anything interesting.

JOYCE: I might as well be dead. (*Pause*) What if you came home and I was dead?

MIKE: Are you queer?

JOYCE: No.

MIKE: (*Pause*) Is your insides playing you up?

JOYCE: I'm all right.

MIKE: Is your liver upset then?

JOYCE: No.

MIKE: It's that fried food you eat. You wolf it down. Put something in the pan and have a fry. That's your motto.

JOYCE: You seem to thrive on it.

MIKE: I'm a man. A man has different glands. You can't go on what I eat.

JOYCE: Oh, well, if you must know, I think it's my nerves.

MIKE: You can't die of nerves.

JOYCE: Can't you?

MIKE: I'm going to the free library tomorrow. I'll look it up.

JOYCE: (*Pause*) What if I were done in?

MIKE: Who'd do you in?

JOYCE: Somebody might. You read of attacks every day on lonely defenseless women.

MIKE: You could call for help.

JOYCE: Who to?

MIKE: Mary.

JOYCE: She's not in. She's working again. I'm alone in the house.

MIKE: You could break a window. That would attract attention.

JOYCE: (*Pause*) Don't go out tomorrow.

MIKE: I can't mope around here. I'm active. It gets on my tits.

(*Joyce closes her book, marking the place. Mike begins to clear the supper things away and puts them into the sink*)

MIKE: Mary used to be on her own. She was all right.

JOYCE: Mary can cope.

MIKE: (*Turns from the sink*) And why's that? Because she's a Catholic. She carries her faith into her private life. That's what we're taught to do. We don't always succeed. But we try. (*He takes off his coat*) Why don't you have a chat with Mary? She'd put you right. Give you the address of a priest with an inquiring mind. He'd stop your maundering. (*He takes off his shoes*) You've a vivid imagination. A fertile mind. An asset in some people. But in your case it's not. (*Pause*) It's in the mind. That's what the Father would say. You'd be better if you'd accept the Communion. That's what you need. I've said so for years.

JOYCE: I'd still be alone.

MIKE: You'd have the Sacrament inside you. That would be something. (*Pause*) Anyway who'd assault you? Who? He'd have to be out of his mind. Look at your face. When did it last see water?

JOYCE: I've been crying.

MIKE: Crying? Are you pregnant?

JOYCE: No. I'm worried.

MIKE: No one would be interested in assaulting you. It's pride to think they would. The idea is farcical. Please don't burden me with it.

(*He takes off his bow tie, goes into the bedroom, turns back the sheets and picks up his pajamas. Joyce comes to the bedroom entrance*)

JOYCE: Mike . . . (*Pause*) A kid came here today.

MIKE: (*Takes off his waistcoat*) One of the Teds?

JOYCE: No. He tried to molest me.

MIKE: These kids see you coming. Why didn't you call for Mary?

JOYCE: She's not in! She's not in! Do I talk for the sake of it? (*Pause*) Mike . . . If he pays another visit—what shall I do? Give me a word of advice?

MIKE: (*Unbuttons his shirt*) Bring me my overcoat, will you? It's raw tonight. We'll need extra on the bed.

Scene Three

Morning. Joyce pauses in cleaning the room.

JOYCE: I can't go to the park. I can't sit on cold stone. I might get piles from the lowered temperature. I wouldn't want them on top of everything else. (*She puts down the duster, apathetically*) I'd try, maybe, a prayer. But the Virgin would turn a deaf ear to a Protestant. (*Pause*) I can't be as alone as all that. Nobody ought to be. It's heartbreaking.

(*She listens. There is silence*)

The number of humiliating admissions I've made. You'd think it would draw me closer to somebody. But it doesn't.

(*Three short rings are given on the doorbell*)

Who's there?

(*No answer*)

What do you want? (*Making up her mind*) I'll answer the door to no one. They can hammer it down. (*Pause*) Is it the milk? (*Calling*) Are you deaf? No, it wouldn't be him. He only rings for his money.

(*She stands behind the door*)

(*Loudly*) Are you the insurance? (*Pause*) But he comes on Friday. This is a Wednesday.

(*She backs away from the door, anxious*)

Nobody comes of a Wednesday. (*She bends down and peeps through the letter-box*) If it's my money you're after, there's not a thing in my purse.

(*She bites her lip, standing in thought*)

(*Loudly*) Are you from the Assistance? They come any time. I've had them on Monday. They come whenever they choose. It's their right. (*With a smile and growing confidence*) You're the Assistance, aren't you? (*Her voice rises*) Are you or aren't you?

(*Glass is heard breaking from the bedroom. She runs to the entrance of the bedroom and leaps back, startled; a piece of brick has been thrown through the window. Joyce stares, her mouth trembling. Another piece of brick hurtles through the window, smashing another pane*)

(*Screaming*) It's him! He's breaking in. God Almighty, what shall I do? He'll murder me! (*She stamps on the floor*) Mary! Mary!

(*She runs to the door, opens it and runs out into the passage. Her frantic tones can be heard crying*)

Mrs. O'Connor! Mrs. O'Connor!

*(She runs back into the room; slams the door shut. The
lock drops with a crash on to the floor. She picks it up
and stares at it and then shrieks with fright)*

It's come off! It's broke!

(She tries to fit the lock back on to the door)

I've told him so often. I've—told him to—mend it!

*(She gives up, breathless. Then she tries to pull the settee
out into the room, but gives up and picks up a chair
which she pushes against the door and sits on)*

He'll easily fling this aside. Oh, Michael, I'm to be murdered
because you're too bone idle to fix a lock.

(There is a prolonged ringing on the doorbell)

Let me alone! I'm going to report you. I've seen them at the
station. They've set a trap. I'm safe in here. We have an extremely strong and reliable Chubb lock on the door. So you're
trapped. Ha, ha! The detectives are watching the house.

*(The front door is kicked. The chair pushes away and
Joyce is flung aside. She backs into the bedroom)*

If it's the gun you want, I don't know where he's put it. He's
taken it. *(Pause)* I may be able to find it. Is that what you
want?

*(Outside the door a burst of music is heard from a tran-
sistor radio. There is knocking. The bell rings. A sudden
silence. Laughter. Silence. A splintering of wood. Joyce
calls shrilly)* I've told my hubby. He's seeing someone.
You'll laugh on the other side of your face!

(Suddenly, giving up all pretence, she bursts into tears)

Go away. There's a good boy. I don't know what you want.
I've no money. Please go away! Please, please, please . . . *(She
sobs)*

Scene Four

*Later. Mike sits at the table reading a newspaper. Joyce
enters in outdoor clothes.*

MIKE: Where've you been? (*He folds up the paper*)

(*Joyce takes off her hat and coat and puts them into the wardrobe*)

JOYCE: Out.

MIKE: Out? What about my tea? It wasn't ready.

JOYCE: I've been walking 'round. I didn't come back till I saw the light in the window.

MIKE: Where did you go?

JOYCE: Into Woolworths.

MIKE: What for?

JOYCE: The people. The lights. The crowds. (*Pause*) That kid came again. He broke two windows today in the bedroom.

MIKE: I thought it was them next door.

JOYCE: Have you seen the banisters? Smashed to bits. Wantonness. I couldn't stop him. (*Lowering her voice*) He pissed on the floor in the passage. I had to clean it up. Been ringing the doorbell half the day. Running up and down the stairs. I'm nearly out of my mind. It didn't stop till four. (*Pause*) I can hardly think with worry.

MIKE: Did you witness him?

JOYCE: I was in here.

MIKE: Did you see him?

JOYCE: (*Furiously*) I won't stand it! I want something done! Look at that lock. Why don't you mend it?

MIKE: I'll try and borrow a set of screws.

JOYCE: You can decide what you're doing. I can't keep pace with the excitement. I'll be in a home.

MIKE: Did he try to get into the room?

JOYCE: No.

MIKE: Could he have got in if he'd wanted?

JOYCE: (*Pause*) Yes.

MIKE: Did he speak?

JOYCE: No.

MIKE: Then how d'you know it was him from yesterday? If you didn't see him and he didn't speak? How d'you know?

(*Silence*)

JOYCE: It must be the same man.

MIKE: Why didn't you go outside and see?

JOYCE: He'd've killed me.

MIKE: How do you know that? You've no evidence to support your theory.

JOYCE: But . . . (*Wide-eyed*) . . . I'd be dead if I'd got evidence.

MIKE: I'd prosecute him on your behalf, Joycie.

(*Joyce blows her nose; she doesn't speak*)

JOYCE: (*At last, wearily*) Will you mend the lock for me? I'll feel safer then.

MIKE: I'll see to it when I get back. (*He goes into the bedroom and picks up his coat from the end of the bed*)

JOYCE: Back? Back from where?

MIKE: (*Entering, putting on his coat*) I'm seeing a man who could put me in touch with something. (*He goes to the sink and puts the flower into his buttonhole*)

JOYCE: I'll go down to Mary. (*Pause*) Would you like a bikky before you go?

MIKE: No. I'll have something on the way.

JOYCE: Is it important tonight?

MIKE: I may be employed to do another job in the van. We're fixing the details.

(*The doorbell is rung violently. Mike puts the silver paper from the flower into the waste bin*)

MIKE: Is that the bell?

JOYCE: Yes.

MIKE: (*Going into the bedroom*) Answer it then. I'm here with you.

(*The bell is rung again. Mike takes a packet of cigarettes from the drawer and fills his cigarette case. Joyce opens the door. Wilson is outside*)

WILSON: (*Smiling*) Are you the lady I saw yesterday?

JOYCE: It's you!

WILSON: You *are* the lady?

JOYCE: What do you mean by pestering me?

WILSON: There's no need to raise your voice.

JOYCE: My husband is in. Coming here, trying your tricks. Making a nuisance. I've only to call and he'll soon put a stop to you. Do you understand?

WILSON: I'm afraid I don't.

JOYCE: Coming here, playing me up. What do you mean by it? It's disgusting. Anyone would think you were a kid. Behaving like that. You know what I mean, don't you? You know. Like an animal. (*Pause*) Are you paying for those windows?

WILSON: I don't know what you're talking about.

JOYCE: You're a liar! A bloody little liar!

WILSON: Don't speak to me like that, lady. I'm not used to it.

JOYCE: I've had enough. I'm putting a stop to this. (*Calls*) Michael!

(*Mike enters from the bedroom. He slips his cigarette case into his pocket*)

JOYCE: Come here. (*To Wilson*) Stay where you are! Stay here!

(*She attempts to grab his arm. He tries to shake her off. She hangs on. He shrugs her away, violently. She comes back. They struggle. Mike goes to the mirror and runs a comb through his hair*)

JOYCE: (*Shouting, excited*) Mike! Michael! (*To Wilson*) I'll have my husband to you. (*Turning, excited*) Where are you, Michael! For God's sake!

(*Mike puts the comb away and strolls to the door*)

MIKE: (*Coolly*) What's the matter?

JOYCE: This is him! The one that's been coming here.

MIKE: (*To Wilson*) What's this, I hear? Have you been annoying my wife?

JOYCE: Yes! He has.

MIKE: (*To Joyce*) Let's hear his version of it (*To Wilson*) Tell me the truth.

WILSON: I wanted a room.

MIKE: We haven't got a room.

WILSON: You're Irish! My mother was Irish. My father was Mediterranean. I have difficulty with rooms for that reason. (*Smiles*) I've walked all the way from the bus station by Victoria. Do you know that district at all?

MIKE: I know King's Cross intimately.

WILSON: Victoria is a different place entirely. In the summer it has a character of its own. Are you a Londoner?

MIKE: No. I was born in the shadow of the hills of Donegal. We had a peat farm. It was the aftermath of the troubles drove us away. Otherwise there'd be people called Mike in Donegal to this day.

WILSON: I love Ireland. I'd go there tomorrow if it wasn't for my dad. He's a hard man to please. My feet are killing me. Could I have a drink of water?

MIKE: Certainly. Come on in.

JOYCE: You're not letting him in?

MIKE: Be quiet. You're making yourself look ridiculous. (*To Wilson*) This way. And take no notice of her. She can't help herself. (*He leads the way into the room*) Get the lad a glass of water, Joycie.

(*Joyce goes to the sink and fills a glass with water*)

MIKE: (*To Wilson*) What part of Ireland is your mother from?

WILSON: Sligo.

MIKE: I once knew a lad from Sligo. Name of Murphy. I wonder if maybe your Ma would've come across him?

WILSON: I'll make inquiries.

MIKE: I'd be obliged if you would. He had dark curly hair and talked with a pronounced brogue. Not an easy man to miss in a crowd.

(*Joyce hands Wilson the glass of water*)

JOYCE: (*To Mike*) What did you let him in for?

MIKE: He isn't a leper.

JOYCE: Ask him.

MIKE: What?

JOYCE: Ask him about his conduct. He won't be able to face it out.

MIKE: (*To Wilson*) About these things she tells me. Did you cheek her yesterday?

WILSON: It depends on which way you look at it. I thought my behavior was exemplary.

MIKE: Did you molest her?

WILSON: (*To Joyce*) What've you been telling him? I never tried to interfere with you, did I?

JOYCE: (*Angry*) Stop using that kind of talk. (*To Mike*) You can see what I had to put up with.

MIKE: That's medical talk, Joycie. You should learn to control your temper. (*To Wilson*) Why did you bring a suitcase with you?

WILSON: I wanted a room. (*Nods to Joyce*) I thought she might change her mind.

JOYCE: Who's she? The cat's mother.

MIKE: (*To Wilson*) Bring it in. You don't want to leave it lying out there.

(*Wilson exits*)

JOYCE: What are you playing at? After what he's done to me?

MIKE: Quiet!

JOYCE: What's his background? He could be anything.

MIKE: Give the lad a chance.

JOYCE: Chance? After what I've been through?

MIKE: Shut up!

JOYCE: (*Bewildered*) Shut up?

MIKE: You're heading for a belt around the ear. Go to Mary. Are you going?

(*Wilson returns with a suitcase*)

MIKE: Put it over there, lad. How about a cup of tea, Joycie?

(*Joyce goes into the bedroom*)

MIKE: She's taken offense. (*Calls*) Did you hear me?
Why don't you show a few manners? (*To Wilson*) What's your
profession?

WILSON: I'm a Gents' Hairdresser.

MIKE: You wouldn't happen to be dabbling with birth-
control devices? That's no way for a Catholic to carry on.

WILSON: I don't handle that part of the trade. My old
man does it. He has the free-thinking frame of mind. I can't
approve, of course. It's the Latin temperament which has been
the curse of our religion all along.

MIKE: The Pope is Italian.

WILSON: You have something there. I'd like to see a
Liffey man on the throne of St. Peter myself. I'd be proud to
hear the Lateran ring with the full-throated blasphemies of our
native land.

MIKE: What are you thinking of? The Vicar of Christ
doesn't blaspheme.

WILSON: He would if he was Irish and drank Guinness.

MIKE: You're a lad after my own heart. You'll not know
me by name, I suppose?

WILSON: I didn't quite catch it.

MIKE: Michael O'Rourke. I was known as Mike or
Mickey O'Rourke in the days when you were a nipper. I used
to be respected in the boxing profession. I was thought to be
heading for the top at one time. Then I had my trouble. (*He
turns to the bedroom and calls*) Isn't that right? Wasn't I handy
with my fists then? In the days after the second German war?
(*Turns back to Wilson*) Ignorant cow. (*Into bedroom*) Are you
going to behave decent?

(*Joyce is sitting on the bed. She gives a toss of her head*)

WILSON: I'll go.

MIKE: Don't let her drive you away. You stay.

(*Joyce picks up a cardigan. She enters from the bedroom*)

JOYCE: (*In a tight, angry voice*) I'm going downstairs!
(*She goes off into the hall, slamming the door behind her*)

MIKE: Take no notice. She'll come round. She's nervous, you know. It's the life she led before I took up with her. I have to watch her. She'd get me into all sorts of trouble. She has no religious feelings. That's the worst of it. She never had the benefit of the upbringing.

WILSON: My mum was brought up by nuns.

MIKE: Is she still alive?

WILSON: She's in the hospital with an infectious disease of the hip-joint. The nuns think the world of her.

MIKE: Is she in pain?

WILSON: She screams out. It's terrible to hear her.

MIKE: I wish I could do something. Would it be any use to burn a candle? I don't think I've the cash on me.

WILSON: Wouldn't the priest lend you the cash?

MIKE: I'd not like to ask. I'd pop across and burn a candle myself. But he might ask questions. It's his business, of course. He's a right to ask. But why should I subject myself to scrutiny? (*Pause*) Is your mother expected to recover?

WILSON: It's touch and go.

MIKE: She's maybe doomed. She's likely to be a candle herself already. She's probably being stripped by the angels as we speak. I suppose we are roasted nude? I've never seen fit to ask. It's not a question you can put to the Father. Though he is a Jesuit. And that makes a difference. (*Pause*) Is your dad in good health?

WILSON: He's fine. (*Pause*) I'm not keeping you, am I?

MIKE: No. (*Pause, looks at his watch*) As a matter of fact you've kept me. I've missed my appointment. I shall have to drop them a line and apologize for my absence. (*He takes off his coat, puts the flower from his buttonhole into a glass, and puts water into the glass; then, putting the glass on to the draining board:*) If you're desperate for a room we could put you up. On the bed-settee. It's quite comfortable.

WILSON: Is it new?

MIKE: No.

WILSON: You surprise me.

MIKE: I bought it a long time ago. I couldn't afford such luxury today. Financially I'm in a bad way.

WILSON: Well, my money will help you out.

MIKE: It's the Assistance Board. I'm not a believer in charity. Unless I need it. With the cost of living being so high I'm greatly in need of a weekly donation from the government. They say my circumstances have altered. I haven't any circumstances to alter. They should know that. I've filled in a form to the effect that I'm a derelict.

WILSON: Yes. My brother and me had the same trouble.

MIKE: They haven't the insight into the human heart that we have in Ireland.

WILSON: We lived in Shepherd's Bush. We had a little room. And our life was made quite comfortable by the N.A.B. for almost a year. We had a lot of friends. All creeds and colors. But no circumstances at all. We were happy, though. We were young. I was seventeen. He was twenty-three. You can't do better for yourself than that, can you? (*He shrugs*) We were bosom friends. I've never told anyone that before. I hope I haven't shocked you.

MIKE: As close as that?

WILSON: We had separate beds—he was a stickler for convention, but that's as far as it went. We spent every night in each other's company. It was the reason we never got any work done.

MIKE: There's no word in the Irish language for what you were doing.

WILSON: In Lapland they have no word for snow.

MIKE: I'd rather not hear. I'm not a priest, you know.

WILSON: I wasn't with him when he died. I'm going round the twist with heartbreak.

MIKE: He's dead?

WILSON: Yes. I thought of topping myself. As a gesture. I would've done, but for my strict upbringing. Suicide is difficult when you've got a pious mum.

MIKE: Kill yourself?

WILSON: I don't want to live, see. That's a crude way of putting it. I've lived among rough people.

MIKE: You won't do it, though?

WILSON: No. I've made a will, of course. In case anything should happen in the future.

MIKE: What might happen?

WILSON: I might get killed.

MIKE: How?

WILSON: I don't know. (*Pause*) In my will I state that I want to be buried with Frank. It's my last request. They'll be bound to honor it. His fiancée won't mind. She's off already with another man. He's not cold and already it's too much trouble for her to put a bunch of flowers on his grave. She's a typical woman. You've met with it yourself?

MIKE: I have. Some of them are unholy bitches.

WILSON: He wouldn't have benefited from her. I was more intimate with him than she was. I used to base my life 'round him. You don't often get that, do you?

MIKE: (*Uneasily*) No.

WILSON: I heard he was a friend of yours. You were pointed out as a man that knew him. (*He takes a snapshot from his pocket and hands it to Mike*) Recognize him?

(*Mike looks at the snapshot*)

MIKE: (*Pause*) He was nice looking.

WILSON: He had personality. That indefinable something. That was taken two days before he was killed. (*Pause*) What's the matter? The light hurting your eyes.

MIKE: (*Hands the snapshot back*) Take it away. It upsets me. The thought of him being dead. He was so young.

WILSON: Do you recognize him?

MIKE: I may have seen him once or twice. I may have spoken to him.

WILSON: A van knocked him down.

MIKE: (*Pause*) Did he say anything? Was there a death-bed scene?

WILSON: He was killed instantaneous. (*Pause*) You recently had a smash-up in your van, didn't you? I checked with the garage. You've had five major repair jobs in under two years. Why don't you learn to drive properly? You're a disgrace to your profession.

MIKE: I feel bad. I'll have to ask you to go now. It's embarrassing to be ill in a stranger's presence.

WILSON: (*Smiles*) I was going to live here, I thought.

MIKE: I've just realized. We can't put you up.

WILSON: Why not?

MIKE: Her aunt may drop in. I'm sorry I raised your hopes.

WILSON: Does she usually come this late?

MIKE: She does.

WILSON: She must be an ignorant kind of woman, turning up in the middle of the night. No consideration for others. What's her name?

MIKE: Snell.

WILSON: What's her first name?

MIKE: Bridie Francine. She uses the second. Everyone knows Francine Snell.

WILSON: I haven't had the pleasure. What does she look like?

MIKE: She has a growth on the side of her neck. She walks with a limp.

WILSON: She sounds a dear old lady. Where does she normally live? When she's not up half the night careening about visiting?

MIKE: In the suburbs. She prefers it to the city center.

WILSON: Well, I'm sorry I can't stay. I must be going then. Before I say goodbye would you mind telling me, as briefly as possible, why you killed my brother.

MIKE: I didn't!

WILSON: You did. You were paid two hundred and fifty quid. Exclusive of repairs to the van.

MIKE: No!

WILSON: It was on October the twenty-first he was killed. What were you doing that day?

MIKE: I was fishing.

WILSON: Where?

MIKE: In the canal.

WILSON: Did you catch much?

MIKE: I put it back. That's the rules. The rules of the club.

WILSON: My brother belonged to the club. He was the best angler you had. He gave out the cards. (*Pause*) What did you catch on the day he died?

MIKE: I can't be expected to remember.

WILSON: Did you have the good fortune to find a salmon on the end of your line?

MIKE: No. Whoever heard of catching salmon in a canal?

WILSON: You killed my brother. Your denials fall on deaf ears. (*Pause*) You're a liar. That's what it amounts to.

MIKE: (*Frightened*) What are you going to do?

WILSON: Nothing I can do, is there? (*He picks up his suitcase and goes to the door*) I'll be off. (*He smiles, deliberately*) Give my love to Maddy.

MIKE: Let me alone. I'm ill. (*Pause*) What did you say?

WILSON: Maddy. Your old scrubber.

MIKE: (*Goes over to Wilson*) Are you asking for a backhander? What is this about Maddy? I don't know any *Maddy*.

WILSON: She lives here.

MIKE: Her name's Joyce. (*Wilson shrugs, smiling*) Out you go, you young whore's get! (*Wilson smiles*) Piss off! Coming here trying to make trouble. I was handy with my fists once. I could make pulp of you.

WILSON: All this energy. Nearly blowing your top. You ought to get it regular. You'd feel better then.

MIKE: Don't come to me with your gutter talk. I won't listen to it.

WILSON: You won't have been capable of a jump since the Festival. It's the usual story.

MIKE: (*Grabs Wilson's arm*) Why did you call her Maddy?

WILSON: She asked me to. In private. It's her trade name.

MIKE: She never saw you till two days ago.

WILSON: She told you that? Do you believe her?

MIKE: Yes.

WILSON: It's your affair. I never believe a woman. I've had experience.

MIKE: The only experience you've had is with your fist.

WILSON: What a coarse remark. How typical. (*He glances to the bedroom*) I wish she'd change the sheets on the bed. Have you noticed? It's a bad sign.

MIKE: If you've had her I'll swing for you.

WILSON: Would you kill me?

MIKE: I would! I'd throttle you with my bare hands. I'd choke the filth out of you.

WILSON: You've got a gun. Kill me with that. (*Pause*) I'll be back tomorrow. Tell Maddy I'll see her.

MIKE: You can believe me. I never murdered your brother. Don't you believe me?

WILSON: No. (*Pause*) I might decide to put Maddy in the pudding club. Just to show my contempt for your way of life. I never take precautions. We're skin to skin. Nature's method.

(*Mike gives a groan of pain. He runs to the drawer, rummages and takes the gun from the drawer*)

MIKE: (*Waving the gun before Wilson*) See this? I'll use it if I catch you with her.

WILSON: How good a shot are you?

MIKE: I'm an expert.

WILSON: The heart is situated . . . (*He points*) . . . just below this badge on my pullover. Don't miss, will you? I don't want to be injured. I want to be dead.

MIKE: You think I'm joking?

WILSON: I hope you're not.

MIKE: You're an ignorant young sod! Like your brother. It must run in the family.

WILSON: Have you noticed that mole she has?

MIKE: Where?

WILSON: In a private place. I don't expect you've looked lately. That's why she's gone for someone younger.

MIKE: (*Screaming*) Get out!

(*Wilson smiles and exits*)

MIKE: (*Softly*) I feel bad. I'm sickening for something. (*He puts the gun away in the drawer*) They think because you're a criminal they can treat you like dirt. Coming here like that. Telling a man to his face. The morals of Nineveh were hardly so lax. (*He sits at the table, closing his eyes*) Oh, but he's playing with fire. I'll shoot him. I'll geld him. I've a clear case. I'm the injured party. I'll have the stones off him if he's done her. (*Pause*) He'll be putting her into a whorehouse next. These kids have only one idea.

(*He goes into the bedroom, picks up his pajamas and slippers, pulls the clothing and a pillow from the bed and enters the main room*)

I'll sleep out here. I can't have her next to me.

(*He sits on the settee and begins to undress*)

Oh, oh! I'm cuckolded. What a spectacle. Yet you'd swear you were safe with her. She's not much of a looker. The sex is rotten. Perfidious. Treacherous. She's old enough to be his mother. (*Pause*) I shouldn't say that. That's a terrible thing to say.

(*He puts on his pajama jacket*)

She's whored herself under two assumed names. Before I met her she was known to the Directory of Directors as Madelein Scott-Palmer. And before that she'd led a loose life as Sarah Fielding. She wasted her auntie's legacy on cards for tobacconists' windows. Oh, it's too much! I'll have to kill her.

(*He puts on his pajama trousers*)

If I kill her I'll have to say goodbye. I'll never see her again. I'd be alone. The pain of it. I never realize the pain. I'm too old to start again. Too old. I love her. My heart aches to admit it. She's all I've got. I want her if she's the biggest old tart since the mother of Solomon.

(*He puts on his slippers*)
What a life it is living in a country full of whores and communists.
>   (*He puts his coat on as a dressing-gown. Joyce enters. She
>   takes off her cardigan*)

JOYCE: Has he gone?

MIKE: (*Looking up, narrowing his eyes*) What d'you mean?

JOYCE: I thought he was staying here.

MIKE: Do you want him to?

JOYCE: Do *I* want him to?

MIKE: (*Nodding his head*) I see your plan. I see it. You've the cunning of Luther. (*Joyce walks past him into the bedroom*) Where are you going?

JOYCE: To bed. I'm not listening to you.

MIKE: What's she up to? (*Pause*) I'll maybe forgive her. Our Lord forgave the woman taken in adultery. But the circumstances were different. (*Pause*) It's a ludicrous business. Ludicrous. The deceit. At her age. She wants somebody younger. At her age they get the itch. It's like a tale told by a commercial traveller. Just for a few minutes' thrill. I don't know what she'd be like if we had a television.

JOYCE: (*Undressing for bed*) Are you giving a recitation out there?

MIKE: (*Entering bedroom*) What?

JOYCE: I thought you were entertaining the troops.

MIKE: I leave that to you. That's more *your* line, isn't it?

JOYCE: What's the matter?

MIKE: You cow! Playing me up.

JOYCE: You shouldn't've invited him in. You upset me.

MIKE: I've heard about you. You'll be taking your clothes off in the street next.

JOYCE: What's got into you?

MIKE: Some men would kill you. You're lucky I'm not some. . . . A fine family! Your mother was doing it in a doorway the night she was killed. If she hadn't been such a wicked old brass she'd've been in the shelter with the rest. Taking the A.R.P. from their duty. Your granny spent Mafeking night on her back. That makes *three* generations of whores. (*He smacks her face. Joyce shrieks with surprise and fright*) I'll murder you! (*He leaps upon her. They fall across the bed*)

JOYCE: (*Shouting*) Mind the fish! You'll upset my gold-fish.

MIKE: (*Standing up, taking off his coat*) What d'you want to keep fish in a bedroom for? It's not hygienic.

(*He gets into bed. Joyce fetches the pillow and blanket from the main room and puts them on the bed*)

JOYCE: What's he been telling you?

MIKE: Did you let him?

JOYCE: (*Indignantly*) He never touched me.

MIKE: You'd have to say that. I don't want to lose you. I don't want to be on my own again. I was so lonely before.

JOYCE: Shall I put your coat on your feet? It's freezing again.

Scene Five

Next morning. Joyce is washing dishes. The doorbell rings. Joyce takes off her gloves and wipes her hands. The door is pushed open and Wilson enters.

JOYCE: What are you doing in here? That door is supposed to be locked.

WILSON: There's no lock.

JOYCE: My husband is downstairs. It's true. This time it's true.

WILSON: I know. I saw him hanging about down there. I told him last night we were having an affair. It didn't inconvenience you in any way? (*He takes off his coat and spreads it on the settee*) You don't want to have an affair with me by any chance?

JOYCE: You're only a little boy.

(*Wilson picks up a chair and wedges it under the handle of the door*)

JOYCE: What are you doing that for?

WILSON: So as when he comes up and tries the handle he'll think we're knocking it off.

JOYCE: (*With distaste*) Don't use expressions like that. I'm not used to it.

WILSON: When you were on the game you must've been.

JOYCE: I never allowed anyone to take liberties with me. My people were good class. (*Pause*) Who told you about me?

WILSON: My brother. He had it off with you after seeing *The Sound of Music*. I waited downstairs. He was as pissed as a . . . He would never have had a prostitute and seen *The Sound of Music* otherwise. (*Loosens his tie*) You're like most women. Here today and gone tomorrow. My brother's fiancée resembled you in many ways. Fickle in her emotions. She was trying on her wedding-gown when we got news of Frank's death. Now she's had it dyed ice-blue and wears it to dinner dances. My only consolation is that she looks hideous in it. But it shows what kind of woman she is, doesn't it? I knew the type by the way she moved her knees up against my thighs at the funeral. I felt like throttling her. A whole hour she was at it. We went the long way round to avoid the procession.

JOYCE: What procession?

WILSON: They were celebrating some victory or other. We heard the bands playing in the distance. The Royal Family were out in full force. Furs and garters flying. My old man was in it. He couldn't come to the funeral because he was on the British Legion float. He represented something. (*He sits, his shoulders hunched, staring into space*) He thought more of tarting himself up than burying his son. All our family seem to be some kind of idiot. If anybody so much as mentions the British

Legion to my dad he goes into a trance. On Armistice Day he takes part in all the rituals. He eats poppies for a week before-hand. I haven't seen him since the funeral. I expect he's in a home by now. (*He stands*) He should be up here.

JOYCE: Who?

WILSON: Your old man. We should have some warmth. Haven't you got an electric fire? I hadn't anticipated being frozen to death.

(*He goes off into the bedroom*)

WILSON: (*Calling from the bedroom*) Are these some kind of carp?

JOYCE: No. Just goldfish.

(*Wilson enters the main room*)

WILSON: You can catch germs from them, you know. (*He takes off his tie*) My brother would've been twenty-four in three days' time. He had plans for a business. (*He kicks off his shoes*) I expect he would have made good sooner or later. He was the go-ahead type. His mentality was fully developed. He used to read a lot about expansion. His death put a stop to that. I don't take after him. Except in the physical sense. (*He sighs and shakes his head*) I get a bit lost without him, I don't mind admitting. (*Pause*) He might have made a lot of money in his own line. It was my ambition to become the brother of a mil-lionaire. (*Pause*) I expect you're bored. You didn't know him. I can't expect you to see my point of view. (*He takes his pullover off, unbuttons his shirt, pins a badge on his shirt above the heart, and unzips his fly*)

JOYCE: Here, what are you doing?

WILSON: It ought to look as if we're on the job when he comes up.

JOYCE: Stop it! Stop it! Whatever will Michael think? He'll think we're carrying on.

WILSON: I banked on him being up here by now. Rattling the door. He's probably gone back on his word.

(*He goes into the bedroom and looks out of the window*)

WILSON: He's not out there now.

(*Joyce picks up his pullover and goes into the bedroom*)

JOYCE: (*Handing him his pullover*) Put your clothes on. Don't be so silly.

WILSON: (*Accepting the pullover*) He won't come up. He won't. I can see this is a failure like everything else.

(*Mike is heard coming up the stairs*)

MIKE: Joycie! Joycie . . .

WILSON: I'm sorry if I've caused trouble. I'm not usually like this. My heart is breaking. I wish I'd been with him when he died.

JOYCE: You poor boy. Oh, you poor boy.

(*She kisses his cheek tenderly. He holds her close. Mike crashes into the room. He advances slowly. Pause. Wilson turns from Joyce, smiles at Mike, and zips up his fly. Mike fires the gun. The shot crashes into the goldfish bowl. Joyce screams. A second shot hits Wilson in the chest. He crashes to the floor on his knees*)

WILSON: My will is in my overcoat pocket. My address in my pocket diary. Remember, will you?

JOYCE: (*To Mike*) What've you done?

WILSON: He took it serious. How charming. (*He coughs, blood spurts from his mouth*) He's a bit of a nutter if you ask me. Am I dying? I think . . . Oh . . .

(*He falls forward. Silence*)

JOYCE: He's fainted.

MIKE: (*Laying the gun aside*) He's dead.

JOYCE: But he can't be. You haven't killed him?

MIKE: Bring a sheet. Cover his body.

JOYCE: I've a bit of sacking somewhere.

MIKE: I said a sheet! Give him the best.

(*He goes into the bedroom and drags a sheet from the bed which he puts over Wilson's body*)

JOYCE: What excuse was there to shoot him?

MIKE: He was misbehaving himself with my wife.

JOYCE: But I'm not your wife. And he wasn't.

MIKE: He called you *Maddy*.

JOYCE: Somebody must've told him about my past. You know what people are. (*Pause*) Did you have anything to do with his brother's death?

MIKE: Yes.

JOYCE: This is what comes of having no regular job. (*Pause*) Is the phone box working by the Nag's Head?

MIKE: Yes.

JOYCE: Go to the telephone box. Dial 999. I'll tell them I was assaulted.

MIKE: (*Horrified*) It'll be in the papers.

JOYCE: Well, perhaps not assaulted. Not completely. You came in just in time.

MIKE: You'll stick by me, Joycie?

JOYCE: Of course, dear. (*She kisses him*) I love you. (*She sees the shattered goldfish bowl*) Oh, look Michael! (*Bursting into tears*) My goldfish! (*She picks up a fish*)

MIKE: One of the bullets must've hit the bowl.

JOYCE: They're dead. Poor things. And I reared them so carefully. And while all this was going on they died.

(*She sobs. Mike puts his arm round her and leads her to the settee. She sits*)

MIKE: Sit down. I'll fetch the police. This has been a crime of passion. They'll understand. They have wives and goldfish of their own.

(*Joyce is too heartbroken to answer. She buries her face in Mike's shoulder. He holds her close*)

Curtain

Israel Horovitz

ACROBATS

Israel Horovitz

Israel Horovitz made his first appearance in *The Best Short Plays* annuals in 1969 with *The Indian Wants the Bronx,* a powerful and terrifying study of violence on a New York street. A striking Off-Broadway success, it also scored heavily in other major American cities, at the Spoleto (Italy) Festival and in numerous foreign countries. The play won a 1968 Drama Desk-Vernon Rice Award (for outstanding contribution to the Off-Broadway theatre) and three "Obies", as well as a commendation from *Newsweek* magazine citing the author as one of the three most original dramatists of the year.

Mr. Horovitz was born in Wakefield, Massachusetts, in 1939. After completing his studies at Harvard College, he journeyed to London to continue his education at the Royal Academy of Dramatic Art and in 1965 became the first American to be chosen as playwright-in-residence with Britain's celebrated Royal Shakespeare Company.

The author's first play, *The Comeback,* was written when he was seventeen; it was produced in Boston in 1960. In the decade that followed, Mr. Horovitz's plays tenanted many stages of the world. Among his works: *Line; Rats; It's Called the Sugar Plum* (paired with *The Indian Wants the Bronx* on the New York stage); *The Death of Bernard the Believer; Chiaroscuro* (the "morning" play of the triple bill by Mr. Horovitz, Terrence McNally and Leonard Melfi, *Morning, Noon and Night,* Henry Miller's Theatre, New York, 1968); *Play for Trees; Leader;* and *The Honest-to-God Schnozzola* for which he won a 1969 Off-Broadway "Obie" Award.

First Season, a collection of Israel Horovitz's short plays, was published in 1968 and his latest effort, *The World's Greatest Play* (whose protagonist, Hero, is born onstage, lives a full and long life onstage and then dies onstage) is scheduled for New York production in 1970. The presentation will be sponsored by Hillard Elkins and directed by Bob Dishy.

A recent recipient of a Rockefeller Foundation Playwriting Fellowship, Mr. Horovitz wrote the screenplay for the film,

The Strawberry Statement (in which he also plays the role of a professor). The film won the *Prix de Jury,* Cannes Film Festival, 1970.

Mr. Horovitz lives in New York City with his wife and their three children. He holds Professorships in the English Departments of City College and New York University. He is a Ph.D. candidate at C.U.N.Y.

An earlier version of "Acrobats" appeared in *Show* magazine.

Author's Note

Acrobats *is a play about dependency. It is a highly stylized work that must be performed as well as acted by actors who also are acrobats. If such a team isn't possible to find, I would accept a pair of acrobats, who also are actors.*

The play is a simple metaphor. It is a puzzle with interlocking, highly-breakable human parts: acrobats, a husband and his wife. For me to discuss my play further is a form of lunacy. To describe what a play is about *is merely to adapt that play into prose form. As you can see by now, I am, not by any stretch of imagination, not even mine, a prose writer. And I do honestly believe (although drama critics seem to disagree) that the restatement of any serious play in* prose *rather than* dramatic *form lessens rather than enhances the value, the impact of that play.*

My thoughts about Acrobats *would fill more pages than the play itself, as well they should. I'll cut off now and let you get on with it.*

Characters:
  MAN, *a nameless, middle-aged acrobat.*
  WOMAN, *his wife, Edna.*

Place:
  Where it actually is happening: on a theatre stage.

Time:
  When it actually is happening: now.

  *The stage is absolutely empty; dark. There is silence for
  a count of five. Bright white light snaps on. The silence
  continues for another count of five. Half a fanfare sounds
  but is instantly switched off.* Note: *The action of the
  play should be punctuated with appropriate fanfares,
  building in rhythm as the play builds, ending in a cre-
  scendo as does the play.*
  *A man enters. He is an acrobat: all rippling muscles
  and a professional smile. He will hold his smile throughout the play, until He can no longer smile. His costume
  is tight white cotton. He walks to the center of the stage
  and neatly, professionally, proceeds to lie on his back on
  the stage floor; his feet facing the audience.*
  There is silence for a count of five.
  *A woman enters. She is his wife: as muscular in the
  way that women are muscular. Her breasts are small, her
  arms and legs thick and strong. She wears a tight white
  cotton acrobat's costume and a solid professional smile.
  She walks to a position just above her husband's head, facing the audience straight-on, neatly. She reaches down to
  her husband with both arms. His hands reach up to her.
  He takes her hands in his, never really looking up nor
  moving his body at all. Suddenly, She seems to dive at his
  head with hers. In an instant, He stiffens his arms and
  She is in a handstand position, locked on his hands.
  Slowly, stiffly, carefully, He rises until He is standing*

> erect. *They are now in a full handstand position. She carefully maneuvers a turn, so both their faces are to the audience. Their smiles are quite fantastic.*
>
> *There is silence as They hold their position. If there is applause from the audience, the silence must be doubled. When the applause has ended, He speaks, never breaking his smile.*

MAN: (*Simply, sternly, flatly*) I want a divorce.

WOMAN: (*An arch whisper*) My hand. Let it go.

MAN: Can you do it? Are you sure you can do it?

WOMAN: Don't be ridiculous.

MAN: I'm here. Don't be frightened.

WOMAN: I'm all right.

MAN: Tell me when.

WOMAN: Okay. (*After a long hold*) Now!

(*He pauses, smiling*)

MAN: Which? Which hand? You didn't tell me. Which hand?

WOMAN: This one.

(*She wiggles her left arm. He slowly, carefully, takes his right arm down. The movement is almost indiscernible at first, then He snaps his arm away from her. She now stands on one hand, resetting her weight on him to maintain the balance. They hold in that position for a count of five. As before, if there is applause, the silence is doubled. When the applause has ended, He speaks*)

MAN: (*Slowly, sternly*) I hate your guts, Edna. I swear to God. I really hate your guts.

WOMAN: Your hand.

MAN: Here.

(*He takes her hand back in his again, and She descends to the stage floor. They step neatly beside each other, holding hands, smiling*)

WOMAN: (*Facing absolutely front*) Who is it?

MAN: Nobody. Don't be ridiculous. There's no one else. You'd like that, wouldn't you? If there were someone else. Sorry, Edna. There's nobody else.

WOMAN: (*After a silent hold*) Ready?

MAN: (*A military reply*) Ready.

(*He bends forward and She leaps so that She is standing on the base of his spine.*)

MAN: (*Bitchy*) I want you off my ass, Edna. I've got to have a life of my own. You wouldn't understand that. (*Pauses*) Ready?

(*They change positions in an amazing move, so that He is now standing on her back*)

WOMAN: Lower.

(*He steps down lower on her back*)

MAN: Sorry.

WOMAN: It's all right.

MAN: (*Walking tiptoe up her back until He stands triumphantly on her shoulders*) Dependency, Edna. That's my problem. I can't fill my life this way . . . with you demanding, demanding. It's gone way beyond. Way beyond. I'm a laughing stock. I'm a jerkoff. I can't decide who I hate more, me or you. I hate both of us. We're really shit, Edna.

WOMAN: Ready?

MAN: Ready.

(*He leaps to the floor. They stand and face the audience again, hand in hand, smiling completely*)

WOMAN: Just tell me when.

MAN: Why not tonight? Right now.

WOMAN: It's all right with me! Believe you me, I couldn't care less. I really don't give a shit.

MAN: You've got a foul mouth.

WOMAN: Ready?

MAN: Lead.

WOMAN: Now!

(*He falls onto his back again and She dives into a hand-stand on his shoulders. His hands are on her shoulders.*

He wriggles in a circle as She does a split in the air)

MAN: Watch your nails.

WOMAN: Sorry.

MAN: It's all right.

WOMAN: What about the children? What will I tell them? Huh? You got an answer for that?

MAN: They're better off with us split up. I swear to God. How do you think they feel? Us fighting all day, all night? Huh? How do you think they feel?

WOMAN: I know how *they* feel, believe me! I've talked to them.

MAN: (*Amazed, rather angry*) You've talked to the kids?

WOMAN: I did.

MAN: You're really a bitch. I swear to God.

WOMAN: You think they're dummies? You think they can't see what's going on with us?

MAN: I just want you off my back. As soon as possible.

WOMAN: Ready?

MAN: Ready.

(*He leaps precisely as She jumps backwards. He falls forward and She leaps on his back. She quickly does a handstand on his back as He bends forward*)

WOMAN: Okay?

MAN: Perfect. Okay for you?

WOMAN: Perfect. Down a little.

(*He wriggles upstage a bit*)

MAN: Funny you should ask *me* "Who is it?" Funny.

WOMAN: We've had that out.

MAN: Well it ain't out of me, believe me. I'm a laughing stock.

WOMAN: I won't get into that with you again.

MAN: The truth. You wouldn't know the truth if you fell on it.

WOMAN: On dead ears. Your lies are falling on dead ears!

MAN: Ready?

WOMAN: Ready.

(*They both leap at the same time and stand facing the audience again. They smile, holding hands*)

MAN: What did you tell them?

WOMAN: That you might be taking a trip.

MAN: You rotten bitch. Rotten dirty bitch!

WOMAN: They asked. They asked me what was happening. They're not babies.

MAN: They are. They are. They're too goddam young to get mixed up in this. They can't understand. Could you? (*Pauses*) I'm a laughing stock. A goddam laughing stock. I really hate your ass, Edna.

WOMAN: Now!

(*They both dive at the stage floor beside each other. They stand on their hands and walk the stage, from side to side, in a comic handstand stroll*)

MAN: I can't walk anywhere . . . do anything . . . without people laughing. I'm funny to people. Funny. Like a humpback, a freak. Everybody knows.

WOMAN: Nobody knows. Nobody knows unless you told them.

MAN: Up.

(*They spring to their feet and stand side by side, holding hands, facing the audience*)

WOMAN: I can't go into that with you. You want to leave, leave. You want to stay, stay. But I can't go into that with you. You understand? (*Pauses*) Ready?

MAN: Ready.

(*She lies back on the stage floor and He does a headstand on her knees*)

MAN: I don't need you.

WOMAN: I don't need you.

(*They continuously, rhythmically, exchange positions. They speak and move in point and counterpoint*)

MAN: I hate your ass.

WOMAN: I hate you more.

MAN: I've never loved you. I never did.

WOMAN: You took advantage.

MAN: Took advantage? That's a laugh. How can you take advantage of a . . .

WOMAN: Of a *what?*

MAN: . . . overpay her??? (*He laughs*) Huh? Answer that one.

WOMAN: You're a shit. A real shit.

MAN: You've got a rotten mouth.

WOMAN: I never did. Never did, 'til I got stuck with you. I'll tell you that.

MAN: You know what I wish? You know what I wish? I wish you were dead. I swear to God. That's what I wish. (*Pauses*) Ready.

(*She leaps onto his back*)

MAN: I really want you off my back, Edna. You're like a lead weight just strapped to me. Strapped to me. I swear to God. I really want you off my back.

WOMAN: Ready?

MAN: Ready.

(*She leaps from his back onto the stage floor. She stands on her hands and He walks her around, holding her feet, so They form a berserk wheelbarrow*)

MAN: I really want you off my back.

WOMAN: You wanna leave, leave. You wanna stay, stay. I personally couldn't care less.

MAN: I hate you, Edna. I hate you.

WOMAN: You said it all ready. You said it.

MAN: And I meant it. I meant it. You'll see after I'm gone. You'll see. Who's gonna tell you when to move? When to think?

WOMAN: Now!

(*He leaps into the air and She does a roll under his legs. He falls forward into a handstand and She walks him around now as the wheelbarrow*)

MAN: When to move? When to think? Who?

WOMAN: Now!

(*They leap into their forward position, holding hands and smiling*)

MAN: You just watch me once I'm free of you, baby. Just watch me. Who I want *when* I want.

WOMAN: Now!

(*He leaps into a handstand and She dives through his legs. They're both walking on their hands again in a reprise of their comic stroll*)

MAN: "Might be taking a trip"!

WOMAN: What should I have said? That you want a divorce?

MAN: Who said that? I didn't say "divorce"! Not me. I hinted maybe, but I never said that. Not divorce. Not me.

WOMAN: (*Showing emotion now*) I said . . . I said . . . divorce.

MAN: When?

WOMAN: In my mind. In my *mind*. I said I want out. I want away from you.

MAN: You're crazy, you know that? What are you gonna do with the kids? Without me? Huh? What are you gonna do? Tell me *that!*

WOMAN: I don't care, that's what. That's what I got to tell you is that I don't care. I slave for *what?* To put your supper on the table? You don't eat it. You eat it and you don't like it. If I didn't put your supper on the table, you'd starve. Why?—because you're too dumb to get your own supper.

MAN: Up your ass, Edna.

WOMAN: Ready?

MAN: Ready.

(*She leaps forward and He leaps onto her back*)

WOMAN: Get out. Just get out. But don't tell anybody you left *me*, because I'll tell 'em all the truth.

MAN: And what's that?

WOMAN: That I threw you out. Threw you right out.

MAN: The hell you threw me out. *I left.*

WOMAN: No chance.

MAN: I left. I walked right out. I'm free. Me. I walked out.

WOMAN: Right out!

MAN: No chance. Right out. I *walked* right out in the . . . into the . .

WOMAN: Garbage.

MAN: . . . Street!

WOMAN: Bullshit!

MAN: Bullshit!

WOMAN: Ready?

MAN: Ready.

(*They leap forward and face the audience. Strained smiles. They don't move*)

MAN: My back. It hurts.

WOMAN: Age.

MAN: Don't be ridiculous.

WOMAN: Age.

MAN: I'm young, Edna. Bitch. Rotten bitch. Rotten-bitch-Edna, I'm young.

WOMAN: Smile, face-front. Bend slow. Touch your toes. It'll unlock. Smile . . .

MAN: (*Following her instructions*) See? I'm touching my toes.

WOMAN: It unlocked.

MAN: Pull your tits up. They're sagging.

WOMAN: Don't be ridiculous.

MAN: Pull them up. They're sagging. Sagging way the hell down, too. Awful to look at, those two sagging glands. M'am—short for mammary. (*Considers it*) Not bad at all. It's a sad, sad sag, Edna-m'am.

WOMAN: Bastard!

(*She rushes at him, fist clenched, trying to punch him. He grabs her fist and They Indian hand-wrestle a bit. The advantage shifts back and forth . . . the fight is fierce . . . but neither seems to be winning, ever, really*)

MAN: Saggy.

WOMAN: Bad-back!

MAN: Sad saggy sacks!

WOMAN: Crack-back. Crack-back. Out of whack.

MAN: Whack this, Edna.

WOMAN: Not for a million dollars!

MAN: You're wrestling a man! A man!

WOMAN: Old. Old. An *old* man!

MAN: The same age, Edna. Precisely and exactly the same goddam age.

WOMAN: Perform.

MAN: Well as ever.

WOMAN: Back locks.

MAN: Sacks sag.

WOMAN: There's still time.

MAN: Goddam right!

WOMAN: There's still time!

MAN: Goddam, goddam right!

WOMAN: For what?

MAN: "For what?" What?

WOMAN: For what? Time? For what?

MAN: Can we stop?

WOMAN: What? Stop what?

MAN: Wrestling.

WOMAN: (*After a long, long silence*) Yes. Tonight. We can stop.

MAN: Are you . . . sure? Are you sure you don't just say "tonight" and not really *mean* "tonight"?

WOMAN: (*With quiet dignity; resignation*) I'm sure. I mean tonight. That's clear enough. Tonight.

MAN: Never to wrestle again, then? Tonight, then? *Never?*

WOMAN: Never.

MAN: You're not frightened to . . . to . . . end it?

WOMAN: The wrestling?

MAN: The wrestling. The balance. That too.

WOMAN: Frightened? No. No, I'm not frightened.

MAN: I wouldn't mind living a bit more. If only it could be . . .

WOMAN: Pleasant?

MAN: Yes. That too.

WOMAN: I'd like to . . .

MAN: End it?

WOMAN: Yes.

MAN: You're sure, then. You're absolutely . . .

WOMAN: Certain?

MAN: Yes?

WOMAN: Yes.

MAN: Ready?

WOMAN: Ready.

(*They begin to do cartwheels, slowly and controlled at first. The dialogue is spaced between the acrobatic movements*)

WOMAN: Tonight then?

MAN: Why not?

WOMAN: This is the last time?

MAN: The last time.

WOMAN: Make it good then. If you can, make it good.

(*Their cartwheels increase furiously*)

MAN: I don't need you.

WOMAN: I don't need you.

MAN: I hate you.

WOMAN: I hate you.

(*Now the cartwheels have lost form. The Man and Woman are in a berserk dance of death. They lift themselves up from the stage floor and flog themselves down again. The thumping and crashing against the stage floor is awful to watch. They gasp and groan in pain*)

MAN: Please . . .

WOMAN: Stop . . .

MAN: God! Oh, God!

WOMAN: Oh my God!

MAN: Please . . .

WOMAN: Please . . .

MAN: Edna? (*He stops and lies as an animal on his haunches, watching her slam herself against the floor, screaming in agony*) Edna! Edna!

WOMAN: Arghhhh! Arrrr! Arghhhh!

(*She moves slowly now as her weight becomes heavier and heavier and the sound of her body hitting the floor more awesome*)

MAN: (*A scream in terror as he realizes*) Ednaaaaaaaa!

(*She lies still. He bangs his body against the floor in a short definite rhythm to his short stabbing cries*)

MAN: Edna. Edna. Edna. Edna. Edna. Edna. Edna. Edna. Edna. Edna. Edna. Edna. Edna. Edna. Edna. Edna.

(*Slowly, as He beats himself against the floor, heaving his body higher each time and heavier with each blow. There is a silence. She raises her head slightly. He raises his head slightly. He stares at her*)

MAN: You're not dead.

WOMAN: (*Softly*) No.

(*The lights fade to blackness*)

The Play Is Over

Ed Bullins

THE
GENTLEMAN CALLER

(A Parable)

Ed Bullins

Ed Bullins made his initial appearance in *The Best Short Plays* annuals in 1969 with his powerful and haunting drama, *Clara's Ole Man*. When the latter opened in New York (with two companion pieces by Mr. Bullins: *The Electronic Nigger* and *A Son, Come Home*) the author was greeted by members of the press with such rare encomiums as: "The American Place Theatre has given a first New York production to another exciting writer. A major new talent. A welcome addition to the ranks of New York playwrights. His plays reveal a gift for creating compelling characters in absorbing situations. The plays are sad, funny, harsh and horrifying."

The triple bill that brought acclaim to Mr. Bullins was so successful in its limited engagement at the American Place Theatre that it later was transferred to the stage of the Martinique where it ran for an additional seventy performances. At season's end, *Newsweek* magazine designated Ed Bullins as "one of the three most original dramatists introduced to New York audiences during the year" and in that same month, he was cited with a Drama Desk-Vernon Rice Award for "outstanding achievement in the Off-Broadway Theatre, 1967–68 season."

Mr. Bullins (b. 1936) is from Philadelphia, "from the underprivileged class, spent most of his adult life in California, in and out of college, in and out of work." His stories, essays and poems have appeared in numerous publications and his plays have been staged in many corners of the world. He is one of the founders of Black Arts/West in San Francisco's Fillmore District, patterned after his close friend LeRoi Jones' Black Arts Repertory Theatre/School in Harlem. As a member of the Black Arts Alliance (an organization of Black Theatre Groups) he has assisted Mr. Jones in film-making and stage productions on the West Coast.

In 1968, Mr. Bullins edited a special issue of *The Drama Review* devoted to Black Theatre which he believes is "such a strong force that just as Black Music changed all American music, Black Theatre will change all American theatre."

When the New Lafayette Theatre moved to its present

Harlem location in 1968, it chose Mr. Bullins' full-length play, *In the Wine Time,* to inaugurate the premises, and for the second time within the year, his work earned an enthusiastic reception. In 1969, the New Lafayette Theatre and Workshop, an all-Black company that presents drama with contemporary themes, received from the Ford Foundation a grant of $529,350 to support (and develop) its professional activities in the Harlem community.

The Gentleman Caller (published here for the first time) formed part of *A Black Quartet* comprised of four short plays by LeRoi Jones, Ronald Milner, Ben Caldwell and Mr. Bullins. Originally presented by the Chelsea Theater Center at the Brooklyn Academy of Music, the exciting response from press and public promptly motivated a transfer (for an indefinite run) to Off-Broadway's Tambellini's Gate Theatre. Richard F. Shepard, in covering the presentation for *The New York Times,* described *The Gentleman Caller* as "a short play that holds the viewer from start to finish."

A collection of the author's works, *Five Plays by Ed Bullins,* was published in 1969, and in its commendation of the volume, *Publisher's Weekly* declared that "Bullins writes a sharp, hard-hitting dialog and is acidly humorous, with an occasional hint of thwarted lyricism breaking through . . . His work shows coherence and power."

Recently, Mr. Bullins became the recipient of a personal Rockefeller Foundation grant "to provide for an uninterrupted period of writing."

Characters:

THE MAID
THE GENTLEMAN
MADAME
MR. MANN

Scene One

A comfortably furnished living room in a fashionable section (if there be any) of a northern American city.

Against the back wall is a gun rack with rifles and shotguns in it. Upon the wall are mounted and stuffed heads of a Blackman, an American Indian, a Viet Namese and a Chinese.

The telephone rings. The Maid enters and answers the phone. She is in the classic image of how a Negro maid is thought to look—large, heavy, black, sometimes (though seldomly) smiling, mostly fussying to herself, but always in her place, at least for the moment.

MAID: Hello? . . . Nawh . . . Madame's not takin' no calls. Sho I'm sho. Nawh . . . nawh . . . can't do dat. (*A knock at the door*) Nawh, sah . . . I can't do dat. Now I gotta hang up now, man. Bye . . . bye, I said.

(*She hangs up. Another knock. She crosses to door, opens it. A well-dressed young man, somewhat blacker than she, stands outside*)

MAID: Deliveries in the rear, boy!

(*She slams the door. Immediately, another knock. The Maid turns back, muttering and scowling, and opens the door. The young man is standing in the same spot*)

MAID: What you messin' wit me fo, boy? Is somethin' da matta wit you?

(*He hands her his card. She reads the piece of paper and looks confused, turning it upside down and peering at its*) *back, and starts to close the door partially, though thinks better of the act, and recovers)*

MAID: Well . . . I guess you should come in. (*She leads him into the room, takes his hat and shows him a chair. Shakes head, to herself)* Uummm uummm . . . don't know what the world is comin' ta dese hare days. Always somethin's else ta mess wit you! (*To the visitor)* What you goin' round messin' things up fo, huh? (*Peeved)* Well, what for? I jest can't understand yous young'uns none. (*Turns; over her shoulder)* I'll go tell the Missy you's here.

(She exits. The Gentleman Caller observes the surroundings and lights a dark cigarette. He looks for a moment at the rifle hung above the mantle. Noises off-stage. Madame's voice is heard warbling "America." The Maid's voice is heard mumbling, or is not heard, being lost in the mumbles, then bursts forth in a vigorous chorus of a Negro spiritual. Silence. The lights brighten to glaring orange and harsh yellow, then dim to accommodate Madame's complexion, and Madame enters. She wears an expensive looking dressing gown. The Gentleman Caller sits with his legs crossed, smoking)

MADAME: So you're here at last! Well, I suspected you'd come like this. When we least expect you or are prepared. My most private leisurely moments . . . and I find you sitting with your legs crossed in my home! Blowing smoke from those terrible imported cigarettes all over my curtains and drapes! (*Frets)* Ohhh . . . now what do you have to say for yourself and how you treat me! . . . How you treat me! . . . No respect in my own home. Come, you, now tell me. What do you have to say for yourself?

(He continues to smoke. She takes a seat across from him)

MADAME: You'll have to wait for my husband. He's in the bathroom . . . Shaving! And if I were him I wouldn't hurry . . . not for you in any case. Ohhh . . . where is everybody! (*She calls)* Mamie . . . Mamie! (*Whining)* Ohhh . . . where is she?

(*The Maid enters*)

MAID: Yas'sum?

MADAME: We'll have tea, Mamie. Unless our gentleman caller prefers something . . . (*He shakes his head*) . . . No, he doesn't . . . so tea will do for the two of us.

MAID: Yas'sum.

MADAME: Mr. Mann will join us later.

MAID: Yas'sum, Mrs. Mann.

(*The Maid exits. Madame appears relieved, more relaxed*)

MADAME: What a blessing Mamie is. (*Broad smile*) I don't know what I'd do without her. (*Warming up*) She's been with the family for years. One of the truly worthwhile possessions my father left us with.

(*The Gentleman uncrosses and recrosses his legs*)

MADAME: (*Rises, walks in back of her chair and touches the fabric*) She's getting old now and times are changing. Yes, changing, quite a bit. And Mamie's getting to be something of an inconvenience . . . but tradition, family sentiments and loyalty are so much better than what the times would declare . . . don't you think so, mister . . . mister . . . (*Nods head*) Oh, I see; I see now.

(*She walks around the room, pulling together drapes, turning on a lamp, lifting a bound book and reading the title*)

MADAME: You're not very conventional, sir, are you? (*Faces him*) Are you surprised that I call you sir? And you have reason to be, for though I'm entirely orthodox, as you can see, I'm not a fool. Now my husband . . . well, that's another matter! But as I said, you're not very conventional. Or are you *too* conventional but in an unsuspecting way . . . your manner, perhaps . . . for one is led to think of its being very different than something usual. Say for instance, an Englishman might look very out of place in the dress of an Eskimo. Unless, of course, he were in the Arctic, or . . . well, enough of that. You're here. And we're here . . . and somehow it all doesn't fit together, the way things are going, I mean, not to our reckoning, at least. (*She sits again*) Take for instance me. That's right, *me*. Wouldn't it be thought odd if I were to sit beside you on a bus when I could more easily have found a seat alone or with someone else? Someone that's . . . well, you know what I'm getting at. Now what would people think? What would they say? And, yes, it's true that I never ride in buses, but it might happen one day, so I must prepare myself, we all must prepare ourselves for the worst, don't you agree? Having seen what you believe is the worst, I know you are in sympathy, aren't you? So, you're not. (*Gesturing*) Now what would they say? The people, I mean. How would I feel about how they'd think? Oh, it's just too horrid to conceive.

(*The Maid enters with a tray. She moves to serve Madame. The phone rings*)

MADAME: The guest first, Mamie, please!

MAID: (*Confused*) But Missy.

MADAME: (*Warning*) Don't question me, Mamie!

MAID: Yas'sum.

MADAME: And answer that telephone, Mamie. Same message, please.

MAID: Yas'sum. (*She lifts phone*) Now lissen, man, I ain't got time fo all dat foolishness, now. She don' wan'na talk ta you. She ain't gonna come and I ain't gonna call her no mo'. Good bye!

(*She hangs up. The tea is served; the Maid exits*)

MADAME: (*To Gentleman*) You know who that is, don't you?

(*He nods*)

MADAME: (*Annoyed*) He shouldn't be so insistent. Mamie should know by now how to handle him! (*Explaining*) This is the trouble with keeping people with you too long. They feel that they can question your authority as if they had some priority. Now I knew how I wanted it all done. (*Becoming more angry*) How dare she question me! Me! How dare she?

(*The Maid returns*) . . .

MAID: (*Worried and sullen*) Is there anything else, ma'am?

MADAME: Is there anything else? You meant to say is there anything wrong, didn't you? Of course there's not! What would make you think that there was anything wrong?

MAID: Why I jest thought there might . . .

MADAME: (*Rises*) How dare you to think! (*Pointing toward exit*) Excuse yourself and leave us, Mamie Lee King. At once! Do you hear?

MAID: (*More sullen; avoiding the Visitor's eyes*) 'Scuse me . . . yawhl. (*She exits*)

MADAME: (*Sits*) How dare she take it upon herself to return? And to ask questions? And to think? Ohhh . . . what are the times coming to? What *are* they coming to? There's only one solution. I have failed to face up to it before now. She must go. (*Arm at her forehead in classic anguish stance*) She must go! (*Calls*) Mamie! Mamie, come here at once!

(*The Maid enters*)

MAID: Yas'sum.

MADAME: You are fired.

MAID: Yas'sum.

MADAME: Get your things and be off at once.

MAID: Yas'sum. (*She turns to go*)

MADAME: Is that all you have to say?

MAID: Yas'sum.

MADAME: Why?

MAID: 'Cause I didn't want to upset lil Missy anymo'.

MADAME: Ohhh, how sweet! You're such a living doll, Mamie! (*To Gentleman*) Isn't that simply divine . . . so innocent . . . so childlike and naive.

MAID: Yas'sum. (*The phone rings; she answers it*) Wha? Ya don' say? Nawh, I ain't gonna call her. Wouldn't if I could. Thank ya, sah. (*She hangs up*)

MADAME: (*Inspired*) You know . . . you know, Mamie, dear . . . I don't think you'd better go after all.

MAID: Nawh, ma'am.

MADAME: In fact, I'm thinking of giving you a two-dollar a month raise. And . . . and . . . now listen to this, Mamie, dear, this is the best . . . and that new black taffeta dress I got for Aunt Hattie's funeral six years ago. Well, that's yours too, dear. Isn't that thrilling for you? Of course I'll have to first talk to my husband, Mr. Mann, about it first and see what he has to say. But you know how much his word means with me . . .

MAID: Yas'sum.

MADAME: (*Warm*) And you know I wouldn't turn you out anyway, don't you, you old actress, you? Why it's right in daddy's will where we are to give you a home until that day when you lay your old grey and black head on the duckdown pillows and rise no more.

MAID: Yas'sum.

MADAME: Now how could I go against daddy's wishes?

MAID: Don' know, ma'am.

MADAME: (*Smiling*) Good. Now go back to your kitchen and wait until I call you.

MAID: (*Stands firm*) Well, ma'am . . .

MADAME: (*Surprised*) What is it, Mamie?

MAID: (*Shuffles from one foot to another*) I guess this is as good a time as any to tell you . . .

MADAME: (*Annoyed*) Tell me what, Mamie?

MAID: I'm quittin'.

MADAME: (*Disbelief*) You're what?

MAID: Quittin'.

MADAME: You're not! (*To Gentleman*) Did you hear what she said? (*He doesn't respond*) You *can't* be leaving, Mamie?

MAID: I'm so too.

MADAME: But you can't!

MAID: Am too.

MADAME: But you can't, Mamie, dear.

MAID: Yas I can.

MADAME: But what about all these years you've spent with me? With us?

MAID: I dunno, ma'am.

MADAME: What about my suckling your big flabby breasts . . .

MAID: They dry now, ma'am.

MADAME: . . . and you raised me as one of your own?

MAID: Dat's cause I's never had time fo mah own, ma'am.

MADAME: And the love and respect I showed you. (*Silence*) And the devotion and loyalty and gratitude you have for me. (*Silence*) What about the will? (*Silence*) Daddy said that if you left that it would be against his wishes and . . .

MAID: (*Loudly*) Yas'sum!

MADAME: (*Pleading*) Then . . .

MAID: I'm quittin'.

MADAME: (*Last resort*) What about your raise and . . .

MAID: Tonight's my last night. (*She exits*)

MADAME: (*Furious*) The idea! (*To Gentleman*) The idea . . . just think of it!

(*Madame paces about the room, mutters, looking off toward where the Maid disappeared. Then, she stops and abruptly turns to the Gentleman and pulls open her dressing gown, revealing that she has nothing beneath the gown save Madame*)

MADAME: Like this?

(*The Gentleman looks at her, expressionless. Madame begins a slow, unfamiliar to her, dance*)

MADAME: Like this, boy? Huh? You want this, boy? You want some of this? Or should I say, *Sir?* (*Mocking*) Sir . . . now how does that sound? Sir? Boy Sir? Sir Boy? Now do you want people to be going around saying "Sir, this . . . Sir that?" Huh? Do you? How about if I said, "Sir, come and get some of this, come get your goodies." How would you like that? (*She moves closer to him, and less clumsy*) Let's leave that kind of Sir stuff to my old hubby. That stupid clunk! We'll just be more . . .

(*The Gentleman rises, turns his back and moves away from Madame, and to the bookcase where he lifts a heavy tome*)

MADAME: (*Covering herself, exasperated*) Why, I never! You're not going to *read* . . . !

(*She attacks him and tries to claw the book from his hands. He shoves her to the floor*)

MADAME: Why *you* . . . *you* . . . !

(*The Gentleman waggles his finger at her, as she rises and pulls the service cord*)

MADAME: (*Anxiously*) Mamie! Mamie! Where are you? Can't you hear me ringing for you? Where is she? She *couldn't* have been serious about leaving. What shall I do? Mr. Mann will help! (*Calls:*) Mr. Mann! Mr. Mann! Come out right away! Do you hear me? At once, Mr. Mann! Ohhh . . . what's wrong with him? Why won't *someone* come? Mr. Mann, you have company . . . a guest. A guest, Mr. Mann. He's waiting for you. Been here a long long time waiting, Mr. Mann. (*She sighs, picks up a cigarette from a jeweled case and lights it. Then pours herself tea, composes herself and sizes up the situation. She sits, blows out smoke and sips tea*) So you don't want me? Hmmmm, times have *really* changed, haven't they? (*Annoyed, calling*) Mr. Mann! Mr. Mann! (*Disgust*) Ohhh, that man! What could he be doing? And for so long? Always pretending to shave! He'll never be without that damn white beard of his . . .

(*The Gentleman moves involuntarily. Madame notices movement*)

MADAME: Say, what goes on . . . ? (*Testing*) All I said was that he'll never be without that damned beard . . .

(*The Gentleman flinches*)

MADAME: . . . of his . . . (*Under her breath*) He'll have it to the day he dies. (*Raises voice*) Oh, I'm beginning to see.

I see now! (*To Gentleman*) You wouldn't want *that,* would you? *Not that?*

(*The Gentleman smiles for the first time*)

MADAME: You would? (*Hilarious*) Oh ha ha ha . . . (*She laughs very unladylike for a full minute*) Oh, you have to be joking! You *must* be. You just can't be serious?

(*The Gentleman nods*)

MADAME: Oh, how marvelous! Ha ha ha . . . heee heee heee . . . Oh, dear! Pardon me, Sir, while I bust a dignified gut! Ha ha . . . and for this you came so . . . ha ha . . . so goddamned far? Oh, my god, how diabolical history is! (*The telephone rings. Catching her breath*) That damned thing again! Doesn't he ever sleep? (*Ignoring phone; to Gentleman*) Don't you want to tell me? No, you don't. But just think of it! With me here thinking . . . thinking . . . that . . . ha ha ha . . . You beautiful young man, you! You've made my day . . . no . . . ha ha . . . my life . . . *complete* . . . ha ha . . . (*Irritated*) Oh, Mamie, come on and answer the phone! (*Laughing more*) Mamie! Mr. Mann! All of you come here! This is simply too too . . . just too marvelous for words! Ha ha ha . . . (*She wipes away tears*) They won't come yet. Still playing their roles. *But if they only knew.* Why doesn't she get that phone? (*Rising*) Here, let me pour you some more tea. (*Touches his hand as she pours*) Isn't there anything else I can get you? Are you comfortable enough? (*She returns to her seat*) My, my. Well, here we are. How nice. It isn't all that stuffy, is it? Really, we do have a certain style about us, wouldn't you admit? A style that we've acquired down through the years . . . from practice, from tradition. From living with certain precepts in mind. It's not all soft, our life, you know. There's a certain rigidness of the spiritual fibers . . . a kinda mystical determinism of the psyche, you might say . . . a certain attitude of predestination . . . a preordained vision of ecclesiastical rank. Keeps one's uppers tight behind his or her straight lip, I might say. In fact, and I shall say, for I know. I'm an expert, a virtual veteran with a daddy who was all blood and entrails . . . all spit, sweat and shit. But that husband of mine . . . *him.* (*Angrily*) Mamie, answer it, please! (*Noise off*) But here they come now. And now we can get down to cases, heh, boy? For this is *your* story, isn't it? Now about you, my good little laddy-buck. About you . . . (*She breaks off. Thoroughly agitated, she rises, lifts phone. Voice of Distinction*) Hello, the Mann residence. Hello? Hello? (*She hangs up*) I wonder why he won't speak to me?

Lights Down

Scene Two

Lights up. Mr. Mann is stretched out in the center of the living room floor, dressed in an Uncle Sam suit, without trousers or shoes; his shorts are cut from an American flag; his socks are star spangled.

Madame circles him, an exceedingly long cigarette holder poised with a brown cigarette in it, her eyes upon the Maid.

The Gentleman stands, looking down at Mr. Mann's beard.

MADAME: (*The interrogator*) And now, Miss Mamie Lee King, dear, you say you found Mr. Mann dead?
MAID: Yas'sum.
MADAME: Dead in the bathroom . . .
MAID: Yas'sum.
MADAME: From a self-inflicted wound in the throat . . .
MAID: Yas'sum.
MADAME: From a straight razor!
MAID: Yas'sum. He cut his throat while sittin' on the toilet seat. I found him dead as a chicken.
MADAME: (*Blows out smoke; with distaste*) Well, so much for details. Now let's see what shall we do? Hmmm.

What do you suggest, Mamie? You always keep a level head in these kinds of emergencies.

(*The Maid ponders. The Gentleman crouches down on all fours and with much trepidation touches Mr. Mann's white beard, appears astounded, and snatches the beard off Mr. Mann's face*)

MADAME: (*To Gentleman*) Yes, it's *false!* Surprised, huh?

MAID: Wahl, dere's only one thing to do, ma'am, as I sees it.

MADAME: Good! Like I always said, you can always be depended upon. You good nigger, you. I don't know *what* Mr. Mann and I would have done without you all these years!

(*She turns to the Gentleman; the Maid goes to the mantle and takes down the gun. The phone begins to ring*)

MADAME: Do you know that even when I was just a little girl I never feared . . . for Mamie was there! She was like the mountains, unchanging. Like time, limitless. Always faithful, always the source of inspiration. Young . . . (*Paternal*) . . . Young man, you can be proud you sprang from her loins. You can be thankful for having the very salt of the earth, the very blood and marrow of the universe as . . .

(*The Maid shoots Madame in the head*)

MAID: (*To Gentleman*) Okay, boy, you grab him and drag him in the hallway! (*She points gun. The Gentleman looks dazed, confused*) Don't you hear me talkin' ta ya? Boy, put down that ole piece of hair; it came from between mah granny's legs, anyway. Now I've taken enough of yo silly behind stuff. Grab his feet like I said!

(*The Gentleman grabs Mr. Mann's feet and drags him off, the beard stuffed in the Gentleman's coat pocket. The Maid drags Madame off by the back of the collar. The telephone continues ringing. A shot is heard off, and the lights turn to red and blues.*

The Maid returns, wearing an exotic gown of her own design. Her bandanna has been taken off; her au naturel hair style complements her strong Black features. She picks up the phone)

MAID: *(Refined)* Hello? Yes, you wish to speak to the madame? *Yes, she is speaking . . .*

(Slow curtain as the Maid speaks into the phone of high finance and earthchanging matters)

Black

Terence Rattigan

ALL ON HER OWN

Terence Rattigan

Terence Rattigan, one of the most successful and popular of Britain's playwrights, was born in London on June 10, 1911. Educated at Harrow and Trinity College, Oxford, he sprang to prominence in 1936 with his comedy *French Without Tears* which ran for over a thousand performances in the West End. Seven years later, he was to duplicate this theatrical feat with *While the Sun Shines,* a West End landmark for 1,154 performances.

Among Mr. Rattigan's other noted plays are: *Flare Path; Love in Idleness* (retitled *O Mistress Mine* for Broadway where it was performed by the Lunts for almost two years); *The Winslow Boy* (recipient of the Ellen Terry Award for the best play produced on the London stage during 1946, it won the 1947–48 New York Drama Critics Circle Award as the season's best foreign play); *The Browning Version* (the Ellen Terry Award play for 1948); *Adventure Story; Who Is Sylvia?; The Deep Blue Sea; The Sleeping Prince; Man and Boy; Separate Tables;* and *Ross.*

The enormity of Mr. Rattigan's popular success has made him wealthy (Tennessee Williams once countered the accusation of being one of the richest living playwrights by saying, "Terence Rattigan makes me look like a pauper.") as well as a frequent target of the new-wing and avant-garde dramatists and critics who regard him as the prototype English playwright of the old school—the school of the 1930's drawing-room comedy, of elegant flippancy and glossy theatrical confections. Yet the true fact is that of the more than twenty plays written by Mr. Rattigan (and by the way, only *three* were written in the thirties) at least ten have not been comedies at all.

A staunch defender of craftsmanship, he has expressed his thoughts on the subject in a preface to the collected edition of his works: "The school of thought that condemns firm dramatic shape derives, I suppose, originally from Chekhov, an author who, in my impertinent view, is not usually properly understood either by his worshippers or his active imitators. I believe that his plays are as firmly shaped as Ibsen's. The stream that seems to meander its casual length along does so between strong artificial banks, most carefully and cunningly contrived by a master craftsman. To admire the stream and ignore the artifice that gave it its course seems to me a grave oversight, and may well have led over the years to the present critical misapprehension by which laziness of construction is thought a virtue and the shapelessness of a play is taken as evidence of artistic integrity."

In addition to his works for the stage, Mr. Rattigan has written more than fifteen major films and a number of original television plays, one of these being *All On Her Own*, here published for the first time. Originally produced on B. B. C. Television in 1968 with Margaret Leighton as star, the presentation garnered much praise. *Plays and Players* magazine said of it, "Rattigan's virtuoso piece, which set Miss Leighton drunkenly interrogating her dead husband in an attempt to find out whether he had killed himself deliberately or not, had the real stuff of drama in it . . . altogether a little gem."

(*Note:* The editor has taken the liberty of deleting technical television terms from the manuscript that were, in the main, set down for the director and camera crew.)

The author, who in 1958 was made a Commander of the British Empire by Queen Elizabeth, soon will be represented again in the West End with his newest play, *Bequest to the Nation,* to be presented by H. M. Tennent, Ltd.

Characters:

ROSEMARY

HOSTESS, *an offstage voice.*

Place:

London; the present.

Rosemary is standing at the door of either a house or a ground-floor flat, speaking to someone who evidently has been her hostess at a party, the noise of which is coming to us from an open window.

ROSEMARY: It's been a marvelously rewarding evening—thank you so very much. Do tell your young guest of honor how brilliant I thought his paper was. I can't say I entirely agreed with all that he said about Kafka, but then that school never has struck much of a chord on my piano. I mean, I don't really believe in "nameless fears"—I don't think there are any fears that can't be named, and once they're named they can be exorcised. Or is that a very silly thing to say?

HOSTESS: Not at all. Not many people take that point of view.

ROSEMARY: Yes. Unfashionable, I agree, but I don't mind that. Well, goodbye again. It really was a heavenly party.

HOSTESS: I'm so glad you enjoyed it.

(Rosemary starts to go, then turns back as the Hostess speaks again)

HOSTESS: I'm sure someone will be going your way in a car.

ROSEMARY: No. I really don't need a lift, thank you. I live across the way.

HOSTESS: Do you live on your own?

ROSEMARY: Yes, all on my own now—since Gregory's death—the boys are still at school.

HOSTESS: Don't you ever feel lonely?

ROSEMARY: No, not a bit lonely. I don't allow myself to be, anyway. The trick is always to have enough to occupy one's mind. I despise loneliness. It's such a defeat. Anyway, who could ever be lonely in Hampstead?

(*She walks off into the darkness. The lights come up slowly to reveal Rosemary's sitting room. The room reflects her tastes which are discreet to the point of gloom. It is evidently a Victorian house and has just been decorated. After a moment, Rosemary comes in, looks around the room appraisingly, adjusting a couple of articles. Then she pours herself a drink and sits down, taking up a book entitled "Guilt and the Human Psyche: A Study of Contemporary Literature." As she opens the book, the ticking of a clock comes to her ears. She glances at the clock: the hands show 11:25. She lowers the book onto her lap*)

ROSEMARY: What time did you die? (*She has spoken conversationally, as if to a person sitting close to her in the room*) Gregory, what time did you die? Wasn't it about now? The police said you'd been dead between eight and nine hours, and it was eight in the morning Mrs. Avon found you over there, on that sofa . . .

(*She stares at the sofa which is very tidy and clean, not looking in the least as though someone had once been found dead on it*)

ROSEMARY: . . . Or just before. Yes, it must have been before, because when she called me down the clock was striking. It's one of those silly things you remember. So it must have been about now you died.

(*The clock strikes the half-hour*)

A woman at a party I've just been to told me quite seriously that she talks to her husband every night at exactly the hour he died. He sends her long messages on a ouija board or something. Well, I haven't got a ouija board, but I'm talking to you Gregory, and at near enough the time you died. You might just answer, you never know, and then I'll have a story to tell at a party, too . . .

(*She lights a cigarette and inhales deeply*)

Talking to a dead you is as good a way as any of talking to myself, I suppose—which is roughly what talking to you alive was too, come to think of it—only I hope you're not listening because that was rude, and I was never rude to you in all our eighteen years, was I?

(*She laughs into her drink*)

Unfailingly polite—wasn't it "unfailingly" you used to say, or "invariably"? . . . No. "Unfailingly". Poor Gregory—how you hated that, didn't you? How you longed for just one honest, vulgar, hammer-and-tongs husband and wifely flamer! But I never gave it to you, did I? I was brought up to be polite, you see—unfailingly polite. Was that so wrong? (*Answering herself*) Yes, it was. It was pretty damn bloody! (*Surprised*) Do you know—talking to you is rather good for me, Gregory. I should do it more often. It might even make me *honest*.

(*She takes another sip of her drink, then again looks over at the sofa*)

Now *you* be honest, Gregory, and tell me if the police and the coroner and the insurance people were right when they said it was a drunken accident, or if *I'm* right now when I say that you killed yourself?

(*She leaves a long pause, almost as if now she half expects to be answered. Then she shakes her head hopelessly, rises and goes to the sofa. She gazes at the sofa for a moment before stretching herself out on it; a movement she performs as if it were in some way mildly blasphemous. She speaks in a gruff, North Country accent*)

But Rosemary, darling, why should I kill myself? I had everything to live for, hadn't I? I'd just sold my business in Huddersfield for a lot of money, and bought a beautiful house in Hampstead, and for the first time in my life could enjoy all the ease and comfort of a charming, civilized, cultured retirement in

ROSEMARY (cont'd.)

London, with my charming, civilized, cultured wife beside me, and my two charming, civilized, cultured sons at Eton. And my wife is still quite young, you know, as wives go, and *still* quite attractive in her way—well, *I* find her so anyway, but I suppose you'd say I was prejudiced about that and always have been. Oh, yes. I was a lucky man when I was alive. There's no doubt at all about it. Why on earth should I have killed myself?

> (*She gets up from the sofa and goes to replenish her drink. In her own voice*)

If I answered that for you, Gregory, would you *still* tell me whether you did? (*After a pause*) Of course you wouldn't . . .

> (*In Gregory's voice*)

But all that happened that night, Rosemary darling, was that after we had that little tiff about whether I couldn't go out on the town with Alf Fairlie from the rugger club instead of going with you to the ballet—which I never did fancy very much, as you know—along with the Fergusons who always treated me like some kind of a nit who'd married a mile above myself. Not the only ones to do that, down here in Hampstead, come to that, which doesn't always seem to put *you* out too much, Rosemary love—be honest now, does it? Is that why we're in Hampstead?

> (*Stridently, in her own voice*)

Oh, my God! That wasn't me. I'm not as honest as that, am I? Gregory, that must have been you! Gregory, are you in this room? (*Looking round, anxiously*) Are you in this room, Gregory? (*More loudly*) *Are you?*

> (*There is no answer and no sign. Rosemary swallows her drink and pours another*)

Let's try again! (*In North Country accent again*) Well, we had this little argie-bargie, love—remember? And afterwards, you went up to bed—never a cross word, mind you—impeccably polite as . . .

> (*In her own voice, excitement mounting*)

It was "impeccably", not "unfailingly" or "invariably". No, it wasn't—it wasn't—but it *was* just then. Gregory, you *are* here! You are, aren't you? You're here, with me, in this room?

> (*Again, there is no answer and no sign. Controlling herself*)

Go on. Go on, Gregory!

> (*She begins to speak again, with a conscious imitation of his accent, carefully contrived at first—as in the two previous "Gregory" speeches—and only later, does her voice quite suddenly seem to become a spontaneous expression of a living personality*)

All right, Rosemary darling, it was like this . . . You went up to bed, see, impeccably polite . . .

> (*In her own voice*)

That was me that time, not you!

> (*In his voice*)

. . . as always, and it was early still—not more than nine o'clock or thereabouts, and so I'm afraid, love, I got myself at that decanter that you're holding now . . . (*Very gently*) . . . going my way, are you, love?

> (*Rosemary slams the decanter down as if she had hardly known she had it in her hand*)

Careful of the whiskey, love. It's bad stuff for widows living on their own. You had two before you went to the party. Not many there, I shouldn't think, knowing those parties—bad Algerian burgundy, I expect—but you probably sneaked yourself an extra glass or so, shouldn't be surprised. And now three since eleven twenty-five.

> (*Rosemary pours some of her drink back into the decanter*)

That's better, Rosemary darling. Can't be too careful, I always say. Look what happened to me that night.

> (*Rosemary, with an effort at control, pours water into her drink and then, as if shrugging off Gregory's presence, deliberately adds to it from the decanter. Still in Gregory's voice*)

ROSEMARY (*cont'd.*)

Think it's not me talking to you? Think it's just you talking to yourself?

(*In her own voice*)

I know it's just me talking to myself—in a bad Huddersfield accent!

(*In his voice*)

I didn't talk in a Huddersfield accent, love. I was born in Newcastle.

(*Sharply, in her own voice*)

Did I know that? Yes, of course, I must have . . .

(*Controlled*)

All right, Gregory. What happened to you that night? Tell me.

(*There is a pause, as if she really were expecting a reply. Then, she laughs*)

Of course! The game is—I begin and then you take over.

(*In his voice*)

Well, Rosemary darling, you'd gone to bed, as I told you, and I got at the decanter and got myself fairly tipsy.

(*In her own voice*)

No, that wasn't your word. What *was* your word? "Whistled," was that it? No—*whoozled!*

(*Unconsciously, in his voice*)

Aren't you going to say "I wish you wouldn't use that awful word, Gregory! If you mean drunk, why don't you *say* drunk?"

(*In her own voice, now stiff with fear*)

Because you *weren't* drunk. When you came up to my room you were quite sober. If you hadn't been, I'd have smelled it on your breath. I knew what whiskey smelled like on your breath; I'd had enough experience of it these last fifteen years . . .

(*In his voice*)

But not much these last ten years, eh love? Not from very close. And not at all *that* night.

(*In her voice*)

You said you wanted to sleep down here. And I told you to please yourself.

(*In his voice*)

Ay, you did. And I pleased myself. It was then, if you want to know, that I got myself really whoozled. *Boy, did I get whoozled!*

(*After a pause; in her own voice*)

You expected to come to bed?

(*In his voice*)

Not expected. *Hoped,* you might say. I'd said I was sorry, hadn't I?

(*Rosemary nods*)

And it *was* a Friday night, after all. I know it wasn't back at Huddersfield, not working on Saturday and all—not working *any* bloody day down here! And I know things like that had—well—lapsed a bit lately between us—but, well, it's always a good way to make up a quarrel, isn't it?

(*Rosemary nods again*)

Don't cry, love. There's no need for that, now. I told you, I didn't *expect.* I only *hoped.*

(*After a long pause; in her own voice*)

What about those pills?

(*In his voice*)

Well, this sofa isn't much of a place to sleep on, you know. A man my size . . .

(*Rosemary's gaze is fixed upon the sofa*)

Oh, very aesthetical and quite the rage in North London, I don't doubt, but not too comfy for a man in a bit of a state. Whoozled I know, but still in quite a state what with one thing and another. So I went up to the bathroom . . .

(*The immediate impression is that Rosemary is listening intently, although of course she continues to speak*)

. . . and I found that bottle of pills that you use. Nembutal or some such name. Little yellow things. And I gave myself enough to make myself sleep—just two or three . . .

ROSEMARY (*cont'd.*)
>   (*Interrupting herself; quietly*)
Six.

>   (*After a pause; in his voice*)

Was it *six?* I told you I was whoozled, didn't I? Well, doesn't that show it was an accident, love? I mean if I'd wanted to kill myself I'd have taken sixteen, wouldn't I?

>   (*There is a pause. Then Rosemary finishes her drink and shrugs hopelessly. In her own voice*)

Not if you wanted me to think it *was* an accident. And to let me have the money from the insurance.

>   (*With a sudden access of real grief*)

Oh, my God, do you think that money could make up for you? Oh, you bloody, bloody fool! (*A moment*) But how were you to know?

>   (*She goes to replenish her drink*)

Yes! Another whiskey. It'll be the last. Oh, Gregory, why did you do it? It's silly to ask you that, isn't it? I know *why* you did it—*if* you did it. *Did you?* No, what's the point! It'll only be my own brain answering for you again, and my brain will go on thinking *no,* and believing *yes*—yes and no, no and—until the end of time.

>   (*After taking a gulp of her drink*)

And when will that be, Gregory? Are you allowed to know these things? And would you tell me if you were? (*A moment*) No, you'd never say anything to hurt me, would you?

>   (*She looks round the room in silence for a moment*)

It doesn't matter. Yes, I'm lonely, Gregory, and I do miss you. Quite terribly I miss you. Does that surprise you? I expect it does. It certainly surprised me . . .

>   (*She finishes her drink*)

So you had everything to live for, did you? Your work, which you loved, finished by me. All your friends lost, and your life uprooted—by me. Your children, whom you could have loved, made to despise you—by me. And a wife—"unfailingly polite" —who only knew she loved you when you were dead, And whom you loved and went on loving in spite of—I can say it. Oh yes, I'm brave enough! In spite of her driving you to your death . . . (*Raising her voice for the first time*) I *did*, Gregory, didn't I?! I want the *real* truth now, and I'm not going to answer for you any longer through *my* brain and with *my* voice! You'll have to find some other way. Open a door, break a window, upset a table! Make some sign! But do *something*, and tell me the *real truth! Did I kill you?*

(*Nothing stirs in the room and there is no sound*)
I killed you, didn't I? Say it, Gregory—*say it!*

(*The clock quietly and musically begins to strike midnight. There is no other sound. Rosemary waits until it is finished, then goes quietly round the room turning off the lights. The last light left burning is by the sofa. Just before she turns it off, she gently puts her hand on the part where Gregory's head might, one night, have lain. Then, she picks up her book, marks the place, closes it and goes toward the stairs. She stops, turns back and pours herself one more drink, before turning again and walking slowly up the stairs to bed*)

Darkness

Benjamin Bradford

WHERE ARE YOU GOING, HOLLIS JAY?

Benjamin Bradford

A new leading Off-Off-Broadway playwright, Benjamin Bradford also happens to be somewhat of a rarity in a milieu where fulsome expletives are swung about with all the subtlety of a head-happy mallet and sexual gymnastics flow swifter than the currents of the Bay of Fundy. It is refreshing indeed, then, to discover a dramatist who conveys youthful sexual arousal with psychological implications (and in-depth characterization) rather than mere sexological scatology; with poetic simplicity instead of pretentious obscurities.

In *Where Are You Going, Hollis Jay?*, Mr. Bradford "analyzes and delineates the great gap that exists in late adolescents between what they are and what they think they are; would like to be." Although the author is American (born in Alexandria, Louisiana, in 1925), the play initially was produced at the University of Kent (Canterbury, England) and subsequently was dispatched to tour other major British universities including Oxford. It won an honored place in the finals of The National Student Drama Festival, 1969, sponsored by the *London Sunday Times* and in covering the event, the esteemed drama critic Harold Hobson described *Where Are You Going, Hollis Jay?* as "a very pleasant play", while Andrew Samuels of the Oxford University magazine found it to be "very funny indeed . . . the laughter is laughter of recognition, an aid in bringing about a tension between actor and audience through which identification and sympathy are created. . . ."

The author (graduate of the Louisiana State University School of Medicine) pursues a dual career. He is a prominent internist (in Paducah, Kentucky, where he resides with his wife and three children) as well as an active playwright. Bradford follows a distinguished line of physicians who proceeded into the realm of creative writing: Anton Chekhov, W. Somerset Maugham, A. J. Cronin, James Bridie, and a number of others. But Bradford, who admits to being equally dedicated to the pursuit of both his professions, does not intend to abandon his medical career: "It was too many years in the making and I not only have the need to create, I have the need to be needed, to protect, to care for."

Among the Benjamin Bradford plays seen Off-Off-Broadway during the past year are: *Geometric Progression; The Anthropologist; Concentric Circles;* and *The Ideal State.* The latter has been optioned for a full-scale Off-Broadway production scheduled for autumn, 1970.

Where Are You Going, Hollis Jay? appears in print for the first time in *The Best Short Plays 1970.*

Characters:
HOLLIS JAY
ELLIE MC KUEN

Scene:
A quiet, wooded garden.
Stone benches on either side of the garden.
There is a sense of peaceful isolation. Occasionally a
slight breeze stirs the trees. It is May and the world is
very new and at its greenest.
Hollis Jay enters somewhat warily, looking from side to
side. He walks with the clumsiness of the final stages of
adolescence. His face is innocent, almost angelic. He is
carrying a slight unbound manuscript and a book.
As the play develops he will be required to use two
voices. His thinking voice is how he hears himself and
is a rich baritone. (These speeches are in quotation marks
AND SMALL CAPITAL LETTERS.) The voice that the world
hears is a little higher pitched.

HOLLIS: "SHE SAID SHE WOULD COME" (*Pause*) "I DON'T
CARE IF SHE . . ." (*Exuberantly*) "GOD, THE WORLD IS BEAUTIFUL!
GREEN, ALL GREEN . . . I AM A DEFINITION. HOW AM I DEFINED?"
(*His nervousness is apparent in the way he now lights a
cigarette, takes a few short puffs, and quickly stomps it
out*)
"I AM DEFINED AS YOUNG. NOT BAD LOOKING AND SMART AS HELL.
THREE-POINT-FOUR. BETTER THAN MOST. I KNOW A LOT OF THINGS. I
GUESS I KNOW MOST EVERYTHING THERE IS TO KNOW. THE REST WILL
BE REVIEW, I GUESS."
(*Mimicking*)
Mr. Jay, we will review the pre-Raphaelite poets this week, and
their contribution to the literature of tomorrow.
(*Proudly*)

"THE LITERATURE OF TOMORROW. THAT'S ME. I'M CLEVER. ELLIE SAID I'M CLEVER. AND I AM. NO, THERE'S NOT MUCH MORE FOR ME TO LEARN. I'M EIGHTEEN. YOU LEARN IT ALL BY THEN OR YOU DON'T LEARN IT AT ALL. SURE THE PROFS KNOW A LOT, BUT JUST THEIR OWN FIELDS. THAT'S ALL. DR. JAMES IS STUPID. THEY'RE ALL A LITTLE STUPID. BUT I'M NOT. WHAT WAS I THINKING A BIT AGO? OH . . . A DEFINITION. I'M AN ANALYST. I ANALYZE. I SEE RIGHT THROUGH PEOPLE. I UNDERSTAND THEM. AND I UNDERSTAND ME. THAT'S THE IMPORTANT THING. I KNOW ME. WHAT MAKES ME GO. NONE OF THIS 'WHERE AM I GOING' STUFF FOR ME. I KNOW WHERE I'M GOING! WHERE'S ELLIE? SHE SAID SHE'D COME."

(A moment)

"I DON'T CARE. SHE DOESN'T MEAN A THING TO ME."

(Pause)

"I'M NOT LIKE MY FATHER. WHY DO THEY ALWAYS SAY THAT TO ME? *Just like his father!* I'M NOT LIKE MY FATHER AT ALL. HE DOESN'T KNOW VERY MUCH. WRONG MOST OF THE TIME. CARING ABOUT CARS AND THINGS. WHATEVER HE KNEW HE'S FORGOTTEN, COMPLETELY FORGOTTEN THE WHOLE THING. I DON'T CARE ABOUT HIM EITHER. A LOT OF THINGS I DON'T CARE ABOUT."

(He sits on a bench)

"THAT'S WHAT MAKES YOU FORGET IT ALL, *caring.* I WON'T EVER CARE ABOUT ANYTHING BUT ME AND WHERE I'M GOING. AND I KNOW THAT. BOY, I SURE KNOW THAT."

(He lights a cigarette)

"SHE OUGHT TO BE HERE. SHE CAN'T AFFORD NOT TO COME. SHE'S NOT GOOD LOOKING ENOUGH. PROBABLY SCARED. SHE THINKS I'LL ATTACK HER HERE IN THE WOODS. SHE WANTS ME TO BE SEXUALLY DEPENDENT. SHE WANTS TO BE THE FLAME AND ME THE BUTTERFLY, DASHING MYSELF TO DEATH ON THE ROCKS OF HER FEMININITY. SHE DOESN'T KNOW ME! WHAT DOES SEX MEAN TO ME? WHAT DOES *anything* MEAN TO ME? SHE'S GOING TO BE VERY SURPRISED IF THAT'S WHAT SHE'S EXPECTING. VERY SURPRISED. I'M COOL AS THEY COME."

(A note of anguish)

"GOD, WHERE AM I GOING? WHY AM I HERE?"

(*He hears a noise from behind the trees*)
Ellie, that you, Ellie?
(*Silence*)
"MUST HAVE BEEN A SQUIRREL. MAYBE PEOPLE WATCHING. SEE HOW I
HANDLE IT, SEE HOW I ACT. WELL THEY DON'T KNOW ME. PEOPLE
WATCHING IS SOMETHING ELSE I DON'T CARE ABOUT. I GUESS SHE
THINKS I'VE BEEN AROUND A LOT AND KNOW HOW AND ALL THAT.
I'LL JUST LET HER THINK THAT. I DON'T CARE WHAT SHE THINKS!
MAYBE SHE JUST LIKES MY MIND. I GUESS IT *is* MY BEST PART."
(*He opens the book and reads aloud*)
What, silent still? and silent all?
Ah! no;—the voices of the dead
Sound like a distant torrent's fall,
    And answer, 'Let one living head,
But one, arise,—we come, we come!'
    'Tis but the living who are dumb.
(*As he closes the book*)
" 'In vain—in vain: strike other chords;' THAT LIVING HEAD. THAT'S
ME. THERE IS NO DOUBT THAT I AM DESTINED FOR GREATNESS. HOW?
TIME WILL SHOW. I KNOW WHERE I'M GOING! WHAT I DON'T KNOW
IS *how* I'M GOING."
(*He quickly lights a cigarette*)
"I'M TRYING TO LOOK CASUAL. I HEAR SOMEONE IN THE BUSHES BE-
HIND ME. IT MIGHT BE HER. NO, SHE WOULD COME FROM THE QUAD-
RANGLE, NOT THE RIVER . . ."
(*Pause; he listens*)
"SOMEONE'S MAKING LOVE BACK THERE. WONDER IF I KNOW THEM?
NO! I'M TOO SOPHISTICATED TO GO BACK THERE AND SEE. THEY MAY
JUST BE TALKING. I SHOULD SEE. I WILL."
(*He rises, goes to the upstage area and calls out*)
Somebody back there?
(*Silence; he moves away*)
"THEY'RE QUIET NOW. I'M SORRY I . . . I WOULDN'T WANT TO IN-
TERRUPT THEM."
(*A moment*)

"THEY'RE WALKING AWAY TOWARD THE RIVER. WELL, I DON'T CARE A LOT ABOUT THEM EITHER. I HOPE THEY DIDN'T RECOGNIZE MY VOICE."

(*He returns to the bench*)

"SHE OUGHT TO BE HERE."

(*He flips open the book*)

'Fill high the cup with Samian wine'

(*He slams the book shut*)

"I GUESS I DRINK TOO MUCH. YOU HAVE TO KEEP ABOVE IT ALL. I CAN DRINK MOST FELLOWS UNDER THE TABLE. I'M NOT ASHAMED OF IT. BOY, I SURPRISED THEM ALL, NIGHT BEFORE LAST! WHAT'S SAMIAN WINE? I'LL LOOK IT UP."

(*A moment*)

"I WISH I'D BEEN QUIET. COULD HAVE LISTENED AND HEARD THEM MAKING LOVE. SOMETIMES I'M *stupid* TOO!"

(*Slight pause*)

"I WONDER WHERE THEY'VE GONE TO FINISH? YES, I WISH I'D SEEN THEM. I'D LIKE TO SEE A GIRL STARK NAKED . . . EVEN WITHOUT SHOES. I BET I'D KNOW WHAT TO DO. I'D DO IT WELL TOO."

(*A moment*)

"EVERYBODY'S BIGGER THAN ME. I HATE THAT DAMN LOCKER ROOM BECAUSE EVERYONE IS BIGGER THAN ME! EVEN THE LITTLE GUYS. WOULD A GIRL LAUGH? IF I WAS STARK NAKED AND WALKING TO HER, WOULD SHE LAUGH?"

(*Brightening*)

"HELL! IT'S NOT WHAT YOU GOT, IT'S THE WAY YOU USE IT. I'VE GOT POWERFUL HIPS. I'LL DO IT IN THE DARK. WON'T EVEN TURN ON THE LIGHTS. THEY'LL FEEL MY HIPS, STRONG AND POUNDING. I'LL GET UP, THEY'LL BE BRUISED, PROBABLY BLEEDING, CRYING FOR MORE."

(*Remembering an old Bogart movie*)

"I'LL SAY SORRY BABY, I'M OUT TO MAKE THE WHOLE GODDAMN WORLD. YOU JUST HAD YOUR SHARE. THEY'LL BEG AND PLEAD. ON THEIR KNEES . . . ON GRASS AND COBBLESTONE, THEY'LL WALK ON THEIR KNEES TO ME. I MIGHT BE GENEROUS. IT WOULD DEPEND ON THE GIRL."

(*Plaintively*)

"I JUST WISH I WERE A LITTLE BIGGER."

(*Quickly*)

"NOT THAT I'M NOT SECURE WITH WHAT I'VE GOT. I'M PLENTY SE-
CURE!"

(*Sound of someone approaching. He stops; now, almost
panicking*)

"WHAT'LL I SAY TO HER? HOW'LL I ACT? GOOD GOD, I WISH I HADN'T
COME!"

(*His voice quavering*)

Ellie?

(*Ellie runs in. She is very young, very pretty. Her movements are quick and she is slightly breathless*)

ELLIE: Am I late, Hollis? I'm sorry, I ran most of the
way. I've never been here. Of course, I've *heard* about it! It's
beautiful.

HOLLIS: (*Deliberately flat*) Yes.

ELLIE: Are you angry because I'm late?

HOLLIS: I just got here myself. (*Then*) "THAT'S A LIE. I'VE
BEEN HERE FOR HOURS AND HAD A LASCIVIOUS EXPERIENCE!" (*A
short pause*) I brought it.

ELLIE: Brought what?

HOLLIS: The paper. (*Wistfully*) "SHE'S FORGOTTEN SHE'S
TO HELP ME WITH MY TERM PAPER."

ELLIE: Oh, of course, Hollis. I'd forgotten it for a moment. (*She is enjoying the quiet beauty of the place*)

HOLLIS: (*Impulsively*) I'm a rotten punctuator! (*Ellie
turns*) I can't punctuate worth a damn. (*He picks up the small
manuscript from the bench*) "SHE DOESN'T CARE ABOUT THE PAPER.
WHAT DOES SHE WANT?"

ELLIE: Let's just sit quiet. Oh, I love it here, Hollis. I'm
so glad you suggested it.

(*Silence. She crosses her feet; looks about rapturously*)

HOLLIS: "WHAT DOES SHE WANT ME TO DO . . ? SIT BESIDE
HER? SWEEP HER IN MY ARMS AND . . . WHAT DOES SHE
WANT?" (*Then*) I don't think it's too good.

ELLIE: What?

HOLLIS: My paper, I . . . I don't think it's very good. "A MASTERPIECE, THAT'S ALL."

ELLIE: (*Absorbed*) I've heard the girls talk about this place. I've always wanted to see it. It has quite a reputation.

HOLLIS: I . . . I asked you here for . . .

ELLIE: What, Hollis?

HOLLIS: My paper! (*He sits shyly on the far end of the bench*)

ELLIE: Some of the girls have been here and made out with some of the fellows. Did you know?

HOLLIS: I guess I knew that. (*Reflectively*) "IF I TOLD HER ABOUT THAT COUPLE—?"

ELLIE: Nice place to study, so quiet.

HOLLIS: There were some others, a while ago. I heard them. Studying, I guess.

ELLIE: (*Turning*) Oh? Who were they?

HOLLIS: I . . . I don't know, I didn't care enough to . . . My paper, want to look at it now?

ELLIE: All right. (*He just looks at her*) Hollis, do you want me to read it or not?

HOLLIS: (*Finally hands her the manuscript*) You . . . you won't like it. (*He rises, starts to move away*) "WHEN SHE READS IT, SHE'LL THINK I'M PURE GENIUS."

ELLIE: Where are you going?

HOLLIS: It embarrasses me to watch someone read what I've written.

ELLIE: Silly, I'm sure it's very good.

HOLLIS: No, it's awful.

ELLIE: (*Reading*) The Parabal of George Gordon, Lord Byron. (*She looks up*) That's not how you spell parable. PARABLE.

HOLLIS: I spelled it that way on purpose. I thought it would catch the eye.

ELLIE: Well, it does but I think you ought to spell it right. Do you have a pencil? (*Hollis searches his pockets and gives her the pencil)* Please sit down, you're making me nervous.

HOLLIS: It makes me nervous to sit down. (*She begins to read as he walks nervously about*) Correct anything you find wrong. I didn't learn to punctuate.

ELLIE: No, you didn't. Or spell. (*She erases and corrects as she reads*)

HOLLIS: "SHE'S BORED. SHE DIDN'T WANT TO COME. HER FRIENDS FORCED HER. THEY ALL LAUGHED ABOUT ME, SAID WHAT A JOKE IT WOULD BE TO MEET ME IN THE GLEN. SHE'S NEVER BEEN HERE BEFORE. PROBABLY A VIRGIN. I'M PRETTY GOOD AT SPOTTING VIRGINS. I'M SURE SHE'S ONE. I CAN TELL BY THE WAY THEY CROSS THEIR FEET. SHE CROSSED HERS THAT WAY. SHE DOESN'T REALLY WANT TO READ THE PAPER. SHE WANTS TO LOSE HER VIRGINITY. PROBABLY THOUGHT I'D BRING A CARAFE OF WINE AND PUT DOWN A BLANKET." (*He lights a cigarette*) "SHOULD I OFFER HER ONE?" (*Too casually*) Do you smoke?

ELLIE: (*Shaking her head*) No . . . thanks.

HOLLIS: "SHE DOESN'T SMOKE. I BET SHE'S A SIGN READER. READS ALL THE SIGNS. SHE MAY BE THE SMARTEST GIRL IN CLASS BUT THAT DOESN'T MEAN SHE'S INTELLIGENT. NO COMMON SENSE. SHE'D BELIEVE ANYTHING YOU TOLD HER. WHAT IF I WALKED UP BEHIND HER AND SAID, 'I HAVE LOVED YOU IN BASIC ENGLISH FOR THE LAST SIX MONTHS? I HAVE BEEN DESPERATE WITH LOVE FOR YOU, AND NOW HERE WE ARE ALONE, JUST YOU AND I . . . YOU AND ME . . ? YOU AND I, AND I LOVE YOU.' GODDAMN. I'M A VIRGIN TOO. I BET I'M THE ONLY BOY VIRGIN OVER TWELVE IN THE WHOLE GODDAMN COUNTRY. IT'S ALL IN OPPORTUNITY. I WAS SHELTERED, NO OPPORTUNITIES." (*Pause*) Ellie?

ELLIE: (*Still reading*) Yes?

HOLLIS: Ellie?

ELLIE: Yes . . .

HOLLIS: I . . . Do you like it?

ELLIE: I think it's good. So far.

HOLLIS: "DAMN RIGHT, IT'S GOOD. *I* WROTE IT. OH, THEY'LL RECOGNIZE ME SOMEDAY. SHE'LL TELL ALL HER OLD GRAY HAIRED FRIENDS." (*He mimics Ellie*) "I SPENT AN HOUR WITH HOLLIS JAY

IN THE WOODS AT COLLEGE. WE WERE FRESHMEN, NAIVE AND INNO-
CENT. TOO BAD. IF I HAD PLAYED MY CARDS RIGHT I COULD HAVE HAD
HIM. IMAGINE HAVING HOLLIS JAY!" (*Strongly*) "AND HER OLD GRAY
HAIRED FRIENDS WILL CRY OVER THE OPPORTUNITY GONE FOREVER.
THEY'LL SMILE A LITTLE SMILE BECAUSE LITTLE ELLIE HAD MORE
THAN THE REST OF THEM." (*A moment*) "WHERE'S THE PLACE IN
GREECE? WHERE THE MONKS ARE? NO WOMEN? I THINK I MAY GO
THERE AND BE CELIBATE. INTERNATIONALLY, I MAY BE KNOWN FOR
MY CELIBACY. SHE READS VERY SLOWLY. SHE'S AWFULLY PRETTY. AND
LITTLE. AND SMART. I COULD PUT MY FINGERS ABOUT HER WAIST . . .
SHE'S VERY LITTLE. GOT A BIG CHEST THOUGH. THAT WAS THE FIRST
THING I NOTICED. THAT BIG CHEST. I'D LIKE TO PUT MY HEAD ON HER
CHEST. LORD GOD, WHAT A PLACE TO REST. I WANT . . ." (*Ellie looks
up, puts the pencil and manuscript on the bench*)

HOLLIS: You hate it!

ELLIE: No, I like it. I like it a lot. It's very good.

HOLLIS: You're trying to be nice to me.

ELLIE: I mean it. It's a fresh idea, a new approach to ro-
manticism . . . if that's how you want to look at it. You write
very well.

HOLLIS: I don't at all. I saw you use the pencil a hundred
times.

ELLIE: You really *can't* punctuate. You didn't make a
single marking right. And *that* took a special talent. It should be
worth an A now. Dr. James hates poor punctuation. Milton could
have given him *Paradise Lost,* and if he hadn't punctuated it
properly . . . an F double minus. You learn a lot about punctuation from Dr. James. Hollis, this is very good. I mean it.
Very original. Thank you for letting me read it.

HOLLIS: Oh . . . thank you for reading it. "DOES SHE
really THINK IT IS ORIGINAL, GOOD? IS SHE BEING NICE? I'D GIVE
EVERYTHING I HAVE IF I COULD LOOK INTO THE MIND OF SOMEONE
AND TELL IF THEY ARE HONEST, IF I COULD TELL WHAT THEY *really*
THINK." Thank you for correcting it.

ELLIE: It's fine now.

HOLLIS: The paper?

ELLIE: The paper.

HOLLIS: (*With increasing shyness*) Thank you for correcting it.

ELLIE: You said that.

HOLLIS: I said that. "I'M CRAZY, I CAN'T TALK." You . . . want to go now?

ELLIE: No, not especially. I like it here very much. I like being with you.

HOLLIS: (*Incredulously*) You like being with me?

ELLIE: Yes. Is that strange? Don't other people like being with you?

HOLLIS: Guess so. (*Exuberantly*) "SHE LIKES BEING WITH ME. SHE SAID THE WORDS. SHE WANTS ME! SHE WANTS *me*. HERE, I WALK ACROSS TO HER, PUT ONE HAND ABOUT HER LITTLE WAIST AND ONE HAND ON HER BREAST . . . NATURE WILL TAKE ITS COURSE."

ELLIE: What are you thinking?

HOLLIS: Nothing.

ELLIE: Of course you are! People always think something.

HOLLIS: About what?

ELLIE: What about what?

HOLLIS: About what we think.

ELLIE: I asked *you* what you were thinking about.

HOLLIS: What did I say?

ELLIE: You said, nothing.

HOLLIS: Then that's what I was thinking. Nothing.

ELLIE: Oh?

HOLLIS: I was thinking that . . . (*Then quickly*) I'd like you to correct all my papers, teach me all about punctuation. Teach me everything.

ELLIE: I don't know everything.

HOLLIS: You do. You do.

ELLIE: I don't. I don't. (*A moment*) You're a funny boy.

HOLLIS: (*Wistfully*) I know it. I know I'm funny.

ELLIE: I mean funny, laugh funny. I've watched you in class. You're amusing.

HOLLIS: "SHE WANTS TO GO TO BED WITH ME." (*He is*

wildly enthusiastic) "SHE WANTS TO HAVE SEXUAL RELATIONS WITH ME! IS THAT WHAT SHE WANTS? NOW?" (*Then, without pausing*) Maybe we'd better leave. Soon be time for dinner.

ELLIE: (*Glances at her wristwatch*) Hollis, it's thirty minutes before dinner.

HOLLIS: (*An embarrassed laugh*) And I thought time flew?

ELLIE: *You're* flying. Do sit down.

HOLLIS: Where?

ELLIE: Anywhere. Preferably here.

(*Pause. Hollis sits; she moves closer to him*)

ELLIE: Isn't that better.

HOLLIS: I . . . I was tired. And didn't know it.

ELLIE: (*Gently sarcastic*) It's been a long day.

HOLLIS: Yeah.

ELLIE: You know, I like it here, really like it.

HOLLIS: The . . . glen?

ELLIE: School. There's so much to do here. I mean, when you get to know people.

HOLLIS: (*Eagerly*) There is a lot to do . . . the library and all.

ELLIE: I don't mean the library. I mean dances and . . .

HOLLIS: And concerts. Do you go to the concerts?

ELLIE: (*Without enthusiasm*) Usually.

HOLLIS: I do too, usually. "MY PALMS ARE PURE SWEAT. I'M SWEATY ALL OVER. SHE'S NOTICED OF COURSE. I'M SOAKED WITH SWEAT. IN A MINUTE MY SHIRT AND PANTS WILL LOOK AS IF I JUMPED INTO THE RIVER AND CAME OUT LIKE NEPTUNE SMILING. LITTLE RIVULETS WILL RUN INTO MY SHOES AND OVERFLOW AND SWEEP ACROSS THE GROUND. SHE'LL THINK I HAVE DIABETES OR SOMETHING."

ELLIE: The dances are fun.

HOLLIS: I don't know.

ELLIE: I wasn't asking you, I was telling. Have you been to any of the dances?

HOLLIS: (*Too quickly*) Sure.

ELLIE: I didn't see you.

HOLLIS: I wasn't there really. I mean, I was there, but I didn't dance. I sort of looked in.

ELLIE: Do you like to dance?

HOLLIS: Sure. (*A moment*) I don't know. I never did.

ELLIE: You don't dance?

HOLLIS: I never have.

ELLIE: Where have you been, Hollis? Where have you been?

HOLLIS: (*Collapsing*) I haven't been anywhere.

ELLIE: (*Taking his face so that he has to look at her*) What have you been doing the last eighteen years?

HOLLIS: Thinking.

ELLIE: (*Laughing*) Thinking?

HOLLIS: Yeah, I think a lot.

ELLIE: Tell me what you think about.

HOLLIS: Lots of things.

ELLIE: Like what?

HOLLIS: Like where I'm going.

ELLIE: (*Softly*) Where are you going, Hollis Jay?

HOLLIS: I don't know. All I've done is think about it.

ELLIE: Well, *I* think you're going to get there. Maybe *you* should spend a little less time thinking about it. Would you like me to teach you?

HOLLIS: What?

ELLIE: To dance.

HOLLIS: Oh, yes.

ELLIE: When?

HOLLIS: Anytime.

ELLIE: Now?

HOLLIS: Here?

ELLIE: Sure. (*She stands*) Stand up.

HOLLIS: "MY GOD, MY GOD."

ELLIE: Stand up. (*She pulls him to his feet*) Are you ready?

(*Hollis backs away from her*)

HOLLIS: "I AM A DEFINITION. I AM A DEFINITION. I AM DE-

FINED AS A QUAKING COWARD. I AM SCARED TO DEATH OF HER. WHAT
DOES SHE WANT OF ME?"

ELLIE: Now, come to me (*She goes to him*) Put your
right arm around my waist . . . like this. (*She puts his right
hand on her back*)

HOLLIS: "MY GOD, MY GOD!"

ELLIE: Fine. Now, take my right hand with your left . . .
That's right.

HOLLIS: (*Pulling away from her*) Suppose somebody sees
us?

ELLIE: Really, Hollis! We're only *dancing*.

HOLLIS: I can't dance, Ellie. I'd feel like a fool. (*He sits*)

ELLIE: You'll never learn unless someone teaches you.
Stand up. (*Hesitantly, he stands*) Try it again. (*He assumes the
position*) Good. Now, I'll hum, and I'll show you how to move
your feet. It's very easy. (*She hums a slow tune*) Watch my
feet . . . and move yours with mine. Good . . . unbend a little.

HOLLIS: "I WASN'T BENDED. I AM A DEFINITION. I AM ME
. . . I LIKE HER. SHE'S EASY TO BE WITH. IF SHE KNOWS WHAT A
PRINCE I AM INSIDE SHE'LL LIKE ME. HOW DO YOU SHOW A PERSON
YOUR INSIDES?" (*He falls awkwardly against her*) Excuse me.

ELLIE: You're doing fine.

HOLLIS: Yeah.

ELLIE: Better.

HOLLIS: "I'M GROSS AND AWKWARD. SHE'S AS GRACEFUL AS
MELPOMONE HURTLING THROUGH THE CLOUDS . . . AS POLYMNIA AT
AULIS." (*He pulls her closely to him*) "MY GOD, I'M GETTING
HARD!" (*He abruptly backs away from her and turns his back*)

ELLIE: That's all there is to dancing. You get better with
time and practice . . . and music helps. Well, what do you
think?

HOLLIS: I think I'd like to take some more lessons. "JESUS
CHRIST, I'M HARD AS A BRICK! GO DOWN, DAMN YOU, GO DOWN!"
Maybe some afternoon you can give me . . . ? "I'M BEGGING
YOU, PLEASE GO DOWN!"

ELLIE: Tomorrow?

HOLLIS: Yeah. Yeah, that'd be fine . . . fine.

ELLIE: The best way to learn is doing it.

HOLLIS: Like at a dance?

ELLIE: Uh-huh.

(*Hollis keeps turning away from her*)

HOLLIS: When's the next dance? "IF IT DOESN'T GO DOWN
PRETTY SOON, I'LL NEVER FACE ANY GIRL. I'LL STAY IN MY ROOM ALL
THE TIME AND IF I HAVE TO GO OUT, I'LL PUT A SACK OVER MY HEAD
. . . OR SOMETHING."

ELLIE: Saturday. Saturday night.

HOLLIS: You going with anyone?

ELLIE: No. No, I don't think so.

HOLLIS: You wouldn't want to go with me?

ELLIE: I would. Hollis, I would.

HOLLIS: But I can't dance and I'm not good.

ELLIE: You'll be fine. You already have a sense of rhythm.
I've known that for months. I've watched you walk.

HOLLIS: "MY GOD, I WAS RIGHT. SHE *wants* ME."

ELLIE: Did you know you walk with a sense of rhythm?

HOLLIS: No, I didn't. "IT TAKES ALL MY BALANCE NOT TO
FALL DOWN. ME, DANCING WITH A GIRL. I'LL HAVE TO WEAR A JOCK
STRAP. OH GOD, THINK ABOUT SOMETHING ELSE! WATER. WATER, COLD,
ICE COLD WATER. CASCADE. LITTLE POOLS FULL OF TROUT LEAPING AT
FLIES THAT COME TOO CLOSE. SOME ARE CAUGHT AND KILLED ON THE
SPOT . . . AND SOME GET AWAY TO DIE IN OTHER PLACES, OTHER
TIMES. NO FLY, HOUSE FLY, HORSE FLY, REALLY CHOOSES HIS DESTINY.
HE FLIES INTO IT. WITHOUT A THOUGHT. GREEN BOTTLE FLIES ARE
USED IN EXPERIMENTS, OR IS IT FRUIT FLIES? TO PROPAGATE FOR SCI-
ENCE. DOES IT MATTER WHETHER YOU PROPAGATE FOR SCIENCE OR
JUST FOR THE FUN OF IT?" (*Anguish*) "NO, OH NO . . ." (*Rapidly*)
"WATER. FALLING WATER, VERY COLD. NIAGARA TOSSING TO THE SEA.
THE LAKEFRONT OF CHICAGO AND DULUTH, MINNESOTA. AND THE
POOR FISH THAT IS CARRIED OVER NIAGARA CAN'T EVER GET BACK TO
LAKE HURON. SOME OF THEM ARE DASHED TO DEATH ON THE ROCKS.
THERE ARE PATTERNS. NO OPPORTUNITIES, ONLY DESTINED AND OR-
DAINED FACTS, AND WE SUBMIT AND THINK WE HAVE A SENSE OF

FREEDOM. IT JUST HAPPENS, THAT'S ALL, JUST HAPPENS. AND THE SMART FISH IS THE ONE THAT LEAPS JUST IN TIME TO KEEP FROM DYING ON THE ROCKS AND SWIMS HAPPILY IN LAKE ONTARIO, AND THE SMART FLY IS THE FLY THAT NEVER GETS TOO CLOSE TO THE SURFACE OF THE WATER AND STILL HAS TIME TO PROPAGATE." What did you say, Ellie?

ELLIE: That you have a fine sense of rhythm.

HOLLIS: (*A shrug of his shoulders*) I've been told that. I'm glad you noticed.

ELLIE: (*Softly*) I'll look forward to the dance . . . Saturday.

HOLLIS: (*Turning to her*) So will I. (*Suddenly*) I like you, Ellie. I have since the first of the year.

ELLIE: Thank you, I'm glad. (*Lightly*) I like you too.

HOLLIS: You do?

ELLIE: Of course, I do. You're smart. You write well. Just a little retarded. You'll catch up fast.

HOLLIS: I will if you teach me.

ELLIE: It's almost time for dinner. (*She starts to go*) I heard the bell.

HOLLIS: I didn't.

ELLIE: You weren't listening. You were thinking.

HOLLIS: I wasn't. I swear.

ELLIE: Thinking's all right, a certain amount, but . . .

HOLLIS: (*Quickly*) I'm going to give it up.

ELLIE: What?

HOLLIS: Thinking! I want to feel, to be human, and, Ellie . . . and . . . (*Reflectively*) "LIKE THAT COUPLE BACK THERE. THEY WERE FEELING SOMETHING."

ELLIE: Will you walk me to the dorm?

HOLLIS: Yeah, I'd like to do that.

(*They turn to go*)

ELLIE: You forgot George Gordon, Lord Byron.

HOLLIS: (*Grinning*) I wasn't thinking.

(*He turns back to get the manuscript and the book*)

ELLIE: You shouldn't ever forget George Gordon, Lord Byron.

(*She exits quickly*)

HOLLIS: No . . . (*Gently triumphant*) "I KNOW WHAT SAMIAN WINE IS! I UNDERSTAND THE PARABLE OF THE FRUIT FLY. I AM, I THINK, FALLING IN LOVE."

Curtain

John Guare

A DAY FOR SURPRISES

John Guare

With the opening of his short play, *Muzeeka,* at the Province-town Playhouse, New York, in the spring of 1968, John Guare (b. 1939) stepped from the environs of Off-Off-Broadway to national attention. *The New York Times* described *Muzeeka* as "beautifully poetic and always meaningful" in its attitude toward the bland society. "Mr. Guare has written with thought, craftsmanship and beauty." The play—originally presented in 1967 at the Eugene O'Neill Memorial Theatre Foundation's Playwrights' Conference, Waterford, Connecticut, and, later, at the Mark Taper Forum, Los Angeles—won a 1968 "Obie" Award for distinguished writing.

In 1969, Mr. Guare moved up another rung on the ladder to prominence with his Broadway production of *Cop-Out,* the collective title of two short plays: *Cop-Out* and *Home Fires.* Although the presentation (with Linda Lavin and Ron Leibman in the leading roles) tarried briefly, at season's end Mr. Guare was cited as the year's "Most Promising Playwright" in the annual New York Critics' Poll conducted by *Variety.* (The author has just completed the screenplay of *Cop-Out,* to be produced by Kaleidoscope Films, Ltd.)

John Guare's other works for the theatre include: *The Loveliest Afternoon of the Year* and *Something I'll Tell You Tuesday,* both presented at the Caffe Cino, New York, 1966; and *The House of Blue Leaves* which originated at the O'Neill Foundation's Playwrights' Conference (1966) and now is scheduled for production in New York.

Mr. Guare recently was appointed to the board of trustees of the American Playwrights Theatre, an organization that makes available new scripts by established playwrights and newcomers to its college and regional theatre members. He also is an active member of the O'Neill Foundation and the New Dramatists Committee, organized in 1950 to give burgeoning playwrights the practical experience and momentum required to develop and perfect their craft. Its alumni includes: William Inge, Robert Anderson, Paddy Chayefsky, James Baldwin, Michael Stewart, William Gibson, Ronald Alexander, Arnold Schulman, James Leo Herlihy, James Goldman, Joseph Kramm, Joseph Hayes, Joe Masteroff, Burt Shevelove and this Editor, among many others.

John Guare's latest play, *A Day for Surprises,* appears in print for the first time anywhere in this collection.

Characters:
A, *a woman*
B, *a man*

Scene:
The pasting room of a very large library.
Time:
The present.

B pasting books. Peace. A Vivaldi runs through his head: "Autumn". We hear it until the door bursts open.
A staggers in: Stravinsky's "Rite of Spring."
His stern look makes her straighten into shape, into the formality he demands of a subordinate.

A: (*A gasp*) Pppppppardon me, Sir . . . bbbbbbbut you have got *have got* to llllloooook out your window!

B: (*With great distaste*) Your paste pot is dried up.

A: Sir, you have got to look out!

B: (*Pasting; muttering*) Less time picking up coffee nerves on coffee breaks, more time collecting overdue fines, we might have more of a library.

A: (*Collapses on her chair in a paroxysm of hysteria*) *Mr. Falanzano, you have got to look out your window!*

B: (*Pasting; laughing*) And you used up your two week vacation? Frazzle frazzle frazzle. Another nightmare year in the overdue fine room.

A: *Sir!*

B: (*Exasperated*) All right, all right.
(*He looks out the window. First left. Then right. He collapses*)

A: (*A last bid for sanity*) Tell me what you see.

B: (*Aghast*) It's what . . . what I *don't* see!

A: *What don't you see?*

B: The lion . . . the lion closest to Forty Second Street.

A: Yes? Yes?

B: (*Grabbing up the phone*) Operator, Operator! (*No response*) The lion closest to . . . (*Click, click, click*) . . . to Forty Second Street is . . .

A: (*Putting the phone down*) It's missing! Isn't it?

B: The stone lion is missing.

A: (*She is calm now*) I know where it is.

B: That stone lion weighs 28,000 pounds!

A: I know where the stone lion is.

(*He looks up at her. Her knowledge stabs her with pain again*)

A: (*Quietly*) The stone lion is in . . . I assume it's the same one . . . there's a lion in the ladies' room and its *eaten* Miss Pringle. (*His hands fly to his face*) It's sitting in the ladies' room with Miss Pringle's feet sticking out of its mouth, out of the lion's mouth. I know it's Miss Pringle as I'd been admiring her blue beaded shoes only this morning, and the way she braided the hair on her legs into the new black lacy stockings. The lion's on its haunches right by the washstand just the way it sits out front . . . only . . . only Miss Pringle's feet are sticking out of its mouth. I ran out of this library screaming. I ran right out onto Fifth Avenue and when I saw the lion closest to Forty Second Street was not there—was absent—was A. W. O. L.—I thought I had gone insane, thought I had snapped! *All this library paste!* Kids sniff this stuff! I thought it had got to me! But you see it too! I'm not alone! Oh God, thank you, Mr. Falanzano! Thank God for you!

(*She hugs him. She is calmed. She hangs onto him. He raises his head. His face is a pitiful sight*)

B: It's eaten Miss Pringle?

(*He leaps up and rushes out of the room*)

A: You stay out of there! That's No Man's Land!

(*He returns with a pair of blue beaded shoes*)

A: (*Chidingly*) You peeked into No Man's Land!

(*She is sufficiently calmed to return to work. She begins*

pasting books with a certain flair that only peace can bring)

A: No need to worry really. (*She thumbs rapidly through an encyclopedia*) It says here—L L L L L L L Linnaeum Linoleum *Lion*—Lion: "after devouring prey, are satiated for two to three weeks." We're safe, Mr. Falanzano—for another couple of weeks anyway!

B: (*Glassy-eyed*) Miss Jepson, I *loved* Miss Pringle.

A: I liked her too, for God's sake, but let's not get all soppy-eyed sentimental.

B: Miss Pringle and I were going to . . . to be married . . .

(*He looks at the shoes, then throws his head down on the desk. He weeps. She is shocked by this disclosure, but quickly recovers*)

A: Well, you sneakies! You and Miss Pringle! Why don't you let anybody *know!* Isn't this a day for surprises! You and Denise Pring . . . It's like all the surprises of the world store themselves up for a day when the one thing you do not need is a surp . . . You and Denise Pring! Sonofagun! Like today. Who needs a surprise today? I was going to go home, curl up with a good book, like any other night, look at the phone and welcome even a Sorry Wrong Number. Guiltily turn on my TV and watch re-runs of beautiful domestic comedies. Father Knows Best. Make Room for Daddy. Hi, Lucy! Hi Doris! Then turn them off because it's time to water my geranium. But today will give me something to think about! A day for surprises! You and Miss Pringle!

B: Me and Miss Pringle.

(*She touches his shoulder comfortingly. He pats her hand. A lion growls ferociously outside the door. They look up. They hold each other. The lion growls fiercely. The lion burps*)

A: Would you like to come over to my place tonight?

B: (*Listening for the lion*) Shhhhhhhh . . .

A: (*Seductively*) Check over some books?

B: (*Uncomfortably*) There's a lion outside the door.

A: (*Snuggling*) Start something between the covers?

B: (*Breaking the embrace*) Miss Jepson, my fiancée is *dead!*

A: What do you want me to do? Start pasting Denise Pringle Memorial Stickers in front of all the Britannicas? I'll do it, but I'm not going to waste my youth weeping over a not-very-attractive girl who was hardly worthy of you! Life has handed us a surprise! There's so few surprises that I want to leap at the present life has given me! You feel so nice—I want to leap before the lion eats me. Those blue beaded shoes! That's not the first time the lion came into the ladies' room and ate one of the staff. Remember Miss Ramirez?

B: And *nobody* reports these horrors?

A: There's a lot of lonely girls in this town, Mr. Falanzano. You know what the biggest lie is? The more the merrier.

B: (*A long pause*) I . . . don't . . . under . . . under . . .

A: (*Petting him*) Shhhhh, Shhhhh, Comfort . . . comfort.

B: . . . understand.

A: I'll sing you a song. A song by Sir Alfred Lord Tennyson. Yes, you'll like that. (*She sings softly*) "Charles gave Elizabeth a dodo"

B: (*Pulling away*) Books . . . poets . . . Alfred Lord Tennyson! I don't want to hear about books!

(*He has a fit and rips all the books in the room into pieces. She tries to restrain him. He sits amid the wreckage of books and pieces of paper snow down upon him. He is angry; she is petrified. He fingers the cover of a book. His voice is cold and repressed and tight*)

B: My whole world was books, Miss Jepson! It always has been. Until. Until. One night, I came back late to the library because I couldn't sleep and wanted a book, needed a book, demanded the company of a volume. And I heard whimpering from the stacks. There was Miss Pringle whom I didn't even know had a passkey, whom I'd never spoken to, even when we met at clearance sales at Marboro Books. There was Miss Pringle, whimpering and holding volumes of Lewis Carroll, Camus, Proust, the *Joy of Cooking* . . . holding these volumes and weeping . . . the overdue cards in the back of the books slipping out like tears that piled up around her ankles, then her knees. I called out, "Miss Pringle!" She stopped and sniffed like a suddenly spied gazelle in some quiet tropical place. "Who is it?" she called out across the black library. "Who is that? I have spent twenty years of my precious life in school and I have just signed up for courses in the fall. If I don't become a member of the human race soon, I'll kill myself. Who is that? Is that *you*, Mr. Falanzano? Please love me! I'm here. I'm ready." And we raced to each other and the wind our two bodies made racing, running to each other, set all the overdue cards flying into the air —overdue cards no longer, but blossoms from a thank-God early spring. Her plea for help had sounded an echo, a Little Sir Echo from my own heart, and I quickly undressed her and then myself and then, while she arranged our things with the neatness that was her trademark and the bane of the overdue fine room, I arranged on the floor of the Neglected Masterpieces Section, a bed—a couch made of photostats of Elizabethan Love Lyrics. She said, "I've never loved anybody so I want this to be good." I said, "Oh, I have never loved anybody before either." So I took a copy of *Love Without Fear* and she took a Modern Manual on How To Do It, and we wrapped—like Christmas packages for people you love—wrapped our bodies, our phosphorescent, glowing, about-to-become-human bodies around each other. And began reading. For the first time in our lives, we wore flesh for clothing instead of baggy tweed. (*Pause*)

After many months of this meeting at night in the stacks, undressing, reading all the books on the Art and Science of Love—boning up, you might say, for our final exam—after many months of this study, we felt we had the system down.

Up. In. Oh Oh Oh. *We* had written that formula down, many times, to make sure we knew it by rote! In the world of sex, you want nothing to go wrong. I bought contraceptives and she bought contraceptives as we had been instructed to do in the New York *Post*'s weekend series, *Stop That Baby*. And we finally felt we were ready. There was a full moon that night. We took a quick gander at *Human Sexual Response* and cleared our throats. The library closed and we came out of our hiding places after the watchmen passed by, and met in the stacks of—The Rare Book Room! To be doubly sure, she had wrapped herself in Saran Wrap from head to toe, and I remembered the lessons I had been taught and pinned the *Playmate of the Month* over her head and finally proceeded. Perhaps some of the one hundred and twenty-seven rubber devices I wore on my erect bookmark dulled some of the sensation. But I must say all went well, as well as chapter seven of *Ideal Marriage* and a pamphlet from the U.S. Government Printing Office had led us to believe. If we had been doing it for credit, I would have given us an A. An A Plus! Well, a B Plus anyway. (*Pause*)

A few weeks later, Miss Pringle came to me with tears in her eyes. *You* were having a coffee break. Tears in her watermark blue eyes. She stood me right here and placed my pasting hand on her womb. I felt a swelling. A distention. Life? Within her? Somehow, despite the one hundred and twenty-seven suits of armor, the eleven diaphragms, the six hundred and eighty-two white pills, the three one-hundred-foot rolls of Saran Wrap, despite all these precautions, somehow *life* had managed to creep—no, triumph through! I loved Miss Pringle! (*Pause*)

She did not want the child. We took a book from the uptown —the Yorkville Branch—where nobody knew us, recognized us. We took out Ann Landers' *Get Rid of That Senior Prom Boo-Boo and Put Yourself into Freshman Honors*. It contained all the information, technical and otherwise, that we needed for getting rid of our child. (*Pause*) What had been our photostatic bed of love became an operating table and I remember seeing through her legs the photostat of a poem by Sir Philip Sidney:

"Ring out your bells
Let mourning shows be spread
For love is dead . . ."

And I who had been so proud of myself for inserting life into
a difficult envelope, proceeded again into Miss Pringle and removed—not a child—not a miniature foetus of me . . . I removed—my hands felt it and pulled out a small, undeveloped
volume of *The Complete Works of Doctor Spock*. Only *this* big.
Time would've gestated it into a full set—time and nature. But
what hurt me was my—my juice of which I'd been so proud,
hubristically proud for leaping so many hurdles like a Kentucky
Derby Day Dark Horse Winner . . . no, an Olympic runner
who finally carries that Torch of Life and plants it in the very
summit of Mount Olympus to claim it for himself—that juice I
bragged to call *triumphant* could only father, only create a dull
set of books! The flour and water of library paste! Not semen at
all! My life has been lived in books. *I had become a book.*
Library paste! We all would've been better off if we'd never
opened a book!

(*A long pause. She begins pasting him with paste from
the paste pot. She pastes her hand to his cheek. She pastes
his hand to her breast. She looks over her shoulder, out the
window*)

A: Look! The lion's walking down the steps, back to its
perch! Isn't that New York for you! Nobody even stops, looks!
They all think it's Candid Camera. You could strut down Fifth
Avenue NUDE and nobody'd even look! I mean, *I'd* look at
you, Mr. Falanzano, with your clothes on or anything!

(*She is at peace; crying and happy. The paste connecting
them begins to harden*)

A: The lion's on its perch now! You'd never even know
he moved. Except for that little piece of pink garter on its tooth,
dangling like a salmon, you'd never even know he moved.

B: You'd never even know he moved.

A: A day for such surprises . . . (*She strokes his hair
and sings softly*)

"Charles gave Elizabeth a dodo
And he never even offered one to me
A lovely lemon colored dodo
With eyes as green as grass could be.
Now it isn't that I'm doubting that Charles loves me
For I know that he would take me out to tea.
But he did give Elizabeth a dodo
And he never even offered one to me."

The lights slowly dim

A. R. Gurney, Jr.
THE LOVE COURSE

A. R. Gurney, Jr.

The Love Course, published here for the first time, is the fourth play by A. R. Gurney, Jr. to be included in *The Best Short Plays* annuals. In the 1969 volume, the author was represented by *The Golden Fleece* which initially was presented in New York in 1968 by the Playwrights Unit, a non-profit experimental organization (founded in 1961 by Edward Albee, Richard Barr and Clinton Wilder) that affords new and promising dramatists an opportunity to see their scripts performed on a professional basis before invited audiences. In June, 1968, *The Golden Fleece* was presented in a full-scale production by the Center Theatre Group at the Mark Taper Forum in Los Angeles and later was taped for transmission by National Educational Television, the first in its series devoted to the American Regional Theatre movement.

Two previous works by the author—*Three People* and *Turn of the Century*—were included in *The Best Short Plays* series when it was under the editorship of Margaret Mayorga.

A native of Buffalo, New York, Mr. Gurney attended Williams College and the Yale School of Drama (under a J. Walter Thompson Playwriting Fellowship, 1957–58). He currently is an Associate Professor of Literature at M. I. T. and lives in West Newton, Massachusetts, with his wife and four children.

Mr. Gurney's drama, *David and Goliath,* was produced Off-Broadway in November, 1968, after a summer tryout presentation at Boston University's Playwrights Workshop in Tanglewood, Massachusetts.

In 1969, Mr. Gurney returned to Off-Broadway with *Tonight In Living Color,* the overall title of a tandem bill comprised of *The Golden Fleece* and *The David Show,* the latter a revised, renamed version of *David and Goliath.*

Among his other produced plays are: *Love in Buffalo; The Comeback; The Rape of Bunny Stuntz; The Problem; The Bridal Dinner;* and *The Open Meeting.*

He also is the co-author of the musical, *Tom Sawyer,* produced at the Kansas City Starlight Theatre; and drama editor of the textbook series, *Adventures in Literature.*

The Love Course had its public baptism in October, 1969, as a staged reading by the Theatre Company of Boston.

Characters:

MISS CARROWAY, *a professor of literature at a large university.*

PROFESSOR BURGESS, *also a professor of literature.*

SALLY, *a student of literature.*

MIKE, *an electrical engineering student.*

Scene:

The entire play takes place in, and during, a class in literature at a university. The audience is to be considered members of the class and the stage should suggest the teaching area: a wooden desk-table, with two or three simple wooden chairs on either side, facing forward. Behind these, a blackboard on which is written a list: Plato, Euripides, Dante, "Tristan et Iseult," Shakespeare, "Madam Bovary," "Wuthering Heights," D. H. Lawrence, John Updike, et al. Bracketing this list, and written in large letters, is "SAVE!!"

After the audience is seated, a loud schoolbell rings. Professor Burgess comes down the aisle toward the stage. He wears a sports jacket and grey flannels, and carries a natty leather briefcase. Sally and Mike, who are sitting toward the front on the aisle, get up to meet him.

SALLY: Professor Burgess . . .

BURGESS: Good afternoon, Sally.

SALLY: This is Mike. Can he audit this class?

BURGESS: Certainly. Hello, Mike.

MIKE: Hello, sir.

(Burgess proceeds to the stage as Miss Carroway comes down the aisle. She carries a stack of well-worn books and wears something simple and slightly old-fashioned. Sally waylays her)

SALLY: Miss Carroway . . .

CARROWAY: Ah, Sally . . .

SALLY: This is the Mike I told you about.

MIKE: I've heard a lot about you, Miss Carroway.

CARROWAY: Good. Fine. Welcome.

(*She moves on toward the stage, acknowledging the audience with soft greetings. She goes onto the stage where Burgess is waiting, a little impatiently. She settles her books on the table as he comes over to speak to her. They converse now in whispers, so that the class can't hear much*)

BURGESS: (*Whispering*) I have to leave in a minute.

CARROWAY: (*Whispering*) What? Surely not *now*.

BURGESS: The faculty meeting . . .

CARROWAY: But this is . . .

BURGESS: I'm sorry.

(*Pause. Carroway looks at him. Thinks*)

BURGESS: (*Indicating class*) You begin.

(*He sits down. Pause. Carroway takes a deep breath, comes downstage, and begins*)

CARROWAY: (*Addressing the audience*) This is our last class on the literature of love. I don't mean simply for this term. This is the last class that Professor Burgess and I will ever teach together. (*She glances at him*) As you may know, I have accepted a position in the English department at Mount Holyoke College for Women. And Professor Burgess intends to join the administration of this university. (*Another glance at him*) I am therefore especially eager on this, our last day, to bring the course together once and for all. I want to resolve, if we possibly can, all the great themes of love which have obsessed us, and the Western world, from February up until now. (*She turns to Burgess*) Professor Burgess, I'm sure you have something to add.

BURGESS: Yes. (*He rises*) A few quick points before I go . . .

CARROWAY: (*To audience*) He has to go to the faculty meeting on the spring riots.

BURGESS: Yes. I have to make a speech.

CARROWAY: Even though this is our last class.

BURGESS: I'm afraid I have to speak.

CARROWAY: Oh, don't be afraid.

BURGESS: (*Irritatedly*) I'm not afraid.

CARROWAY: I am naturally . . . very disappointed, that's all.

BURGESS: Surely you can handle this yourself. A quick review, a few questions, the examination topic . . .

CARROWAY: I had planned to do more. In our last class. (*She lights a cigarette from a brisk little lighter, spews out the smoke*) Go on. Say goodby to us.

BURGESS: (*After a pause, to audience*) Last fall, when Miss Carroway asked me to join her in teaching this course, I must confess I had some trepidations. She proposed that we deal with the literature of love from Plato all the way to the present. I'm a Renaissance man, and Miss Carroway specializes in the Romantic period. Neither one of us had ever before focused on so specific a topic from so broad a perspective. And neither one of us had ever taught—in tandem before.

CARROWAY: You are apologizing for the course.

BURGESS: I am not. I'm simply saying . . .

CARROWAY: You are apologizing for what we have done.

BURGESS: Dear lady, I am not! I've loved the Love Course! I mean, it has been just the sort of course that students have been asking for. Exciting, relevant, and close to the bone! (*Pause*) I am simply responding to criticism which has arisen on the outside.

CARROWAY: What criticism?

BURGESS: We have been accused, by some of our colleagues, of . . .

CARROWAY: Of what? Of *what?*

BURGESS: Of biting off more than we could chew.

CARROWAY: (*Laughing*) Oh dear . . .

BURGESS: We've been accused, by some students, of straying from the syllabus . . .

CARROWAY: Oh dear, oh dear . . .

BURGESS: People say that all we've done is carry on a private dialogue in public!

CARROWAY: And have you regretted it, Professor Burgess?

BURGESS: Not for a moment! I'm simply . . . saying . . . that some people have called our Love Course a little erotic—I mean, erratic.

CARROWAY: (*Laughing*) Oh dear, oh dear, oh dear. Perhaps you'd *better* go to that meeting.

BURGESS: (*A little irritated*) I will. (*To audience*) Good luck to all on the exam. (*He starts out*)

CARROWAY: (*Suddenly getting up*) I had planned . . . (*Burgess stops, out of politeness*) I had planned . . . to read and discuss the first few lines of Shakespeare's *Antony and Cleopatra*.

BURGESS: Ah.

CARROWAY: It says worlds about what we've been up to.

BURGESS: (*To audience*) I love the first scene of *Antony and Cleopatra*.

CARROWAY: I know you do.

BURGESS: "Here   is   my   space . . . Kingdoms   are clay . . ."

CARROWAY: Exactly.

BURGESS: (*To audience*) I once wrote an article on that first scene.

CARROWAY: (*To audience*) "In his salad days, When he was green in judgment, cold in blood."

BURGESS: It was a good article.

CARROWAY: (*Pause*) Much better, perhaps, than some of your recent, earnest memoranda on so-called student grievances.

BURGESS: One tries to do both, these days.

CARROWAY: If one can. If one doesn't neglect Shakespeare for the sake of campus politics!

BURGESS: (*Pause. He comes to a decision; calls out, into audience*) Someone . . . will someone do me a favor? Will someone run over to the faculty meeting . . .

CARROWAY: Someone not regularly in the class . . .

BURGESS: . . . and tell the Chairman of the meeting . . .

CARROWAY: I want my regular students here.

BURGESS: Someone who is auditing, then.

SALLY: (*Rises; calls out*) Mike will do it.

BURGESS: Who's Mike?

MIKE: (*Rises*) I'm Mike.

SALLY: He's here with *me*.

BURGESS: Ah, yes. Then, Mike, would you run over and tell the Chairman . . .

CARROWAY: Say he has a class.

BURGESS: Say I'll be there soon.

CARROWAY: In an hour.

BURGESS: In a minute.

SALLY: (*Nudging Mike*) Go on, Mike. Do it.

MIKE: O.K.

(*He exits up the aisle. Sally sits down. Burgess goes to his briefcase, and begins looking through it*)

BURGESS: Now where's my Shakespeare?

CARROWAY: I have mine. Look on with me.

(*She holds out her book. He joins her*)

BURGESS: All these notes . . .

CARROWAY: Oh, I plan my classes. I prepare . . .

BURGESS: I can see that.

CARROWAY: Well . . . (*To audience*) After some preliminary—and I've always felt, unnecessary talk—Antony and Cleopatra enter, and take the stage. (*She reads*) "If it be love indeed, tell me how much."

BURGESS: (*Reading*) "There's beggary in the love that can be reckon'd."

CARROWAY: "I'll set a bourn how far to be belov'd."

BURGESS: "Then must thou needs find out new heaven, new earth."

CARROWAY: (*To audience*) She is asking him to declare his love.

BURGESS: (*To audience*) Which he refuses to do.

CARROWAY: (*To Burgess*) Why?

BURGESS: Because to describe something is to . . . limit

it. It's beggary—base and contemptible—to pin down their love.

CARROWAY: So she says she'll make up new rules, new boundaries. "I'll set a bourn," she says.

BURGESS: And he replies that she'd have to invent an entirely new world—"new heaven, new earth"—to encompass their love.

CARROWAY: (*Pause*) Yes. (*Then, quickly, to audience*) But you see, they *have* described their love by *refusing* to describe it.

BURGESS: But we know it can't last. Not in this world.

CARROWAY: So they create their own world . . . through language . . .

BURGESS: Which can't last, either.

CARROWAY: Oh yes.

BURGESS: Oh no. The real world intrudes almost immediately. A messenger arrives from Rome.

CARROWAY: Who tells us that the real world is falling apart.

BURGESS: Not falling apart . . .

CARROWAY: Oh yes, oh yes. And we also hear . . . for the first time . . . that there's a wife. (*She glances at him, then reads*) "Fulvia perchance is angry" . . . and later, "The shrill-tongued Fulvia scolds . . ." (*To audience*) Fulvia being the wife. (*Reading*) "Thou blushest, Antony . . ."

BURGESS: (*Quickly*) But Antony replies—in some of Shakespeare's most sweeping poetry . . .

(*He walks downstage, recites from memory*)
BURGESS:
"Let Rome in Tiber melt and the wide arch
Of the rang'd empire fall! Here is my space.
Kingdoms are clay . . . The nobleness of life
Is to do thus . . ."

(*He glances at Carroway; then to audience*)
And at this point he kisses her . . . according to the First Folio edition.

(*Mike returns down the aisle. He calls up to the stage*)

MIKE: Professor Burgess . . .

(*Burgess looks out*)

MIKE: They want you there.

BURGESS: Then I'll go.

CARROWAY: Give your little spiel and then come back.

BURGESS: There won't be time.

CARROWAY: Oh certainly. Gallop, run, jog!

BURGESS: (*Angrily*) I don't . . . jog! (*He turns to audience*) I probably won't see you again, so . . .

CARROWAY: You will, you will. Antony comes back, and so will you! Go on. Go!

(*Burgess looks at her, then exits quickly through the aisle. Carroway watches him go, smiles, then hastily closes her Shakespeare and places it beside the stack of books. She takes up another book, old, leathery, and worn. She gazes at it affectionately, then calls out*)

CARROWAY: You . . . young man . . . Mike.

MIKE: (*Rises*) Me?

CARROWAY: Would you like an excuse to go back to that presumably crucial meeting?

MIKE: O.K.

CARROWAY: Good. Then come up here.

(*Mike comes up on stage*)

CARROWAY: Now. See this book? This is my annotated version of *Wuthering Heights*. I used this when I wrote my biography of Emily Brontë. (*Mike nods mechanically*) Take it to the faculty meeting. Give it to Professor Burgess. Tell him I plan to end the class reading from this. (*She takes a hairpin out of her hair, puts it in the book*) Reading here. At this point. (*Mike takes the book, starts off*) Tell him . . . (*Mike stops*) . . . we began the class in *his* field; I'd like to end it in *mine*.

MIKE: O.K.

(*He exits through the aisle*)

CARROWAY: (*To audience*) Now. While we're waiting, let's be aggressively Socratic. Come up here, Sally, where we can all see and hear you.

(*Sally leaves her seat and comes up on stage*)

CARROWAY: Sally has been loyal from the beginning. Sally has loved this course. Indeed, when my contract was terminated, Sally wrote a letter in protest on my behalf. So let's listen, and learn from Sally. (*She gestures for Sally to sit down*) Sally, why did you sign up for the Love Course?

SALLY: To learn about love.

CARROWAY: Have you ever been in love?

SALLY: Yes. (*A moment, then:*) No.

CARROWAY: That young man . . .

SALLY: Mike?

CARROWAY: Are you in love with Mike?

SALLY: I thought I was. (*Pause*) But now I don't think so.

CARROWAY: Would you *like* to be in love?

SALLY: Oh yes.

CARROWAY: Why?

SALLY: Because . . . oh because . . . it sounds so . . . great.

CARROWAY: Have you read all the books on the reading list, Sally?

SALLY: Oh yes.

CARROWAY: Did you like them?

SALLY: Most of them. Yes.

CARROWAY: Did you find anything in common with all of these books?

SALLY: (*Scrutinizes the blackboard*) It's hard to keep all of them in mind.

CARROWAY: Oh the mind, the mind. Forget the mind, Sally! By now, these books should be in our *blood!* What are these books all *about,* Sally?

SALLY: Love.

CARROWAY: That's obvious. But what *kind* of love?

SALLY: (*Closing her eyes; thinking*) Most of the books are about, well, adultery.

CARROWAY: Yes . . .

SALLY: And most of them . . . are about death.

CARROWAY: Precisely! (*She strides to the blackboard, begins ticking off the books*) Phaedra, Beatrice, Isolde, Juliet, Emma Bovary, Catherine Earnshaw—all the great women die for love!

SALLY: Is that . . . true?

CARROWAY: *True?* Why, there it is!

SALLY: (*Looking at the board*) Lady Chatterley doesn't die.

CARROWAY: (*Contemptuously*) Oh well. Lawrence . . .

SALLY: And in the modern books, in John Updike and . . . others . . . people don't die.

CARROWAY: They *do,* Sally. They die the *modern* death. They die spiritually. Oh yes. Name a book, name a love story worthy of that name, which does not end with the death of the lady!

SALLY: (*Pause*) I can't.

CARROWAY: And so love in the western world ends in what?

SALLY: Death.

CARROWAY: And do you *still* want to fall in love, Sally?

SALLY: Yes.

CARROWAY: With your . . . Mike?

SALLY: Maybe.

CARROWAY: Why?

SALLY: Because it must be worth it.

CARROWAY: Yes. Yes, I think so. Yes. I hope so. Yes. Despite all the risks, it must be worth it. (*Mike returns; she sees him*) Ah! Our messenger from Rome. (*As Mike starts to take his seat*) No, no! Don't sit *down.* Come up here. Tell us how things are in the real world.

(*Mike reluctantly comes up onto the stage*)

CARROWAY: Tell us about the faculty meeting. What was the issue today? Who was interrupting whom? Who's in, who's out? Speak.

MIKE: There was a lot going on.

CARROWAY: Oh, I'm sure! (*As Sally makes a move to leave the stage*) No. Stay, Sally! (*She quickly turns to Mike*) Now, how about Professor Burgess's speech? Was it heart-rending or simply earth-shattering?

MIKE: He hasn't spoken yet.

CARROWAY: Not *yet*?

MIKE: Not while I was there.

CARROWAY: Why didn't he ask for the floor? And speak! And leave! He has a class!

MIKE: Some students were speaking.

CARROWAY: Students? Speaking? At a faculty meeting? Good God, do they know *how*? (*A moment*) Well, well? Did you give him my book? Did you tell him what I told you to tell him?

MIKE: Yes.

CARROWAY: And is he coming back? What did he say?

MIKE: He said thank you.

CARROWAY: He said . . .

MIKE: Thank you.

CARROWAY: (*Sarcastically; to audience*) Oh, these long-winded messengers! (*She wheels on Mike*) Did he look at the particular passage?

MIKE: He glanced at it. And then handed the book to his wife.

CARROWAY: (*A long pause*) His wife . . .

MIKE: The lady sitting next to him. I *think* it was his wife. Doesn't she teach in the Political Science department?

CARROWAY: No! She does *not* teach in the Political Science department. She is *connected* to the Political Science department by some academic nepotism we will not go into. But she does not *teach* there. Unless you call sitting around in some seminar with two or three graduate students—unless you call *that* teaching. Which I do not. This, *this* . . . is teaching! (*Mike attempts to leave*) Wait! I said, *wait*. (*Mike stops*) So. His wife was there. At this so-called faculty meeting. Sitting next to him. Listening to students speak.

MIKE: Yes.

CARROWAY: How about his children? Were his children there, too? Apparently *everyone* goes to faculty meetings these days. Was the row filled with Burgess children? Did the children speak?

MIKE: No. (*Again, he makes an attempt to leave*)

CARROWAY: Why are you slinking away?

MIKE: I'm not slinking.

CARROWAY: (*Infinitely patient*) His wife took the book. Then what did she do?

MIKE: Do?

CARROWAY: (*To audience*)
"By heaven, he echoes me
As if there were a monster in his thought
Too hideous to be shown." *Othello*. Act Three.

(*Suddenly turning on Mike*) What did the wife do with my book? Great heavens, have you ever taken a literature course in your *life*? Are you incapable of description? What are you studying to *be*?

SALLY: Miss Carroway, he's just visiting the course. He . . .

CARROWAY: Sally, I am educating your lover. You'll thank me for it one day! (*To Mike*) What do you want to be, sir?

MIKE: (*Quietly*) An electrical engineer.

CARROWAY: Ah. Then we can look forward to more, and better, television sets. In the meantime, see if you can possibly *engineer* for us a description of what happened to my own, personal copy of *Wuthering Heights!*

(*Pause; they face each other*)

MIKE: She took it . . .

CARROWAY: Yesss. We know that.

MIKE: (*Doggedly*) And then she smiled.

CARROWAY: She smiled?

MIKE: Uh-huh.

CARROWAY: Was that grunt meant to be affirmative?

MIKE: (*Shouting*) *She smiled!* At the book!

CARROWAY: (*Now grimly*) I am going to the faculty meeting.

SALLY: Miss Carroway . . .

CARROWAY: To retrieve my book. (*She hastens off the stage, starts up the aisle*)

SALLY: But Miss Carroway . . .

CARROWAY: I am *going* to the faculty meeting! I am going to retrieve my book. And I am going to speak. (*She stops, turns*) Sally! Take the class. Read your excellent paper on Eleanor of Aquitaine, and the Troubadour Poets. *There* was a woman who knew about love! (*She exits flamboyantly*)

SALLY: (*Calling after her*) But I didn't *bring* that paper!

MIKE: (*Starting off*) Bitch!

SALLY: She's not!

MIKE: Come on. Let's go to that meeting.

SALLY: She asked me to take the class.

MIKE: *I'm* going, then. (*He leaves the stage, starts up the aisle*)

SALLY: Mike! Oh thanks a lot, Mike! I mean, thanks a lot! (*To audience*) Some man. Some friend. Just . . . *leaving* me up here. Oh boy.

MIKE: (*Calling back to her*) This is your course, not mine! I don't even belong here!

SALLY: That's right! Which is sad! Because you, *especially*, could learn so much from it.

MIKE: (*Stopping*) O.K. (*He marches back down the aisle*) O.K. (*He goes onto the stage, grabs a chair, slams it downstage, and sits*) O.K. Teach me.

SALLY: *Teach* you?

MIKE: (*Raising his hand*) I have a few questions, teacher. You drag me here, you set me up as a messenger boy, you let your pal Carroway give me a hard time, and now you say I've got a lot to learn. O.K. So can I ask a few questions, Teach? May I, Teach? May I?

SALLY: Of course. Ask away.

MIKE: First question. What is so goddam *great* about this class?

SALLY: Burgess and Carroway, that's what! Burgess and Carroway.

MIKE: And what's so great about them?

SALLY: If you can't feel it, I can't explain it.

MIKE: I had to cut my major to come here. I could have learned more there.

SALLY: About *computers*.

MIKE: What's wrong with computers?

SALLY: (*To audience*) He loves computers.

MIKE: I like computers.

SALLY: You should learn about *people*.

MIKE: I know a thing or two.

SALLY: You should learn about *love*.

MIKE: I know a thing or two.

SALLY: You should learn about *me*.

MIKE: I know about you.

SALLY: You don't! You don't. You don't know me at all!

MIKE: O.K., then. Second question: why did you move out on me?

SALLY: (*Embarrassed*) Oh Mike . . .

MIKE: I want to learn, Teach! You moved out of my pad and back into the girls' dorm. *Why?*

SALLY: (*Under her breath*) Mike, this is a *class!*

MIKE: You take this course, and suddenly you pack your bags and you move *out!* Why?

SALLY: I moved out because . . . (*Pause; then to audience*) I decided not to share a room with Mike because I decided I didn't love him.

MIKE: That's not what you told me.

SALLY: Oh *Mike!*

MIKE: (*To audience*) She told me . . . (*Gestures to blackboard*) She was reading that Tristan and Isolde . . . and she told me that Tristan and Isolde slept with a sword between them, and she moved back into the girls' dorm!

SALLY: You make it sound so . . . dumb!

MIKE: It *is* dumb. We had a good thing going, 'til you took this goddam love course!

SALLY: It was not a good thing.

MIKE: It *was* a good thing.

SALLY: It was never love.

MIKE: I don't care what it was, but we had . . .

SALLY: What, *what* did we have?

MIKE: I won't say.

SALLY: Because you can't. Because you can't find the words. Because it wasn't love.

MIKE: I can find the words.

SALLY: Then let's hear them. Let's hear what we had. (*To audience*) Oh you see! He can't even *talk*. He wouldn't read one of these books on that list! I mean, we had nothing to *say* to each other! (*Turns to Mike*) Where is the language of love? What did we ever have?

MIKE: We had tremendous times in bed, baby, and don't you ever forget it!

SALLY: (*After a moment, quietly*) That's not enough.

MIKE: (*With a sigh*) O.K. Third question. Are you coming back?

SALLY: (*Helplessly, indicating audience*) Mike . . .

MIKE: Are you going to be with me this summer?

SALLY: I don't know.

MIKE: Do you want me to marry you?

SALLY: No.

MIKE: Because that's a giant step, teacher, and I'm not about to take it at this point in my bright, young life.

SALLY: Neither am I. Oh God, neither am I!

MIKE: O.K., so then tell the class *why* you moved out on a guy who made you happy all spring long and who wants to keep it going in the summer! Tell the class!

SALLY: Because I want . . . more. Because there should be . . . more. Even in the summer, there should be more.

MIKE: Then I'm not your man.

(*Miss Carroway returns hurriedly down the aisle, clutching her book. She comes up onto the stage, panting*)

CARROWAY: (*To Sally and Mike*) Shoo, shoo! Out of my way, children! I have something to say!

(*Sally and Mike promptly leave the stage, return to their seats in the audience*)

CARROWAY: Class! I have just been . . . (*She searches for the word*) . . . magnificent! I have just been superb! Oh, I wish you all could have been there, following me into that faculty meeting like a Greek chorus! Then you would have heard me sing my swan song! Oh yes! The ugly duckling has at last spread her wings, and sung a huge, full-throated threnody! Let me tell you what I said and did . . .

(*Burgess storms down the aisle onto the stage. Carroway draws herself up to face him*)

BURGESS: (*With great self-control*) I'd like to speak to you alone!

CARROWAY: I am teaching a class.

BURGESS: I would like a minute with you alone.

CARROWAY: This is the last class.

BURGESS: (*Exploding*) You *lied* to them!

CARROWAY: That was no lie!

BURGESS: You said we were lovers!

CARROWAY: Which is true!

BURGESS: Not true at all!

CARROWAY: Ever since Plato we've been in love!

BURGESS: You're insane!

CARROWAY: As all true lovers are!

BURGESS: (*Turning to audience*) We never even *met* outside of class!

CARROWAY: (*To audience*) We never had to! Here's where we met! (*To Burgess*) *Here is our space!* (*He moves uncomfortably away from her*) Oh admit it! Think of Plato, think of the *Symposium*. (*She recites*) "There are those who are pregnant in soul . . . And these people maintain a much closer communion than the parents of children . . . They share between them children more beautiful and more immortal." (*She gazes at him*) That is how we were in class. And that is what Plato calls love. And we based the course on it. We taught it. And it's true. Or if it isn't, then this whole semester has been one long lie. (*Pause*) So say what you think.

BURGESS: (*Turning; slowly*) I think . . . that you're a silly academic spinster. I think you made a fool of yourself and of me and of my wife in front of the entire college community. They're still laughing out there, at both of us. And I think they're laughing in here as well.

CARROWAY: (*Aghast*) No . . .

BURGESS: Yes. I'm sorry, but that's the truth. And now I think we should dismiss the class. And I'm going to insist that you write an open letter to the chairman of the faculty explaining your remarks and apologizing for them.

CARROWAY: (*Reeling*) No, No, No! Someone . . . Sally . . . help me!

(*She rushes off, through the aisle. Sally leaps out of her seat and shouts up at Burgess*)

SALLY: You are a stupid, *stupid, stupid man!*

(*She dashes out after Carroway; Mike dashes out after Sally*)

BURGESS: (*To audience*) Class dismissed! (*He starts out, stops*) I said, class dismissed. (*Pause*) Oh look: she barged, she *barged* into the meeting! In the middle of some remarks by the chairman. And she insisted on sitting next to me. I was in the center of the row. With my wife. But in came Carroway. People had to get up and make room for her. Professor Segal, who uses crutches, had to move for her. So she could sit next to me! (*Pause*)

But that wasn't enough. Oh no! She leaned across me and in loud whispers demanded that my wife give her back her book. My wife, when she finally understood, complied. But not before the chairman had stopped his speech, and everyone in the room was watching this ludicrous little scene! But even *that* wasn't enough for your Miss Carroway! Suddenly, she was on her feet, launching into a monstrous defense of the classroom experience, shouting that there wouldn't *be* any student unrest, there wouldn't *be* any faculty meetings, there wouldn't be any *war*—if you please—if we all stayed in the classroom where we belonged! (*Pause*)

And finally, as the chairman was banging his gavel and everyone in the room was pleading with her to sit down, she turned on me. She announced that she, that I, that you! . . . had learned more about love this term than we had ever known before. And she recommended that every member of the faculty take this course. She recommended particularly that my *wife* take it! And then she walked out, sliding sideways down that long, long row. And we all sat stupefied and . . . I rose to reply. But I couldn't even make myself heard. Because of the laughter. Gales of laughter, waves of laughter, even old Professor Kurtz of Physics, who has never cracked a smile, was shaking in his chair. And so I too, like your dear, dear Miss Carroway, had to edge my way out of that room. And come here.

(*Sally appears in the aisle*)

SALLY: Miss Carroway is dying!

BURGESS: Miss Carroway is *not* dying.

SALLY: She says she's dying. And I believe her.

BURGESS: She is naturally upset.

SALLY: She is dying the modern death! She is dying spiritually!

BURGESS: (*Calls out*) Where's that student? Where's that Mike?

MIKE: (*From rear of the theatre*) Right here.

BURGESS: Go find out what the story is, Mike!

MIKE: O.K. (*He goes*)

SALLY: (*Coming angrily up onto the stage*) I know what the story is. The story is—you killed her!

BURGESS: Because I asked for an apology?

SALLY: Because you voted against her tenure! (*To audience*) He did! She just told me. He voted against her contract! And now she's going to die! In Holyoke!

BURGESS: All right. I voted against her. Sally, I *had* to! She's not for this particular place. She has no sense of . . . where we *are!* (*To audience*) She wanted to stop with *Wuthering Heights,* you know. "It's all there," she said. Marx, Freud, Marcuse—they mean nothing to her. I had to beg her to teach Lawrence. And you might recall what a disaster *that* class was!

SALLY: You sent her away!

BURGESS: Because she is too *much!* Can you imagine her here for twenty more *years?*

SALLY: Yes! I can! I can imagine her here forever!

BURGESS: Well I can't! I'm sorry, but I can't.

(*Mike returns down the aisle toward the stage*)

MIKE: Sir . . .

BURGESS: How is she, Mike?

MIKE: She's O.K.

BURGESS: Of course she is.

MIKE: She's sitting in the lounge smoking like a chimney.

BURGESS: Thanks, Mike.

MIKE: And sir, your wife is waiting. She has the car, and she wants to go home.

BURGESS: Then that's it, class. There's my ride. (*Burgess grabs his briefcase*)

SALLY: (*Blocking his way*) You're running out? Without even apologizing to Miss Carroway?

BURGESS: I'll see her on the way out.

SALLY: No. Here! In front of us.

BURGESS: (*A moment; then, as he puts down his briefcase with a sigh*) Tell Miss Carroway I am waiting for her to return to the class. For mutual apologies. And mutual goodbyes.

SALLY: Gladly! (*She hurries off, through the aisle*)

BURGESS: And Mike, ask my wife to wait a moment while I . . .

MIKE: O.K. (*He goes*)

BURGESS: (*To audience*) You see? The course ends with the wife waiting offstage. We've forgotten wives in this course. We've forgotten marriage. (*He goes to blackboard*) Where is the *Odyssey,* where is Tolstoy on this list? Where are the Andromaches, the Penelopes, the Portias? How can we talk about marriage? Where's that Mike?

MIKE: (*Returning*) Here, sir.

BURGESS: Come up here, Mike! I want a *man* up here!

(*Mike comes up onto the stage*)

BURGESS: Sit down, Mike. (*Burgess gives him a chair; he grabs another chair, faces him*) Now we're talking about marriage, Mike. Look at me. I'm a married man. Do I seem happy, Mike? (*Mike looks at him*) Be frank, Mike. Do I seem happy?

MIKE: No sir.

BURGESS: (*Getting up, pacing*) You are right! I am not happy. Not here. But *there,* out there, where my wife is waiting in the car, there I'm happy, Mike. I am eager, Mike, I am eager to walk out of here and get into that car and kiss my wife and drive home and hug my children! That's where I'm happy! Do you believe it, Mike? (*Mike tries to say "No"*) Believe it, Mike. Believe it! Now you—you live with Sally, don't you?

MIKE: Well, we . . .

BURGESS: Sure you do. All you kids shack up. "Let copulation thrive!" But you're not happy with her, are you, Mike?

MIKE: Well, I . . .

BURGESS: No, you're not happy, and she's not happy, and it's a mess! And now I'll tell you how to clean it up. Marry her, Mike.

MIKE: Hold it . . .

BURGESS: Marry her, Mike! That's where it's at, my friend. Get married, buddy. There is a richness, a thickness in the married state which goes far, far beyond the excruciating self-tortures we've gotten into here. Oh get married, Mike. Have babies. Join the human race.

MIKE: I'm too young to die.

BURGESS: Die? You *live,* my friend. You stretch, you expand. Do you know the Rolling Stones, Mike?

MIKE: Of course I know the . . .

BURGESS: My kids introduced me to the Rolling Stones. My wife introduced me to tennis. They all bring things *in,* Mike. Oh, there's a resonance in marriage which all these books can never teach you . . .

SALLY: (*Returning, down the aisle*) Miss Carroway wants to teach *Wuthering Heights.*

BURGESS: Tell Miss Carroway I will simply shake hands and say goodbye.

SALLY: I'll tell her you don't *dare* teach *Wuthering Heights.*

(*She hastens out again*)

BURGESS: See, Mike? She's turning sour. Too many books. Now listen, go tell my wife that I have just sung her a love song. Ask her to wait a little longer. Then go ask that girl to marry you.

MIKE: I'll go tell your wife.

(*He rushes off*)

BURGESS: (*To audience*) Now I'm sorry about what's happened today. I lose my head in here with Miss Carroway. That's what this class does. Never, never, in all my fifteen years of teaching, have I ever gone so . . . far . . . out . . . (*Pause*) Remember the class on *Madame Bovary?* Oh my God, what a class! We flew, we *flew* in that class! It was too much, of course. Much too much. So I will apologize to Miss Carroway and say goodbye. Next year, I'll be sitting in the dean's office. I can do more there in these troubled times.

(*Sally and Mike enter in either aisle*)

SALLY & MIKE: (*Simultaneously*) Miss Carroway . . . Your wife . . .

(*They glare at each other*)

SALLY: (*Determinedly*) Miss Carroway says it's *Wuthering Heights* or nothing!

MIKE: Your wife says the children have to eat!

BURGESS: Tell Miss Carroway . . . tell Miss Carroway I will spend a few moments on *Wuthering Heights.*

SALLY: Good. (*She goes*)

BURGESS: (*To Mike*) Tell my wife . . . tell my wife just . . . please.

MIKE: O.K. (*Mike goes*)

BURGESS: (*To audience*) *Wuthering Heights* it is, then. Just a quick crack at it. For old time's sake. It won't be *Madame Bovary.* No, no. I'm getting too old for *Madame Bovary.*

SALLY: (*From rear of the theatre*) Miss Carroway is ready to teach.

(*Miss Carroway enters, down the aisle, slowly, melodramatically, with Sally behind her. Burgess watches her nervously. She carries her book. She mounts the stage, goes behind the desk, taking her time, lighting a cigarette with her brisk little lighter. She puffs noisily and then addresses the audience; Sally returns to her seat*)

CARROWAY: We thought we might read and discuss the final confrontation between Catherine Earnshaw and Heathcliffe in Emily Brontë's *Wuthering Heights*. (*To Burgess*) Are we agreed?

BURGESS: Agreed.

CARROWAY: (*Opening her book*) I have my book. You can look on with me.

BURGESS: No, no. (*He rummages quickly in his briefcase*) I think I have my own. (*He pulls out a bright paperback which should contrast with her old leathery volume*) I do have my own.

CARROWAY: I begin on page ninety-six.

BURGESS: (*Shuffling through the pages nervously; to audience*) For those who have the Norton Critical Edition, we're on page 132.

CARROWAY: (*To audience*) Cathy is dying because of Heathcliffe . . .

BURGESS: (*To audience*) Not just because of Heathcliffe . . .

CARROWAY: (*Grimly*) She *thinks* because of Heathcliffe. And that's the important thing. What she thinks.

BURGESS: (*Nodding, looking at her*) Yes. All right.

(*He sits some distance away from her. Carroway turns to the audience*)

CARROWAY: Heathcliffe, after *years* of separation, has found his way to the dying Cathy's room. (*She reads*) "And he could hardly bear, for downright agony, to look into her face . . . there was no prospect of ultimate recovery . . . she was fated, sure to die." (*She turns to Burgess*) Read.

BURGESS: " 'Oh Cathy! Oh, my life! how can I bear it?' was the first sentence he uttered, in a tone . . ."

CARROWAY: (*Interrupting him*) Just read Heathcliffe. Sally! Come up, and read the Narrator.

(*Sally comes up onto the stage. Carroway hands her the book*)

CARROWAY: Read there, Sally.

SALLY: (*Reading prosaically*) "And now he stared at her so earnestly that I thought the very intensity of his gaze would bring tears into his eyes. But they . . ."

CARROWAY: (*Interrupting her*) "They burned with anguish, they did not melt." (*With passion; to Burgess*) "You have broken my heart, Heathcliffe. You have killed me—and thriven on it, I think. How strong you are! How many years do you mean to live after I am gone?"

(*Pause. Burgess looks at her, then searches in his book for a response. She smiles, turns to Sally*)

CARROWAY: Continue.

SALLY: "Heathcliffe had knelt on one knee to embrace her . . ."

CARROWAY: (*To Burgess*) Do it.

BURGESS: (*Shaking his head, embarrassed*) I'm not going to . . .

CARROWAY: (*Blithely*) Go on, Sally.

SALLY: "Heathcliffe had knelt on one knee to embrace her; he attempted to rise, but she seized his hair, and kept him down."

CARROWAY: (*Reciting from memory*) "I wish I could hold you till we were both dead! I shouldn't care what you suffered. I care nothing for your sufferings. Why shouldn't you suffer? I do!"

(*Mike enters quickly down the aisle and comes to the edge of the stage*)

MIKE: Sir . . .

(*He beckons to Burgess, who rises and comes forward. He whispers something to Burgess. Burgess nods. Mike leaves*)

CARROWAY: What?

BURGESS: (*Returning to his chair*) My wife wants me to know she's watching from the rear.

CARROWAY: Good! (*She continues to recite by memory*) "Will you be happy when I am in the earth? Will you say twenty years hence, 'That's the grave of Catherine Earnshaw. I loved her long ago . . . I've loved many others since. My children are dearer to me than she was.' Will you say so, Heathcliffe?"

BURGESS: (*Reading very quietly*) "Don't torture me until I'm as mad as yourself."

CARROWAY: Louder. Not everyone can hear.

BURGESS: (*Very loud*) "Don't torture me until I'm as mad as yourself!"

CARROWAY: (*Calmly; to Sally*) Read.

SALLY: "The two, to a cool spectator, made a strange and fearful picture."

CARROWAY: Skip to "she retained . . ."

SALLY: Um. (*Finds the place*) "She retained in her closed fingers a portion of the locks she had been grasping . . ."

CARROWAY: (*Looking at Burgess*) Yes!

BURGESS: (*After a glance; reading desperately*) "You know you lie to say I have killed you. Is it not sufficient for your infernal selfishness that while you are at peace, I shall writhe in the torments of hell?"

CARROWAY: "I shall not be at peace."

(*Mike returns, again to the edge of the stage. Burgess promptly rises. Mike whispers to him, then goes*)

CARROWAY: What now?

BURGESS: My wife has just left.

CARROWAY: Run after her.

BURGESS: No! . . . Yes! . . . No! . . . Oh my God, why, why am I here? I've just missed my ride! I'll probably miss a meal! There will be hell to pay when I get home!

CARROWAY: The shrill-tongued Fulvia scolds!

BURGESS: (*Wheeling on her*) No! She laughs! She laughs at you! She laughs at *me* when I mention you! Oh what have you done to me? Woman, you have seduced me! With *books!* We have rolled in them, we have wallowed in them like lascivious Turks! Right now, I should be home! I should be holding in my hand a cool, dry Martini, with beaded bubbles winking at the brim!

CARROWAY: Keats!

BURGESS: Yes, *Keats!* And Wagner! And Brontë! Oh lady, you are holding me in thrall! I'm drowning!

CARROWAY: Then swim to the dean's office! Lie panting there, on that desert island! Or else come with me!

BURGESS: Where? Where are we going?

(*Pause. Carroway closes her eyes and recites*)

CARROWAY: "Heathcliffe, forgive me. Come here and kneel down. You never harmed me in your life. Nay, if you nurse anger, that will be worse to remember than my harsh words! Won't you come here? Do!"

SALLY: (*Reading*) "Heathcliffe went to the back of her chair."

BURGESS: (*To Carroway; carefully*) I'll come up to Holyoke. Commute. Once a week. To teach the course.

CARROWAY: (*Shaking her head*) Go on, Sally.

SALLY: "He leaned over, but not so far as to let her see his face . . ."

BURGESS: All right, then! You could come down here. Be a visiting lecturer. We'll do it that way.

CARROWAY: (*Shaking her head*) Sally . . .

SALLY: "She bent round to look at him; he would not permit it; turning abruptly, he walked to the fireplace, where he stood, silent, with his back toward us."

(*Burgess has followed these directions, though not so mechanically as to make them comic. Now he turns on Carroway*)

BURGESS: All right! I'll do what I can to have you reinstated here. I'll speak to the chairman. I'll start *something* going!

CARROWAY: (*Reciting*) "Oh you see, he would not relent

a moment to keep me out of my grave! *That* is how I'm loved!"

BURGESS: *What do you want then?*

CARROWAY: (*Reciting; more to herself*) "Well, never mind! That is not *my* Heathcliffe. I shall love mine yet; and take him with me—he's in my soul."

BURGESS: Would you tell me what you want, please?

CARROWAY: (*Going right on*) "And the thing that irks me most is this shattered prison. I'm wearying to escape into that glorious world, not seeing it dimly through tears, and yearning for it through the walls of an aching heart; but really with it, and in it."

BURGESS: For God's sake, tell me what you *want!*

CARROWAY: (*To Sally*) Read.

SALLY: "In her eagerness she rose and supported herself on the arm of the chair." (*Carroway does*) "At that earnest appeal, he turned to her, looking absolutely desperate." (*Burgess does*) "His eyes wide, and wet at last, flashed fiercely on her; his breast heaved convulsively. An instant they held asunder; and then how they met I hardly saw, but Catherine made a spring, and he caught her, and they were locked in an embrace from which I thought my mistress would never be released alive."

(*Sally looks up. They are kissing, frantically. The book slowly lowers in Sally's hand*)

SALLY: (*Softly*) Miss . . . Carroway.

(*Then, suddenly, the schoolbell rings. Carroway breaks away*)

BURGESS: (*Huskily*) I meant what I said about getting you back here!

CARROWAY: Don't be silly! (*She briskly begins stacking her books*)

BURGESS: I want to teach this course again!

CARROWAY: Once is enough. (*She turns to audience*) Now. The examination topic. I thought Plato. (*To Burgess*) Is Plato all right with you? (*Burgess nods vaguely; she turns to the audience again*) Plato it is, then. The ending of the *Sym-*

posium. Where Socrates suggests that tragedy and comedy are ultimately the same thing. (*To Burgess*) I think that ties the knot, don't you?

(*Burgess nods again, ineptly. Carroway finishes stacking her books*)

CARROWAY: May I take you anywhere, Sally?

SALLY: Me? No.

(*She returns the copy of* Wuthering Heights; *Carroway places it on the top of her stack*)

SALLY: Mike? I . . . I left my Plato in your pad!

MIKE: (*From the aisle*) Come and get it!

(*Sally rushes off the stage to Mike's side. Carroway gathers her stack of books lovingly into her arms; she holds her one free hand out to Burgess*)

CARROWAY: Goodbye, Professor Burgess.

BURGESS: (*Mechanically, shaking hands*) Goodbye, Professor Carroway.

(*Miss Carroway exits briskly down the aisle. Burgess sits stunned, as the stage blacks out*)

The End

Martin Duberman

THE RECORDER:
A HISTORY

Martin Duberman

Although Martin Duberman admitted to an interviewer only a short while ago that "there are times when I have trouble deciding which I am, historian or playwright," he successfully has juxtaposed both careers by discovering "there is a feedback between history and the theatre", and the cord that binds his two selves is "curiosity about the inner worlds of people."

A professor of American History at Princeton University, Martin Duberman was born in 1930 in New York City and grew up there and in Mount Vernon, New York. He received his B.A. from Yale University and his M.A. and Ph.D. from Harvard. He is the author of two distinguished biographies: *Charles Francis Adams, 1807–1886,* which was awarded the prestigious Bancroft Prize in 1962; and *James Russell Lowell,* a nominee for the National Book Award in 1966. A collection of his essays, *The Uncompleted Past,* was published in 1969 (*The New York Times* defined it as "a remarkable intellectual autobiography"), and in 1965, he edited *The Antislavery Vanguard: New Essays on the Abolitionists.*

The author became enamored with the theatre at the age of seventeen when he performed the juvenile lead in a summer stock rendering of Thornton Wilder's *Our Town.* "At any rate, I wound up at Yale, where I did some acting and directing and where I also became fascinated by American history."

The elusiveness of truth and the enigma of history are the pervading themes of Mr. Duberman's double bill, *The Memory Bank.* Comprised of two short plays, *The Recorder: A History* (here published for the first time) and *The Electric Map,* the presentation opened on January 11, 1970 at the Off-Broadway Tambellini's Gate Theatre. Clive Barnes found the plays to be "exquisitely wrought" and "one of the season's better moments ... it is good to spend the evening with a professional playwright of Mr. Duberman's quality." The reviewer for *Variety* reported that the plays were of "rare taste and craftsmanship" and the author's point, "history is how you elect to see past events," was admirably proven in *The Recorder.* Martin Gottfried summed up the evening as "engrossing and literate theatre," and his fellow first-night juror George Oppenheimer hailed it as "a dramatically exciting evening . . . *The Recorder* has a prying life of its own."

Mr. Duberman's first play, *In White America,* opened in October, 1963, at the Off-Broadway Sheridan Square Playhouse. It enjoyed a run of 500 performances, two national tours, a large number of foreign productions and won the 1963–64 Drama Desk-Vernon Rice Award. His short play, *Metaphors,* was presented as part of *Collision Course* at the Café au Go Go in 1968; *Groups* was given in a workshop production at the Loft Theatre, 1969; and later in that same year, the Actors Studio reinaugurated its playwright's unit with a production of his play, *The Colonial Dudes.*

The author (who also served two years as drama critic for *The Partisan Review* and currently is covering the theatre for the newly-resuscitated *Show* magazine) has a new full-length play tentatively titled *Payments* under option for New York presentation in 1970. For the foreseeable future, "I'm writing a history of Black Mountain College, an experimental school and community that existed from 1933 to 1956. And as I've been working, a play about a Utopian community—that's what Black Mountain was, in a way—is taking shape in my mind."

A play for two men and a tape recorder. The recorder is on the table. Smyth is fiddling with it as the curtain rises.

SMYTH: Huh! You'd think after a couple of hundred times I'd be able to thread the damn thing.

ANDREWS: Take your time.

SMYTH: To tell you the truth, I'd just about given up hope that you'd see me. I'm grateful to you for letting me come by.

ANDREWS: I admire persistence.

SMYTH: I didn't mean to plague you.

ANDREWS: It was my secretaries you plagued. But eventually word does filter through to me.

SMYTH: When you didn't answer my third letter, I got a bit rattled.

ANDREWS: I was making inquiries.

SMYTH: I understand. You must get all kinds of requests.

ANDREWS: All kinds.

SMYTH: (*Still fiddling with machine*) Damn! I seem to be all thumbs today.

ANDREWS: You have quite a reputation for one so young.

SMYTH: Thank you.

ANDREWS: This book, of course, will boost it still further.

SMYTH: I hadn't thought of it that way.

ANDREWS: Oh my! Pure as well as accomplished.

SMYTH: I think the book will be timely.

ANDREWS: You've talked to many others, have you?

SMYTH: Oh, literally hundreds, sir. You're the last.

ANDREWS: (*Pointing to the tape recorder*) And did you cart *that* with you everywhere?

SMYTH: Yes. It's not very heavy. Ah! There. That does

it. (*He looks up at Andrews*) I hope this isn't going to bother you too much.

ANDREWS: Can't really tell. I've never used one before. I do feel self-conscious.

SMYTH: You'll forget it's there after a few minutes. That's the theory anyway. Frankly, I've never gotten used to it.

ANDREWS: Then why do you use it?

SMYTH: I want to get what you say straight. I've got a rotten memory. Funny in a historian, isn't it? Can't keep a fact in my head. It's safer using the machine. That way, I'll be sure it's accurate.

ANDREWS: But it might not come out right. I *am* a little nervous.

SMYTH: About the machine?

ANDREWS: No, about it coming out right. I've forgotten a lot. I hope that the . . . (*Pause*) . . . talking . . . (*Pause*) will bring back . . .

SMYTH: Don't worry. You'll relax once we get started.
(*A strained pause*)

ANDREWS: Shall I talk now?

SMYTH: I haven't turned it on. All set?

ANDREWS: I suppose.

SMYTH: Let's start right in then.

ANDREWS: Fine.

SMYTH: I'll stop it after a minute just to be sure we're recording.
(*He turns the recorder on, returns to his seat*)

SMYTH: Any time you're ready.

ANDREWS: Should I just talk?

SMYTH: Whatever makes you most comfortable.

ANDREWS: Is it recording?

SMYTH: Should be. Would it help if I asked direct questions?

ANDREWS: What do you particularly want to know?

SMYTH: Well, I guess most crucial would be—it's so hard to know what's finally going to be important. Why not just start talking about him. Anything you happen to remember.

ANDREWS: I remember next to nothing about his early life.

SMYTH: Anything. It might be important.

ANDREWS: You mean like his schooling?

SMYTH: If that's as far back as you can go.

ANDREWS: (*After a pause*) I can see him on a beach. He was three or four. Beautiful baby. Snow-white hair.

SMYTH: With his family?

ANDREWS: I suppose so. There's something about his sister. Probably not true. I shouldn't say it.

SMYTH: Please. You have my promise. This is strictly for my own information. Not a word will go into print without your permission.

ANDREWS: I believe you. Still, one can't be sure. I do feel a responsibility.

SMYTH: I know what you mean. It's important to get everything as accurate as possible. That's why I use the machine. I don't want to have to rely on memory.

ANDREWS: Well. There was some story about his sister at the beach. They loved each other very much, you know. Everyone in the family said so, always. She was left to take care of him for a while. I don't think she was more than eight. He was very fair-skinned. She kept pouring water over his little body. To keep him cool, you know. She'd go back and forth to the ocean, filling her pail. Kept pouring it over him. He got a very nasty burn. Second degree, I think they said. She was only trying to keep him cool. Poor child.

SMYTH: Who?

ANDREWS: *Who?*

SMYTH: You said, "poor child". I wasn't sure who you meant.

ANDREWS: Oh. Him. I suppose. I did say, "poor child"?

SMYTH: Yes. I'm quite sure.

ANDREWS: Curious. (*Brightening*) Well if I did, it'll be on the machine.

SMYTH: Oh, Christ! I forgot to check if we're recording! (*He jumps up, goes to machine and clicks it off*)

SMYTH: I'll just go back a bit. To be sure we're recording. This machine is bad on reproducing voices. You won't sound a bit like yourself.

ANDREWS: I've never heard myself.

SMYTH: Then you won't know how differently you sound.

ANDREWS: You'll be able to tell, though.

SMYTH: (*As he starts to rewind*) When I bought this machine I looked for one with a sensitive pick-up. So that people wouldn't have to hold the mike in front of them. This one's very good. You can put it in the corner of a room and speak in your normal voice and it picks it right up. But the quality of the sound isn't so hot. Since I'm not recording music, though, I don't care. As long as the typist can hear the words.

ANDREWS: It must have been expensive.

SMYTH: (*Stopping the recorder*) That's more than enough. Remember, it won't sound like you. I mean the quality. Your voice has a lot more resonance. (*He turns on the machine*)

MACHINE: "She'd go back and forth to the ocean, filling her pail. Kept pouring it over him. He got a very nasty burn. Second degree, I think they said. She was only trying to keep him cool. Poor child."

(*Smyth clicks off the machine*)

SMYTH: There's the "poor child."

ANDREWS: Yes. You were right. It *didn't* sound like me.

SMYTH: But you'd never heard yourself.

ANDREWS: You know, what I thought I'd sound like. (*Pause*) It's working then?

SMYTH: Yes. We'll be able to relax now. I won't stop it again. (*He clicks the machine back on and returns to his seat*) Now let's see . . . where were we?

ANDREWS: I'm not happy about that.

SMYTH: But that's not the way you *really* sound.

ANDREWS: Not my *voice*. The story about the beach. I'm not at all sure it's true.

SMYTH: Can you recall when you first heard it?

ANDREWS: Heard it? I was *there.*

SMYTH: On the beach?

ANDREWS: No, of course not. But it was re-told in his family a thousand times. You must have heard it yourself.

SMYTH: I have, in fact. But your version is different. My accounts involved his mother, not the sister.

ANDREWS: That's absurd. A grown woman would never have done such a thing.

SMYTH: It does seem improbable. How did the mother strike you?

ANDREWS: Certainly not cruel. Far from cruel. She adored the boy. She was very beautiful.

SMYTH: What's your first memory of her?

(*Andrews thinks; then becomes embarrassed, agitated*)

ANDREWS: This kind of raking up. I really have my doubts, you know. What's the point?

SMYTH: I'm trying to understand what made him tick. I want to find out everything I can.

(*Pause*)

ANDREWS: I only remember a few things. Without all the rest, they can't be trusted. They'll loom too large.

SMYTH: Each person remembers a little. I put it all to-gether. (*The machine squeaks*) Hmm. I can't figure that out. It happens at the damndest times. No pattern to it.

ANDREWS: Maybe it needs oil.

SMYTH: Oh, no! The manual says never to oil it. It has a sealed lubrication system.

(*The machine squeaks again. Smyth gets up*)

ANDREWS: Then maybe it isn't level. The least thing throws them off. Maybe you'd better take notes instead.

SMYTH: Let's try moving it. (*He clicks the machine off*)

ANDREWS: Watch the cord. It's going to pull the micro-phone out.

SMYTH: Oh, yes. Thank you. (*He readjusts the cord, then turns machine back on; listens for a few seconds*) Seems okay.

You were right about leveling. Seems to have done it. (*He goes to his seat*) You were going to tell me your first recollections of the mother.

ANDREWS: I think I was not going to tell you.

SMYTH: I give you my word this is all strictly confidential.

ANDREWS: (*Looking at the machine*) Notes are better. That's all they are, and everyone knows it—traces. They can be denied, destroyed.

SMYTH: The tape is yours. I'll have it typed up, and then I'll send you both the tape and the typescript.

ANDREWS: How will I know there isn't a carbon?

SMYTH: (*Embarrassed*) I guess you'll have to take my word.

ANDREWS: I don't even know you. Not really, that is.

SMYTH: It does come down to trust.

(*Pause*)

ANDREWS: You *will* ask my permission if you want to quote something from your carbon?

SMYTH: You have my word.

ANDREWS: Mm-hmm. (*A long pause. It should not be clear if, in what follows, Andrews is deliberately inventing or telling the truth as he remembers it*) Well. The boy was a good deal older. Thirteen or fourteen. He got the idea one day to write a story.

SMYTH: Excuse me. I had hoped you would tell me about his mother.

ANDREWS: I'm about to.

SMYTH: Oh, I'm sorry. I didn't mean to interrupt.

ANDREWS: It was a moralistic little tale. About a girl named Jane who tried to be good but couldn't. He was very excited when he finished writing it and ran in to show it to his mother. She read it and then turned to him angrily. "You should be outside playing with the rest of the boys in the street," she said. "If you were a real boy, that's where you'd be." The boy looked as if he would faint.

SMYTH: Could you backtrack just a bit? There's something I didn't get.

ANDREWS: You don't have to. The machine will.

SMYTH: Just to get it straight myself, for the conversation.

ANDREWS: So you can ask the right questions.

SMYTH: Exactly.

ANDREWS: He had written a little story about Jane, you see.

SMYTH: No, I understand *that* part. I meant the mother's anger. Why was she angry? What was she angry at?

ANDREWS: I really don't know. Maybe *she* didn't.

SMYTH: But what would you guess?

ANDREWS: I couldn't begin to.

SMYTH: (*Pressing him*) Was she worried that he might not be—well—what do you call it—a "regular fellow"?

ANDREWS: Maybe.

SMYTH: You think that did worry her?

ANDREWS: Maybe. Otherwise why would she have said it?

SMYTH: Said what?

ANDREWS: About playing in the street more.

SMYTH: She wanted him to play in the street more. With the rest of the boys.

ANDREWS: No, it seems to me that's exactly what worried her. He was out in the street so much with *that* kind of boy.

SMYTH: What kind?

ANDREWS: The ones he would play with.

SMYTH: I'm afraid you've lost me.

ANDREWS: Oh, well.

(*Pause*)

SMYTH: You think then—just to clear this up—that his mother disapproved of the crowd of boys he was hanging out with. On the streets.

ANDREWS: I really couldn't say. It was so long ago.

SMYTH: I know how hard it is to recall these things. It must be forty years ago, isn't it? At least.

ANDREWS: I should think. Something like that. You probably know better than I.

SMYTH: Sometimes I think I know him very well. Then it turns out there are whole episodes I've never even heard of. This story about Jane, for example.

ANDREWS: Remember, I didn't want to tell it. I have no confidence in it.

SMYTH: Why don't we try it again. If you don't mind. Tell it to me again.

ANDREWS: (*Sighs*) It's like this. He was not the sort of boy—mind you, this is only as I remember him—who was much for the usual horseplay and sports. Now and then he'd enjoy it. In fact he was a good athlete. Quite good, now that I think about it. He used to win cups in summer camp. Best all-around midget. That sort of thing. But he liked other things, too. Words, any kind of words. In books, in talk. He liked putting words together.

SMYTH: So he started to write stories.

ANDREWS: Yes. There we are. He wrote that story about Jane. He must have been a tot still. Couldn't have been more than seven.

SMYTH: This is the same story about Jane you just described? The moralistic one?

ANDREWS: (*Surprised*) Were there *two* Jane stories? Huh! I'd always assumed there'd only been the one?

SMYTH: I didn't know of any. That is before today.

ANDREWS: Then why do you refer to two?

SMYTH: The first one you said he wrote when he was about thirteen or fourteen. And now this last one you mentioned you said he wrote when he was about seven.

ANDREWS: I only know of one Jane story.

SMYTH: But you did say earlier he had been thirteen or fourteen.

ANDREWS: Not as I remember. I don't see how I could have.

SMYTH: I could've sworn you said thirteen or fourteen. Well, no matter. The machine will have it in any case.

ANDREWS: Perhaps we should rewind and see.

SMYTH: It would be difficult to find the exact spot. I can sort it all out later. It's all there. Anyway, you are now sure he was about seven when he wrote that story.

ANDREWS: Yes, quite sure. I can't swear to it, of course. You know what funny tricks memory can play. But I am reasonably sure he was seven.

SMYTH: Fine. Let's get back then to his mother's reaction. Apparently she didn't like his playing in the streets so much.

ANDREWS: In truth, I think it depended on the boys he was with. Actually, he had several sets of friends. Some the mother liked and some she didn't.

SMYTH: Which did she like?

ANDREWS: (*Thinking*) I wish I could be sure. It seems to me the one she really *didn't* like was the girl across the street.

SMYTH: Not Jane?

ANDREWS: No, no. You've got that wrong. The *story* was about a girl named Jane.

SMYTH: That's what I'd thought.

ANDREWS: Yes, that's right. The *story* was about a girl named Jane.

SMYTH: And the girl across the street?

ANDREWS: Quite something else. She had her hooks into him, you know. Girls aren't very old when they start thinking of marriage.

SMYTH: Yes, but seven . . . !

ANDREWS: The suburbs. You know how it is. In any case, I wouldn't say seven. No, I couldn't be sure of seven. Not the girl across the street.

SMYTH: She was older then?

ANDREWS: Yes, that was part of the trouble. She was much too old for him. Kept him inside all the time. That's what the mother objected to, you see.

SMYTH: She wanted him out in the street with the boys.

ANDREWS: Right. Playing games. That sort of thing.

SMYTH: Would he and the girl write together?

ANDREWS: They mostly played bridge. Even at lunchtime, during school break. Bridge, bridge, bridge. Became very good at it. A lifelong hobby of his.

SMYTH: Yes, I'd heard that.

ANDREWS: He put himself through college playing bridge.

SMYTH: Really? But he didn't need to do that. He was a wealthy boy.

ANDREWS: He wanted to do it. (*Pause*) Bridge is an intricate game. (*Pause*) Do you play?

SMYTH: No, not very well. (*Pause*) You were roommates in college, weren't you?

ANDREWS: Yes. That is, after the freshman year. That may be the most interesting story of all. No memory problem there.

SMYTH: Good.

ANDREWS: But it is painful for me to recall.

SMYTH: I understand. (*Andrews is silent; then, in an attempt to coax him*) Painful episodes are often important.

ANDREWS: For your book, you mean.

SMYTH: Yes, exactly. (*Pause*) But you know I once dropped this whole project. Gave it up entirely for three months. It was after I talked to a woman in Delaware. The more she talked about the "good old days", the more she drank. By the time it was over I couldn't make any sense of what she was saying. I felt terrible, encouraging her to look back. It was like picking scabs off old wounds.

ANDREWS: Inhuman. Why do you do it?

SMYTH: We have to find out the truth.

ANDREWS: For posterity, I suppose.

SMYTH: We must hold on to past experience. It's all we

have to guide us. Without it we'd be like amnesia victims, no moorings at all.

ANDREWS: Each day would be brand new.

SMYTH: Exactly. Think how disconcerting that would be. Having to start fresh each day. (*Noises from the machine. The reel has come to an end*) The reel has ended. (*He goes to the machine and starts to turn over the reel*)

ANDREWS: It must have missed that last part. About amnesia.

SMYTH: That doesn't matter. It was just me, gabbing. (*Laughs*) I'm not interested in recording me.

ANDREWS: Those reels aren't very long.

SMYTH: They come in various lengths. I put on a short one. I wasn't sure how long we'd be. (*Trying to charm him into further reminiscence*) But you're a mine of information!

ANDREWS: No one was closer to him, after all.

SMYTH: (*Finishing up with the machine*) That does it. I've turned it over to the other side. (*He goes back to his seat*)

ANDREWS: Is the machine on?

SMYTH: Yes. Just pick up where you were.

ANDREWS: We were talking about bridge, weren't we?

SMYTH: No, we'd finished with that.

ANDREWS: Oh, had we?

SMYTH: I know—we were talking about college! Something you said was very vivid.

ANDREWS: I doubt if it's the sort of thing you want. After all, he's a public figure. This is pretty private stuff. As I say, we were close.

SMYTH: I promise you it will stay private. I want to know everything I can, but I certainly don't intend printing everything.

ANDREWS: Then why know it?

SMYTH: I want to understand why he acted the way he did.

ANDREWS: Just describe his actions, his public career. That's what's important. That's what's affected history.

SMYTH: But it all might have happened differently. I mean, if he'd been a different kind of man. He might have made different decisions, affected history differently.

ANDREWS: Historians shouldn't deal in "ifs", it seems to me. If he'd been different he wouldn't have affected history at all. If he'd been able to screw that girl he'd never have been a public figure.

SMYTH: The girl across the street?

ANDREWS: No, the girl in college. Joan I think her name was. Maybe I'm thinking of Jane again. Joan? Yes, Joan. She came up for the big freshman weekend. Very sexed-up girl. Everybody knew it. They'd been dating off and on. This was supposed to be the big culmination. She'd promised him that if he invited her up for the weekend, she'd have sex with him. He'd told everybody. It was like the wedding night. Everybody knew they were going to do it. There was practically a crowd waiting for them when they came out of the room.

SMYTH: What room?

ANDREWS: Don't know. Funny, everything else is so vivid. Some freshman's room. We had a big party there after the dance. About a dozen couples. Lots of drinking. Something called "purple passion"—gin and grape juice. There was a huge vat of it. An aluminum vat. With large cakes of ice floating in it. We slopped the stuff down. One girl got sick, I remember. Vomited down the stairwell. Quite a sight. Splashed down the stairs.

SMYTH: It wasn't Joan?

ANDREWS: No, no. They were curled up on the floor. Making out. Everybody was. But we had our eyes on them. We were all virgins—except Joan. It was a different generation, you know. He was going to be the first. That night. We could hardly wait. Finally they got up and went into the back room. I think three of us had orgasms on the spot.

SMYTH: Doesn't sound like the kids nowadays.

ANDREWS: Sex was a big deal for us. It took a lot of planning and work. Sometimes we had to throw in an engagement ring. The kids today would think we're crazy. For them it's like taking a leak.

SMYTH: They wouldn't believe your freshman prom.

ANDREWS: They'd believe it. They just wouldn't care. All those fools in the past. Bury it, forget it. You don't expect them to read your book, do you?

SMYTH: I don't know. I never thought about it. I guess not.

ANDREWS: Why would they? What's it got to tell them?

SMYTH: It could show them how differently people behave.

ANDREWS: So?

SMYTH: It would open up a range of possibilities.

(*Andrews laughs*)

ANDREWS: We all know there are insane asylums. But we don't keep visiting them. Who's going to read your book?

SMYTH: Non-fiction sells well. Better than fiction.

ANDREWS: (*Thoughtfully*) I wonder where Joan would fit.

SMYTH: You didn't make her up!

ANDREWS: I told you how vivid she was. I can see her coming out of that room. Strange expression on her face. Hard to read. Something like his mother's when she saw that story about Jane. His face was less complicated. He was upset. Very upset.

SMYTH: Did he say why?

ANDREWS: Not then. Nobody really questioned them. But he said something to a few of us that they had decided to wait, that Joan was having a period, something like that. (*He looks at the machine*) Hasn't the tape ended?

SMYTH: (*Getting half out of the chair, to check the machine*) No, we've still got a ways yet.

ANDREWS: This side seems longer than the other.

SMYTH: It does, doesn't it.

ANDREWS: We must be on pot.

SMYTH: I beg your pardon?

ANDREWS: Pot distorts the sense of time. Haven't you ever smoked?

SMYTH: No. Have you?

ANDREWS: No. Well, what else do you want for the time capsule?

SMYTH: Did he say anything to you later about Joan?

ANDREWS: He said they'd made out on the floor. That he'd come in his handkerchief. She'd understood. She had been very understanding.

(*Pause*)

SMYTH: (*Embarrassed; confused*) What is it she had been understanding about?

ANDREWS: About his being afraid. She said it didn't matter that he couldn't get an erection. That often happened the first time. No, wait a minute. I think I've got that confused. That wasn't part of the episode with Joan. It seems to me it was earlier. No, perhaps later. With that call girl, I think it was, in Florida. The taxi driver had taken them to this little house on the outskirts of Palm Beach. Yes, it was a house, not a call girl. All the girls—there must have been five or six—were sitting around a small room rocking slowly on their chairs. Nobody said anything. We sat down. The girls just kept rocking. Finally one of them broke into a laugh. "Come on, boys," she said, "make a choice. We can't spend the whole day." I grabbed the girl nearest me and we went into a back room. She dropped her robe as soon as we got into the room. Then she asked me what I wanted. Everything had a different price. "Round the world" was the big one. I think it cost twenty dollars. I told her I only had seven dollars on me. She didn't believe me, so I let her look in my wallet. She said for seven dollars she could only screw me. We tried for what seemed like hours. And we weren't on pot. Finally she said she'd blow me a little to help me work it up, but that I wasn't to tell the madame or any of my friends or she'd catch hell—for seven bucks she was supposed to give me a straight screw and that was it. The blow job didn't help. She was nice about it. Said not to worry, that married men often came in and couldn't do it either. She squirted some kind of ointment around the opening of my cock. Then she wrapped it in gauze, and put a rubber band around it. She said when my friends saw it they'd think I had screwed her.

(*A long pause: Smyth is nonplussed; Andrews sits very calmly*)

ANDREWS: I really can't see why you want to know all this.

SMYTH: (*Confused; hesitant*) Well . . . it's fascinating. It . . . uh . . . helps to explain a great deal.

ANDREWS: It does? Like what?

SMYTH: I think it tells me a lot about your—about the —relations with women. I mean, tying that in with writing the story about Jane. And his inability to have intercourse with Joan.

ANDREWS: He had intercourse with Joan. On the floor. I told you that.

SMYTH: Didn't he say they had decided to wait? That Joan was having a period?

ANDREWS: That's what the handkerchief was for.

(*Noises from the machine; the tape has ended*)

SMYTH: Damn! What a time for the tape to end.

ANDREWS: About time. We've been here forever. She was a very moralistic girl, that Jane. (*Laughs; then almost to himself*) Mary Jane. (*To Smyth, who is at the machine*) Would you do me a favor and backtrack a bit? I'd like to hear that section on the freshman party. I want to be sure I got it straight.

SMYTH: (*Starts to rewind the machine*) Of course. I'd be glad to. (*A short pause while machine rewinds. Nervously*) It won't take more than a few moments. (*He stops the machine after a few more seconds, then starts it forward again*)

MACHINE: "She kept pouring water over his little body . . ."

SMYTH: (*Startled; stops machine*) I thought that section was on the *other* side. That was all much earlier.

(*Andrews sits quietly. Smyth again rewinds the machine for a few seconds, then starts it forward*)

MACHINE: ". . . something to a few of us that they had decided to wait; that Joan was having a period . . ."
(*A slight pause: then a female voice is heard on the tape*)
FEMALE VOICE: "We can't spend the whole day."
(*Andrews looks up startled; Smyth stops the machine*)
ANDREWS: Who was that?
SMYTH: (*Laughs*) Sorry. That sometimes happens. I re-use the tapes after the typist makes a transcript. Sometimes they don't erase fully. That bit must have been left in from the last interview. But you *had* said they decided to wait. You see, it is as I remembered it—they did not have intercourse. I thought that was what you'd said.
ANDREWS: They did have intercourse, as I've already told you. But not to climax. The handkerchief. I was quite distinct about that.
SMYTH: (*Nervously*) Tapes don't lie.
ANDREWS: Neither do I.
SMYTH: (*Placating*) Why don't we just try it from scratch. I'll put on a fresh reel or we can record right over the first version.
ANDREWS: Frankly, this is getting a little tedious. It was, after all, a minor incident. I probably should never have mentioned it. You'll be making too much of it—that he was impotent, or afraid of women, or God knows what.
SMYTH: No, nothing like that.
ANDREWS: Then what will you say?
SMYTH: Well, to the extent that I understand it . . .
ANDREWS: Don't be modest. It's unbecoming in an historian. Makes people doubt your word.
SMYTH: Well, it seems to me . . .
ANDREWS: Bad start. (*Peremptorily*) Who was Jane?
SMYTH: Jane was a fictional character about whom he once wrote. When he was a child.
ANDREWS: Good. Turn on the tape recorder. (*Smyth hesitantly complies*) Now come sit down. (*Smyth returns to his chair*) Who was the real-life character?

SMYTH: Joan?

ANDREWS: You're sure you don't want to say his mother?

SMYTH: (*Hesitantly*) Quite sure.

ANDREWS: You don't sound sure.

SMYTH: (*More firmly*) I'm quite sure. Joan was very real to him. You made her sound very real.

ANDREWS: What made her so real?

SMYTH: Her kindness.

ANDREWS: Is the recorder on?

SMYTH: Yes.

ANDREWS: You're quite sure?

SMYTH: Yes.

ANDREWS: In what way was she kind?

SMYTH: She read to him. Moralistic little tales. Useful, though, when a child is growing up. And they would play games. Card games, like bridge. They were very close throughout childhood. Very close.

ANDREWS: You have the feel of it. That girl was important to him. How about as they got older?

SMYTH: He went off to college, as boys do.

ANDREWS: (*Laughs*) That's a nice phrase, "As boys do." I'd keep that in the book if I were you. Don't worry. The machine's got it.

SMYTH: When it came time for the freshman dance, he didn't know whether to invite her up for it or not.

ANDREWS: I don't remember saying that.

SMYTH: Those weren't your exact words. It was the impression I got. Call it intuition.

ANDREWS: (*Brooding about it*) Yes, yes, I'd say you were right. You've got the essence of it. Truth of mood I suppose you'd call it. Rather than truth of fact. That's very important in good historical writing. You have to be able to recreate the spirit of the times. That's much more important than getting every little fact right. Any fool can check names and dates.

SMYTH: It's the difference between pedantry and poetry.

ANDREWS: Well said.

smyth: (*Very pleased*) But the weekend was a disaster. (*A little alarmed at his own audacity*) That is, looking at it overall.

andrews: *Hmm.* Very perceptive.

smyth: (*Elated*) They had hoped it would prove the consummation of the relationship. But they went to a wild party with friends after the dance. Had too much gin. Besides, there was too much fuss about the whole thing. Almost all their friends knew they were planning to have intercourse.

andrews: Right. That, I think, *is* the key.

smyth: It was like performing on a stage. Enough to inhibit anyone. When the time came he was impotent. She was kind about it. Very kind, really. She fondled him, told him not to worry. That made it worse.

(*Andrews looks up with sharp interest*)

andrews: Oh?

smyth: It reminded him of the one time he had gone to a whore house. He had been impotent there, too. And the prostitute had been very understanding. She had even put a kind of bandage on his penis, so that his friends would think he had screwed himself bloody.

andrews: (*Delighted*) Excellent!

smyth: The memory was very painful. When Joan fondled his penis, it brought the whole episode back. He was groggy anyway, from the gin. So he couldn't perform. He told her he'd been having too much sex recently—yes, he frankly confessed that he had been screwing himself bloody.

andrews: Splendid!

smyth: She felt sorry for him. And angry. They never saw each other again. He did that to people. He went on to fame and fortune. They disappeared from history.

andrews: You've really extracted the essence. (*Pause*) Play back the very last few lines, would you? You put that so well, I'd like to try to remember it.

(*Smyth goes to the machine, starts to rewind*)

andrews: Besides, I haven't heard how *your* voice sounds.

SMYTH: (*Stopping machine*) That should do it. (*Smyth presses the forward button*)

MACHINE: ". . . again. He did that to people. He went on to fame and fortune. They disappeared from history."

(*Another voice comes on the machine*)

MACHINE: "You've really extracted the essence."

ANDREWS: Good Lord, it doesn't sound a bit like you. You're right. The reproduction is very poor.

(*Smyth stops the machine*)

SMYTH: That last bit was *you*.

ANDREWS: Which bit?

SMYTH: "You've really extracted the essence."

ANDREWS: I shouldn't be surprised. Good thing we had the machine here to get it all down. (*He rises*) Well then. I think you have all you need.

SMYTH: (*Hesitantly*) I'd hoped you might tell me a little more about what he was like to live with.

ANDREWS: No, that's a complicated story. Not easy to grasp.

SMYTH: Perhaps another time.

ANDREWS: Perhaps. When we're fresh. It *is* an important story. Very important.

SMYTH: Then may I call you again?

ANDREWS: We might have dinner. In two weeks, say.

SMYTH: That will be marvelous.

ANDREWS: Yes, two weeks from tonight should be fine. Come by at seven.

SMYTH: I certainly appreciate it.

ANDREWS: My pleasure.

(*A pause, while Smyth gathers up the cord, microphone, etc.*)

ANDREWS: Interesting business, this looking back. Surprising how much it can stir up after all these years.

SMYTH: (*Sententiously*) Well, the only way to free ourselves from the past is to learn it.

ANDREWS: We've got you people to thank for that. (*He*

looks at the tape recorder; laughs) That is, you and the tape recorder. You're going to set all of us free. (*Pause*) In two weeks, then.

SMYTH: Two weeks.

Blackout

Brian Gear

A PRETTY ROW
OF PRETTY RIBBONS

Brian Gear

Brian Gear was an actor, journalist and copywriter before turning his creative attention to plays and broadcasting. He held a fellowship in playwriting at Bristol University (1965–67) and it was during this period that he wrote *A Pretty Row of Pretty Ribbons*.

Originally conceived as a television drama (produced twice on the B.B.C. Television Network, England), Mr. Gear enthusiastically took hold of this editor's suggestion and transformed his successful television script into a short play for the stage. The publication of *A Pretty Row of Pretty Ribbons* in this anthology marks its debut in print as well as the American introduction to its British-born (1936) author.

Now a regular broadcaster on the arts for the B.B.C., Mr. Gear has adapted three well-known novels for radio. One of these, Hugh Walpole's *The Cathedral,* was serialized throughout Britain in 1969.

The Sky Is Green, an earlier play by Mr. Gear, won the play competition and Peggy Ashcroft Prize at the inaugural of the new theatre at Croydon (a city near London) named for the noted star who, in 1956, was created a Dame of the Order of the British Empire by Queen Elizabeth. The play later was performed in Berlin, Rio de Janeiro and several other international capitals.

Mr. Gear, who lives in Bristol, cheerfully admits that "he would write more if he was not so fond of listening to music and wasting time. . . ."

Characters:
A GIRL

A MAN

Scene:
A house in England; the present.

The drawing room. Leading off it, a hall. Also visible: the front door to the house and a little of the garden.

The drawing room is expensively and conservatively furnished. A large coal fire, glass and china ornaments, family portraits and photographs, soft lamps, heavy drapes and comfortable chairs and sofas. A grand piano in one corner. Piled in great confusion on one of the sofas: a girl's school-hat, scarf, gym-slip, overflowing shoulder strap bag, pencil box, hockey stick, plimsolls, sketch pad, music book and a pile of exercise and story books.

It is about half-past seven on a winter evening; the drapes are open and the lights are on. Outside, it is damp and foggy.

A transistor radio is quietly playing "pop" music. A chair is drawn up to a table with homework spread out on it. A pretty upper-middle-class Girl of about thirteen is standing on another chair, admiring herself in the large mirror over the fireplace. She wears an expensive dress and an Alice-band in her long hair. She looks a "knock-out" and she knows it. Having turned this way and that to see as much of the dress as possible, she smiles a smile of great feminine pleasure at her reflection. As she is doing this, a Man's face peers in through the window, unseen by the Girl. The face vanishes and after a few seconds, the Man comes round the side of the house to the front door. He is about forty, wears a beret, an assortment of old clothes, and Wellington boots. He has a very full carrier bag tucked under one arm.

The Man stands looking at the door for a moment, then presses the bell. The Girl is startled by the loud

*ring. Guilty! She jumps off the chair and quickly steps
into her shoes. She switches off the radio, and waits. The
The Man rings again, more incessantly. The Girl fingers
the dress with an anxious expression. The Man looks
through the letter drop into the empty hall and calls out.*

MAN: Anybody at home?
(*At the sound of the unfamiliar voice, the Girl's ex-
pression changes to one of irritation at this intrusion by a
person obviously of little consequence. But at least, now it
doesn't matter about the dress! The Man rings again.
Reluctantly, the Girl opens the double doors of the draw-
ing room and goes into the hall. The Man, seeing this,
hastily withdraws from the letter drop*)
MAN: Is anybody there? It's important.
GIRL: (*Hesitantly*) Who is it?
MAN: Is the—er—lady in?
GIRL: Which lady d'you want?
MAN: Is that a little girl in there?
GIRL: D'you mean . . . my mother?
MAN: (*Losing patience*) Can't you open the door?
GIRL: I'm not allowed to let strangers in.
MAN: You on your own, then?
GIRL: What d'you want?
MAN: Can't explain through a coupla inches solid wood,
can I? 'Sides, it's cold out here.
(*Hesitantly, the Girl goes to the door and opens it a
fraction*)
GIRL: Yes?
(*The Man gazes at her for a second, before replying*)
MAN: Oh—er, is your mother in?
GIRL: No, I'm afraid she's not.
MAN: Not in?
GIRL: No.
MAN: Oh, dear. Your dad, then—is he . . . ?

GIRL: No.

(*The Man impulsively steps inside, taking the Girl by surprise, and shuts the door behind him. She backs away, alarmed. Having gained this point, he can afford to reassure her with a smile*)

MAN: I'm lettin' all the cold in. Don't want that, do we?

GIRL: (*On the verge of being frightened*) Will you kindly say what it is you want?

MAN: Well, your mother, see, she said to come back this evening. I spoke to her this afternoon and she said to come back . . .

GIRL: Yes, but what about?

MAN: Well, the garden. I'm looking for a job, see, and she . . .

GIRL: You want a job as a gardener?

MAN: Yes, I thought, see . . .

GIRL: But we already have a man comes three days a week. Are you sure it was here?

MAN: Oh, yes, I saw your mother—a nice lady, a very nice lady—and she said to come back this evening. Call at the house . . .

GIRL: She hasn't mentioned it.

MAN: . . . And she'd, like, give me an answer.

GIRL: Well, really, I don't know what . . .

MAN: I s'pose I couldn't hang on, could I? You know, wait for a bit?

GIRL: Can't you come back in the morning?

MAN: Oh, but I've walked all over from Walton Bay. 'Sides, it might be too late in the morning, the job might be . . .

GIRL: I'm sure if my mother said she'd . . .

MAN: It's ever so cold out. And foggy. Haven't you heard the foghorns in the channel?

GIRL: If you don't mind . . .

MAN: (*Nods towards the drawing room*) Bet you got a nice old fire going in there. Just for a few minutes, eh? Then if she hasn't come, I'll go away again.

GIRL: I'm not supposed to . . .

MAN: Cross my heart and hope to die. That's what you say, isn't it? Cross my heart?

GIRL: I'm sorry, but . . .

MAN: I don't suppose your mother'd be very pleased to hear you turned me away. Not after she was so particler I called. (*Pause*)

GIRL: All right, then. Five minutes. But *only* five, remember.

MAN: Oh, ta. I didn't think you'd see me shivering outside on a night like this—you look a nice kind little girl.

(*He's started to cross the hall to the drawing room*)

GIRL: D'you mind wiping your feet?

MAN: (*Stopping*) Eh?

GIRL: You're getting dirt on the floor.

MAN: Oh, dear, I *am* sorry. Oh, that is careless. Tell you what, I'll just slip these off for a minute. (*As he removes his Wellington boots*) Then I shan't make a mess on your lovely floor. And your mummy won't be cross when she gets back. There! How's that?

GIRL: You can leave your bag out here, too, if you like.

MAN: Oh, no, I'll keep that with me, if that's all the same to you. I never let that out of my sight! (*Going through the double doors to the drawing room*) Through here, is it?

GIRL: (*Following*) Wouldn't you like to take your coat off?

MAN: Oh, I'll see how warm it is first. *What* did you say your name was?

GIRL: I'm afraid I'm rather busy.

MAN: (*Looking around*) Oh, yes. Oh, yes, very fine. Very fine indeed! All this is very much to my taste.

GIRL: It is now nearly twenty-five to eight. At twenty, you go. Is that clear?

MAN: Eh? Oh. Just a minute. I must check that. (*He fumbles for a watch in his top jacket pocket*) Just make sure I agree. Oh yes, that's all right. I never like to go by other people's time, you know—not if I can help it. That's that then. Well, now. This looks a nice comfy . . . (*In front of him, with its back towards him, is a wing chair. He's about to sit in it when he realizes it has an occupant—a large teddy bear*) Cor, bless me! He's a beauty, isn't he? (*Chuckles*) Nearly set on him. What's *his* name, then? Teddy?

GIRL: Mr. Periwinkle.

MAN: Who?

GIRL: Periwinkle.

MAN: That's a funny name for a teddy bear. (*He starts to lift the teddy bear out of the chair*)

GIRL: Just what do you think you're doing?

MAN: Sitting down . . .

GIRL: That is *Mr. Periwinkle's* chair! (*Indicating the plainest possible chair*) *You* may sit *here*.

MAN: No, no, I'll—just have a little look round, if it's all the same to you.

(*He begins to wander about the room, examining all the ornaments and furniture as though he were going to buy them*)

MAN: Lovely place you've got here, eh? I've—er—I've always appreciated the finer things in life, you know—all this sort of thing. But it's not always given to those who appreciate, is it? I mean, I expect *you* take all this stuff for granted, all this beautiful furniture and stuff. But *I* don't. *I* don't. I've been starved of all this sort of thing.

GIRL: D'you mind not walking round all the time? You make a draft.

(*Coming closer to her*)

MAN: Oh, yes, that *is* a pretty ribbon you've got. I can see that properly now. I thought through the window that looked a very . . .

GIRL: (*Incredulously*) You mean you were looking in through the window?

MAN: You know how you do, just to see if there's anyone at home? *I* saw you, admiring yourself in the mirror!

GIRL: Well, really!

MAN: And a very pretty picture you made, if I may say so.

GIRL: You may not!

MAN: Oh, I don't mean no offense. I mean, speak as I find, that's me. And I just thought—well, very nice in there. Warm, pretty little girl . . .

GIRL: I am *not* lit . . .

MAN: Oh, yes, very charming! A charming little scene. Cor, when I think of my old home! Not everyone lives like you, you know. Not everyone's got a lovely room like this, with all these chairs and sofas and tables and bits and pieces. Bric-a-brac, they call it. And that piano. (*He's been wandering around again, and has now found her homework. He flips through a book*) What's all this, then?

GIRL: Put that down! (*She hastens over and snatches the book from him*)

MAN: I'm sorry.

GIRL: (*Tidying the books into a pile*) It is very *rude* to read other people's notebooks!

MAN: (*As he prowls around again*) 'Course, *you'll* never want for anything. Not like some people. Cor, you don't know how lucky you are! It makes me quite angry sometimes, it does. Chairs for teddy bears, while there's some haven't got a dry roof over their heads. (*He discovers some family photographs*) Eh! Who's this, then? Who's *this* little girl?

GIRL: That's my cousin.

MAN: What's *she* called? I don't see any snaps of you about.

GIRL: Anyone can have their photograph taken. *I'm* going to sit for a *painter*.

MAN: What, Sir Joshua Reynolds and all? (*Chuckles*) Cor, it isn't half hot in here. Why d'you want to keep it so hot in here?

GIRL: You could always take your coat off. *And* your beret.

MAN: What? Oh. (*He removes his raincoat and throws it over the back of a chair. He keeps his beret on*) Doesn't matter about me outside, so long as *you're* roasting away in here. I can see the way your mind works, all right.

GIRL: It seems to me, you think too much altogether!

MAN: Ah, that's what they all say. "You think too much." You take life too seriously. And you know who always tells me that? *Your* lot, *your* sort—people with big warm rooms.

GIRL: Your friends must tell you so, too.

MAN: I don't have any friends any more. I keep to myself. Anyway, life *is* serious. Well, come on, then. Don't leave all the talking to me. What d'you do at school?

GIRL: Strange though it may seem, we do lessons.

MAN: Ah, yes, but a young lady in your position—I mean —would do *special* lessons—posture and riding and that sort of thing.

GIRL: Yes.

MAN: Oh. (*Pause*) Tell me about it. About riding.

GIRL: What is there to tell?

MAN: What's it like?

GIRL: (*Losing her patience*) What d'you mean, what's it like? It's like riding, of course! What d'you think?

MAN: Yes, but . . . I've never been on a 'orse. I don't know what it feels like. Being up there, with that great animal under you.

GIRL: We have quite small horses, actually.

MAN: Do you?

GIRL: They breed them specially.

MAN: Is that a fact? What's yours called?

GIRL: It's not always the same one.

MAN: Oh. Oh. Well. When you're not riding, what d'you do?

GIRL: You want to know an awful lot, don't you?

MAN: I'm interested.

GIRL: Well, *I'm* not.

MAN: Oh, *go* on. I'm enjoying it. You're entertaining me very nicely indeed, you really are.

GIRL: I'm so glad.

MAN: D'you do dancing?

GIRL: Yes.

MAN: All that Grecian stuff?

GIRL: Yes!

MAN: You must look very pretty, in all that diaphraneous material.

GIRL: The word is *diaphanous*.

MAN: All floating and trailing after you, like in the adverts. D'you like that? Being all free and your limbs all exposed to the air?

GIRL: If you mean legs, why don't you say so?

MAN: It's a very personal thing, of course, but *I* prefer the word limbs.

GIRL: You've had your five minutes.

MAN: What?

GIRL: You said you'd go after five minutes.

MAN: Already?

(*She goes to the double doors and opens them*)

MAN: Oh—you're not *really* going to make me go, are you?

GIRL: I'll tell my mother you called. Perhaps there's a telephone number you could leave?

MAN: You're making the room all cold. I can't bear cold rooms. Even Mr. Periwinkle says he's coming out in goose pimples. (*He crosses to her; takes out his watch and shows it to her*) Look! Look at my watch. Just the *same* as when I came in. No time's passed at all. Now let's just shut this door . . . (*He reaches behind her and shuts the double doors. She draws back, towards the fireplace*) . . . and you come and sit down and tell me all about yourself. (*He sits; she doesn't move*) Come on! Over here by me.

(*A moment; then she slowly goes and sits in another chair*)

GIRL: I prefer it *here.*

MAN: All right, then. I don't mind. Now then. I expect you do all right in exams, don't you? (*Silence*) I say, I expect you . . .

GIRL: I heard you the first time!

MAN: Well, you didn't say anything. I thought . . .

GIRL: I didn't choose to.

MAN: It's not very polite to ignore someone when they speak to you, is it?

GIRL: That depends on the "someone."

MAN: I mean, I thought you'd *like* to tell me how you get on at school and everything. I mean, here am I, taking an interest, all agog as you might say, to hear your examination results, and you can't even put yourself out to answer a civil question.

GIRL: Well, since you insist on knowing, I usually come *first* in everything.

MAN: (*Wonderstruck*) *Everything?*

GIRL: Everything except domestic science.

MAN: Why aren't you first in that?

GIRL: Because I'm not interested in it!

MAN: Oh? And what do you do apart from, you know, school things?

GIRL: I can sing, paint, dance, write poetry and stories— and last term I gave a piano recital in the school concert.

MAN: Oh, that's marvelous! Would you play something for me? Now?

GIRL: Certainly not!

MAN: Oh, but I'm ever so fond of music—good stuff, mind. Not this pop stuff you get everywhere these days.

GIRL: (*Airily*) I quite like some of it.

MAN: "The Rustle of Spring"—can you play that? I bet that's a hard one, isn't it?

GIRL: Not particularly. Of course, you might think it was, if you didn't know anything about it.

MAN: Oh. Yes. Well. Sport, then. You any good at sport?

GIRL: Yes. *Very* good. At *everything*.

MAN: (*In raptures*) Oh! Oh, it must be marvelous to be you! Clever, artistic, good at games and everything. I bet you're popular, aren't you? I bet you've got a *lot* of friends.

GIRL: Oh, dozens!

MAN: D'you treat *them* like this? All haughty?

GIRL: Haughty?

MAN: Oh, I don't *mind*. I quite like it. I mean, it's only how you *should* be to someone like me, isn't it? It's only right and proper. Just as it's only right and proper that *I* should offer *you* my unstinted admiration. Don't look so surprised! It's only natural that somebody like *me*, who can't do *anything*, should bow the knee as it were, to somebody like *you* who can do pretty near *everything*. I mean, it's only natural.

GIRL: Yes, now you come to mention it, I suppose it is.

MAN: (*Rises*) Haven't you ever noticed, when you've been in places like, er, the thee-etter—you go to the thee-etter, of course?—or at the seaside, or in a caffy, haven't you ever noticed, there's always a little boy—a very dull little boy—who's eating his heart out in admiration of you? One might almost say, not to put too fine a point on it, with *love* for you?

GIRL: Really?

MAN: I don't suppose you've thought much *of* him, have you?

GIRL: Usually, I haven't thought of him at all.

MAN: What d'you think of him now, then?

(*She rises. There is a pause*)

GIRL: It's quite obvious my mother won't be back for ages, and I expect you'll want to be getting off . . .

MAN: Oh, no. I'm enjoying myself. I'm having a lovely time, I really am.

GIRL: That's not quite the point. I've a skirt that needs mending, and . . .

MAN: You could give that to the maid, couldn't you?

GIRL: We haven't got a maid. You seem to think this is Buckingham Palace.

MAN: No maid? Oh, dear. But you must have someone in to help out. I mean, big place like this . . .

GIRL: My aunty keeps house for us, not that it's any business of yours.

MAN: Oh, and where's she? Your aunty?

GIRL: She's . . . (*Hesitates*)

MAN: What?

GIRL: Nothing.

MAN: She's not in, is she?

GIRL: She . . .

MAN: The pictures? Gone to the pictures, has she?

GIRL: I'm asking you to go. Will you *please* go now?

MAN: What? You want me to go? I was just beginning to feel as though I belong.

GIRL: Or do I have to call the police?

(*Sound of a distant foghorn from the channel. Pause; then*)

MAN: They always make the silence seem deeper, don't they? Nice and cozy in *here*, though.

(*He walks abruptly, almost angrily, to the windows and draws the heavy drapes shut*)

GIRL: (*Outraged*) How dare you shut those . . .

(*During his next speech, she realizes that he stands outside the usual area of sanity. The question she's asking herself is, how far?*)

MAN: What I do, I walk round in the fog—it has to be foggy—till it's right in my bones, till I'm chill to the very marrow, and then I look for a house, a house like this one. I look for the gates first—big gates, it must have, and a long drive. Then I come up the drive, with my parcel under my arm and the bushes all looming up at me, until I see the lights, and then the front door, and then I lift the knocker, and I go rat-tat-tat-tat-tat or press the bell until someone answers, and then I say . . .

GIRL: (*Desperately; to stop him*) Would you like a cup of tea?

(*Long pause*)

MAN: Oh, er, yes. That would be lovely. You haven't, er, you haven't got very, very thin sandwiches? And some ice cream to follow?

GIRL: I think there are some chocolate biscuits.

MAN: Oh? Oh, well, I expect they'll be quite nice.

(*She crosses quickly to the doors*)

MAN: Where are you going?

GIRL: To the kitchen, of course!

MAN: I'll come with you.

(*She opens the doors*)

GIRL: You do not accompany your hostess to the kitchen! Just sit down and wait till I bring it to you.

(*She goes out and shuts the doors behind her. He immediately rushes over and listens at the doors. She tiptoes to the telephone in the hall and lifts the receiver. The bell rings once. He flings open the doors, hastens to her and snatches the phone out of her hand*)

GIRL: How dare you!

(*He slams the receiver down*)

MAN: You were getting the police, weren't you?

GIRL: I was trying to ask my mother to come home and see you!

MAN: Don't you lie to me! You were telephoning the police, you were!

GIRL: You're not an easy guest, you know!

MAN: D'you *always* ring for the police if you don't like your guests? That's lovely manners, that is!

GIRL: You're a fine one to talk about *manners*!

MAN: Get back in that droring room!

GIRL: Don't you order me about!

MAN: Get back in there!

GIRL: No!

(*He raises his arm; threateningly*)

MAN: D'you want me to take my hand to you?

GIRL: (*Pause; then, quietly:*) You're a boorish . . .

(*She turns and goes into the drawing room. He follows and shuts the doors behind them*)

MAN: That's better! That's much better.

(*She goes to a chair. She is having a job not to cry*)

GIRL: I shall sit here until my mother comes home, and I shan't say another word. You can jolly well entertain yourself!

MAN: What d'you want to go and do a thing like that for? Just when we were getting on, just when I was beginning to feel . . . at home. (*Pause*) I didn't think you'd go and do a thing like that. You might have got me into trouble, you might. . . . Still, no harm done. . . . I'm sorry I got angry. . . . Really. (*Pause*) Would you like to see my uniform? (*Not the merest flicker of interest. He starts to get something out of his carrier bag*) It's in my bag, look. It ought to be hung up, really, not all bundled up like this in this old carrier bag. This carrier bag, in fact—this carrier bag just isn't good enough. Not for a uniform with medals, it isn't.

GIRL: What did you get those for? *Distinguished gardening?*

MAN: Coh, hoo! You're a sharp one, aren't you, eh? You don't miss a trick, do you? But don't you look down on me just 'cause I'm slow, just 'cause I've only got filthy old clothes. I might be dirt, see, but I've had *friends,* I've had clever friends. Oh, yes! I had a very clever friend in the insti—tute. Brilliant pianist, he was. You'd've been interested. They got Erdelstein—some such name— you know, the conductor?—come and hear him. And funny thing was this friend of mine, he couldn't read a note of music, not a note. Did it all like walking. Like you and I walk, he could sit down in front of all them little black and white notes, and then this lovely sound would come out. And this man . . . was my friend. You, er, you sure you wouldn't like to play a little piece for me?

(*Pause*)

GIRL: In the what? In the *what* did you say?

MAN: In the institute.

GIRL: Didn't you nearly say "institution"?

MAN: Oh, no, no, no, no! Nothing like that, the very idea . . .

GIRL: What then? What *sort* of institute? Not one for studying music?

MAN: T.B. I was head gardener.

GIRL: D'you often go into other people's houses and act as if the whole place was your own?

MAN: Don't you want to see my uniform, then? I'll put it on for you, look.

(*He starts to put it on*)

GIRL: What do you do? When you've got in, what *do* you do?

MAN: Do? I don't do anything. I just enjoy myself. And then I go home.

GIRL: Aren't you ever caught?

MAN: Not yet.

GIRL: You *didn't* see my mother this afternoon, did you?

MAN: There! What d'you think of that? My uniform.

(*It is an old park-keeper's tunic: so much too big for him that it easily fits over his own clothes. And pinned to the breast: a handful of girls' hair ribbons. The Girl tries to suppress a giggle*)

MAN: Don't you laugh!

GIRL: What is it? I mean, what's it of?

MAN: Oh, it's—ceremonial.

GIRL: But it's only an old jacket! And what are all those ribbons?

MAN: Wait a minute. There's a 'at. (*He plunges into the carrier again*)

GIRL: There's what?

MAN: (*Holding up a battered peaked cap*) Peak cap. (*He puts it on over his beret*) See?

GIRL: What will you do if my mother walks in and finds you all got up like that?

MAN: I'll ask her if she wants a gardener! (*The Girl bursts into hysterical laughter: it stops dead on his next word*) Now you listen to me, Miss High-and-Mighty! When I was a little boy, I used to spend hours peeping through hedges at big houses. I used to think how nice it must be for rich little girls— all those big rooms to sit in. Well, I got tired of that! Now I come in and I *use* those rooms. I look at *your* walls and sit on *your* chairs and warm myself at *your* fire. Just to have a taste of what it must be like! (*Pause*) And before I go, I always take a little souvenir, a little something to look at, to remind me I really been there. (*Pause*) Would you very kindly—give me your hair ribbon?

GIRL: My . . . ?

MAN: Then I can go, see.

GIRL: Is that all?

MAN: It's pretty. And it's yours.

GIRL: And if I give it to you, you'll *really go?*

MAN: It's what I wanted from the start! Only, I couldn't say so, straight out. I had to get to know you a bit, or it wouldn't mean anything.

GIRL: Well, if that's all . . .

(*She starts to remove her Alice-band*)

MAN: *No!* I forgot to say—I must take it off myself! You *must* let me take it off myself!

GIRL: (*Frightened*) Please! Let *me* give it to you. Wouldn't you rather I gave it to you?

MAN: It won't be any good unless *I* take it. I'll get angry if you don't let me. I'll get angry again!

GIRL: (*Pause*) All right.

MAN: Come to me, then. Come over here to me. (*She goes to him*) Now kneel down in front of me.

GIRL: Kneel?

MAN: You must kneel to me! (*She kneels*) That's better. It's such a pretty ribbon.

(*He reaches out to take the ribbon. As his hands come close to her head*)

GIRL: You know I've been teasing you, don't you? I've been teasing you all the time. All that stuff I told you about being rich and clever was just a pack of lies.

MAN: (*Slowly*) Then what are you doing here? In this posh house?

GIRL: I'm—I'm the poor relation. It's *my* mother that looks after the house.

MAN: But you're still rich.

GIRL: Oh, no! Mummy says life would be very different if it weren't for . . .

MAN: What about your dad?

GIRL: He's . . . dead.

MAN: But that's not a *poor* girl's dress you're wearing! I know about these things.

GIRL: Oh, but it's not mine! It's my cousin's. There'd be a terrible row if I was caught in it. Even *she's* not supposed to wear it until her party.

MAN: Why didn't you tell me all this when I first came in?

GIRL: I was . . . pretending.

MAN: But you *can* do all those things. I mean, you *are* clever, at least . . .

GIRL: No. Just ordinary.

MAN: I don't believe it! I mean, I'm an *authority*. I'd have taken you for genuine anywhere.

GIRL: You should see Julia.

MAN: How do I know there *is* a Julia?

(*She quickly gets up and goes to books on sofa*)

GIRL: I can prove it! Here's one of her books. Now look at the name inside! "J.M.E. Webster, Lower Fourth." That's Julia. Now look at this one! (*She snatches an exercise book from the pile of homework and shows it to him*) "Susan Brown, Form 3B, Rough Notes." *Now* will you believe me?

MAN: You *must* be Julia, you *must*! I was going to add your ribbon to my collection.

GIRL: Don't you want it now?

MAN: Oh, no! It wouldn't be the same, would it? I think, if you don't mind, I'll be getting along now. Soon as I've got my uniform put away.

(*He tears off the cap and the jacket and stuffs them back into the bag*)

GIRL: Don't forget your coat—your raincoat.

MAN: (*Taking it off the back of the chair*) Oh. Ta. Yes. You don't mind if I dash off like this, only it's getting towards bedtime, see, and I've got to hurry.

(*He opens the double doors, proceeds into the hall with his bag and starts to put on his Wellingtons. The Girl follows him*)

GIRL: I'll see you out.

MAN: I'll just step into my Wellys. I wouldn't like to go without I've made my position clear. I like your ribbon. I like it very much. It's the prettiest ribbon I ever seen. But there'd always be that doubt, that naggin' suspicion, that p'raps it wasn't quite of the best. I mean, *I take a pride in my ribbons.* You do understand, don't you?

GIRL: Oh, yes! I quite understand.

MAN: I don't mean to be rude or anything. It's just a question of . . . *standards.*

(*He opens the front door*)

MAN: Still foggy. Well. Bye-bye.

GIRL: Goodbye.

(*The Man leaves the house and starts to move a few steps away. The Girl quickly shuts the front door, fastening the bolts, top and bottom. The Man stops and looks back, thinking what a perfect setting it was. He shakes his head sadly. The Girl has a sudden thought. She rushes back into the drawing room, hastens to the piano and gives a faultless performance of "The Rustle of Spring." The Man's mouth drops open and stays open, as he stares disbelievingly at the front door*)

The curtain falls

Martin Sherman

THINGS WENT BADLY IN WESTPHALIA

Martin Sherman

Martin Sherman makes his debut in print with the publication in this annual of *Things Went Badly in Westphalia,* his satirical "nightmare vision" of the temper of our times.

Born in Philadelphia, Pennsylvania, in 1940, the author is a graduate of Boston University's Division of Theatre Arts. Originally oriented toward a career as an actor, Mr. Sherman soon swung over from the interpretative to the creative echelon of the theatre. His initial effort as "author and lyricist" culminated in a revue, *Eight at Nine,* for The Poet's Theatre, Cambridge, Massachusetts.

In 1963, Mr. Sherman traveled westward to Mills College, Oakland, California. There he officiated as playwright-in-residence and during his tenure on campus, his rock musical, *A Solitary Thing,* was performed.

Two of his plays, *Fat Tuesday* and *The Night Before Paris* (the latter with Sylvia Miles in the leading role) were presented at the Actors Studio in 1968. In the same year, the Herbert Berghof Playwrights Foundation produced another of his plays, *Next Year In Jerusalem,* directed by Walt Witcover and featuring Anna Sten, Boris Tumarin and Terry Kiser.

In 1969, Mr. Sherman contributed the libretto to the musical, *Change,* a BMI Music Theatre Workshop presentation with a cast headed by Bernadette Peters and David Cryer. *Change* presently is scheduled for an Off-Broadway opening in September, 1970.

Mr. Sherman also fashioned the lyrics (to the music of Stanley Silverman) for the interpolated songs in The Repertory Theatre of Lincoln Center's 1965 production of William Wycherley's Restoration comedy, *The Country Wife.*

" 'What country can this be' said one to the other. 'It must be unknown to the rest of the world, because everything is so different from what we are used to. It is probably the country where all goes well; for there must obviously be such a place. And whatever Professor Pangloss might say, I often noticed that things went badly in Westphalia.' "

Candide
Voltaire

Characters:

JOSHUA
JOANNE
SENATOR
SENATOR'S WIFE
MODERATOR
FACELESS MAN
A STATE TROOPER
A BOY
DENNIS
THE GRAND WIZAR
GOVERNOR OF NEW ORLEANS
NEW ORLEANS TROOPER
ROCK AND ROLL COMBO
LISA
THE CYCLIST
FIRST INDIAN
SECOND INDIAN
POLICEMAN
PRISONER
FIRST MUTANT
SECOND MUTANT
THIRD MUTANT
FOURTH MUTANT
ANNOUNCERS, CAMERAMEN, STATE TROOPERS
SENATOR'S AIDES, NEWSCASTERS
KNIGHTS OF GANYMEDE
NEW ORLEANS RESIDENTS

HELL-RIDERS
GUARDS
PRISONERS
MUTANTS
FLOWER PEOPLE

Author's Note:

There are many characters in the play. It has been designed, however, so that it may be performed with a minimum of fifteen players for a number of the roles can be doubled or trebled. There also are many changes of locale; it is hoped that these will be "suggested" by the designer but not literally executed.

A single light is on Joshua. He is long-haired, intense, in his twenties. He plays a guitar and sings.

JOSHUA:
"By the waters of Babylon
There we sat down
Yea we wept
When we remembered Zion."

(Lights rise on a political rally. Joshua is on a platform, performing. Joanne, fresh and unspoiled, is standing with him, playing a guitar. A young Senator is sitting in the center of the platform with his Wife, Bodyguards and Aides, some of whom are Negro. There are signs that proclaim "Save" and there are balloons hanging from above. Television cameras move in and out. Joshua is finishing his song)

JOSHUA: "But

I like it here in Babylon
I have a gal in Babylon

We all make love in Babylon
(And what is wrong with that?)"

I want to stay in Babylon
I have my friends in Babylon
We all turn on in Babylon
(And what is wrong with that?)
            JOSHUA and JOANNE:
"There are moments in time
And you have to grab them
Before they turn to dust."
            JOSHUA:
"I found the sea in Babylon
And dreamt a dream of Babylon
Bright golden dream of Babylon
(And what is wrong with that?)

I want to stay in Babylon
And sing my song in Babylon
For hope lives on in Babylon
(And what is wrong with that?)
Ain't nothing wrong with that."
            (*The crowd cheers. The Moderator of the rally rises, joins
            in the applause*)
            MODERATOR: Joshua! Joshua and Joanne!

            JOSHUA: (*Takes the microphone and acknowledges the
applause*) Thank you. Look, they wanted me to say a few words,
but . . . I don't know. Words are things I write down and sing;
that's all I really know about. They want me to tell you *why* I
came here. Well, I came—Joanne and I came—because we could
not stay away, because we felt there was hope again. We know
the kind of nightmare that's happened since the killings in
Washington, but we know too that our country must be put
back together. We must try to have a Union again, and a President and a Congress and a Court. And it can happen again. Despite all the senseless events of the past few months, it *can* happen

because there is one person left who can lead us, who can restore form to this land and to our lives, who can make my songs make sense once again. There *is* hope; *he* is our hope! Look, I've made a speech; I didn't want to do that, but it's what I feel, it's what I believe . . .

(*He hands the microphone back to the Moderator. The crowd cheers again*)

MODERATOR: I was going to introduce the Senator myself, but I don't think I have to now. Joshua's words are better than anything I could say. So—here he is!

(*The Senator rises. Cheers. The balloons drift down. The Senator and his wife wave to the people. Finally he tries to quiet them. He holds up his hands and prepares to speak. Suddenly, a Man with undefined features appears at the rear of the platform. He hurls knives, one after another. The Senator falls forward, a knife in his back. The Senator's wife screams and reaches for him, but she too is struck in the back. She falls beside her husband. Two of the Senator's black aides also are hit. The crowd screams. There is pandemonium, panic. The faceless man disappears. Joshua grabs Joanne and clings to her. The television cameras swing in for close-ups of the bodies. The lights begin to fade. Discordant voices are heard*)

ANNOUNCER: Ladies and gentlemen, it appears that . . .

AIDE: Oh my God! Give him air! Give him air!

ANNOUNCER: The victim of an unknown . . .

AIDE: Is there a doctor in the house?

ANNOUNCER: At the bottom of your screen you can see . . .

AIDE: Get these cameras out of here!

ANNOUNCER: The eighteenth, no, the nineteenth major political assassination this spring . . .

AIDE: Goddamn bastard, Goddamn dirty bastard!

ANNOUNCER: If one of the Senator's aides is available for comment . . .

AIDE: For Christ sake, somebody help!

(*The voices drift away. A spot remains on Joshua and Joanne, still clinging to one another. She is crying; he tries to comfort her. Complete darkness. News items flash on and off. Voices overlap*)

FIRST NEWSCASTER: As news of the latest event spread across . . .

SECOND NEWSCASTER: The State of New York declared itself a Republic early this morning, following the lead of . . .

THIRD NEWSCASTER: The people of Harlem seceded from The Republic of New York and became their own . . .

FOURTH NEWSCASTER: The Governor of White New York pledged to destroy the terrorists, but meanwhile urged all citizens to remain indoors . . .

(*The lights rise on a bedroom. Joshua is asleep. Joanne sits on the edge of the bed; plays her guitar and sings*)

JOANNE:

"The face
The face on my pillow
Is handsome
Oh so handsome
And it smiles a secret smile
A hint of something deep
Deep beneath the smile
Morning is the gentlest season of love.

The face.
The face that I stare at
Is childlike
Yes, it's childlike
And it dreams a foolish dream
A sense of something bright
Bright beneath the dream
Morning is the gentlest season of love.

The face
The face on my pillow
So handsome

Oh so handsome
So very handsome . . ."

JOSHUA: (*Sits up*) That's a beautiful song.

JOANNE: I know. Did you write it about yourself?

JOSHUA: (*Kisses her*) You. I changed the gender. (*He lies back and closes his eyes*) What time is it?

JOANNE: Does it matter?

JOSHUA: What's wrong?

JOANNE: I'm tired of this room. I wish we could . . .

JOSHUA: What?

JOANNE: Throw a few bombs.

JOSHUA: (*Sits up*) Who at?

JOANNE: Anyone. Well. The White Vigilante Committee would be a good start. We could escape across The Wall to Afro-Harlem and join the blacks.

JOSHUA: We're not black.

JOANNE: It doesn't matter.

JOSHUA: It does. (*He closes his eyes*)

JOANNE: Don't sleep . . . (*She runs her hand through his hair*) I was proud of you last week, when you made that speech . . .

JOSHUA: I got carried away. I'm not a revolutionist.

(*He gets out of bed and does push-ups on the floor*)

JOANNE: You're a poet of the revolution.

JOSHUA: Yeah? Well, I don't throw bombs. I sing songs.

JOANNE: And your songs keep saying that things are going to get better. Well, we can *do* something; we can *make* things better. If we went across The Wall . . .

JOSHUA: No. If we stay in this room and just love each other then things will get better, you'll see . . .

JOANNE: You're a fool.

JOSHUA: (*Examines himself in mirror*) Maybe. (*Joanne puts her hand in front of mirror*) Hey!

JOANNE: Look at *me!*

JOSHUA: Do you really want to go across The Wall?

JOANNE: Yes.

JOSHUA: Suppose I scrape my knee?

JOANNE: (*Laughs*) I'll nurse it.

JOSHUA: We're better off in this room. You and me.

JOANNE: We can't stay here forever. (*Pause*) I've lasted longer than anyone, haven't I?

JOSHUA: Yes.

JOANNE: Don't worry. I'll hold on tight.

JOSHUA: O.K. As long as you know. I fall in love five times a day; I can't help it. There are so many beautiful people. I think I'm just scared to death of being alone.

JOANNE: I know.

JOSHUA: Do you want to stay in this room or do you want to go out and throw bombs? (*Silence*) Well?

JOANNE: (*Softly*) Don't leave me.

JOSHUA: (*Kisses her*) Joanne?

JOANNE: What?

JOSHUA: I know you don't believe it, but I couldn't live without you.

(*There is a loud explosion. The stage is filled with smoke. A siren is heard. A red light flashes on and off. The siren is deafening. The smoke begins to clear. A television camera appears. An Announcer clutches a microphone*)

ANNOUNCER: One of the many bombings that have erupted in the city . . .

(*Joshua is lying on the ground. There is only debris—and space—behind him. His face is cut and bleeding*)

ANNOUNCER: It is believed there are no survivors . . .

(*Armed, helmeted State Troopers arrive. A crowd gathers. Stretchers are hustled by. The red light still flashes*)

TROOPER: (*To the Announcer*) Blacks have done this! Bombs are going off all over town. And we will not stand for it! If we have to burn the ghetto to the ground—*they will pay for this!*

(*Joshua begins to crawl away*)

JOSHUA: Joanne . . . ?

(*A Trooper drags in a young, struggling black Boy*)

ANNOUNCER: A Negro has been captured . . .

BOY: Keep your hands off me! I didn't do anything, mister. It wasn't me . . .

ANNOUNCER: The crowd is shouting for his death!

(*Joshua rises*)

JOSHUA: Joanne . . . ?

(*The Trooper raises his gun, points it at the Boy's head, about to fire. Joshua, in a blind haze, stumbles against the Trooper, knocking the gun from his hand*)

TROOPER: What the hell . . . !

(*The Troopers grab Joshua*)

TROOPER: Damn nigger-lover!

ANNOUNCER: Increasingly, more and more nigger-lovers have been captured in the city . . .

TROOPER: Bring the branding iron! (*A Trooper hands him a branding iron*) Hold that nigger-lover still! (*He brands a large N-L on Joshua's chest. Joshua screams. The crowd cheers*) Now get him out of here!

(*A Trooper drags Joshua away*)

ANNOUNCER: And the execution will go on after all . . .

TROOPER: (*To Troopers; indicating the Boy*) Turn him over! (*The Troopers do so*) Say your prayers, boy . . .

BOY: The Lord is my shepherd, I shall not want, he maketh me to lie down in green pastures, he leadeth me beside the still waters . .

TROOPER: Hold him! Hold . . . hold . . . (*He raises the branding iron*)

BOY: . . . He restoreth my soul; he leadeth me in the paths of righteousness for His name's sake . . .

TROOPER: O.K., now . . . spread him . . . right . . . now . . . now . . .

BOY: Yea though I walk through the valley of the shadow of . . .

TROOPER: *Now!*

(*He starts to apply the branding iron to the Boy. The lights swiftly black out but the Boy's screams still can be heard. The red light flashes. The siren blasts and then drifts off into the distance. A recording is played of Joshua singing)*

JOSHUA:

"Joanne clings to my chest when we sleep
She's afraid that I'll leave
She's afraid to believe
The truth.
I'll never leave
I'll never leave Joanne.

Joanne whispers my name in the dark
And that makes the night real
Much less reason to feel
Afraid.
I'll never leave
I'll never leave Joanne.

Joanne wakes before dawn to make sure
That it wasn't a dream
Things are what they seem
To be.
I'll never leave
I'll never leave Joanne."

(The recording fades as the lights come up on a field. Joshua stumbles on and collapses against a rock. The cuts on his face have formed several large scars. He is partially in shock. Two young men enter, carrying a large sack. They sneak up behind Joshua and throw the sack over his head)

FIRST MAN: We've got one! We've got one!

(They carry the struggling sack off. Blackout. Male voices, some of them rather high-pitched, are heard singing)

VOICES:

"We shall overcome
We shall overcome
We shall overcome someday

Deep in my heart
I do believe
We shall overcome someday . . ."

> (*Lights rise on a group of Men, hands clasped, swaying in a circle. They wear little white hoods above their eyes and flowing white gowns with slits up the legs. Their leader, The Grand Wizar, stands in the center of the circle. They continue to sing*)

MEN:

"Boys and boys together
Boys and boys together
Boys and boys together someday
Deep in my heart
I do believe
We shall overcome someday."

> (*The Grand Wizar starts an incantation. The men sway in ecstasy as they listen*)

GRAND WIZAR: And The Knights of Ganymede shall spread their word for they are the Chosen Ones . . .

KNIGHTS: Yes, yes!

GRAND WIZAR: I speak for the oppressed. The black man is blessed with the ghetto. But *what* in the city was ours? We, the Chosen Ones, have left the corrupt world of the straight. We follow our own path, wandering like nomads across the land, awaiting the day of redemption when the world acknowledges *our* truth as theirs.

KNIGHTS: Hallellujah!

GRAND WIZAR: And The Knights of Ganymede shall scatter their beauty across the earth and be blessed with eternal peace.

> (*One of the Knights begins to sing*)

KNIGHT:

"Go down Moses
Way down in Egypt land
Tell ol' Pharaoh
Let my people go."

KNIGHTS: Amen! Amen!

GRAND WIZAR: (*Moves out of the circle*) And now we shall tend to our needs. (*Claps his hands*) Bring in the plunder. (*The two young men with the sack lead Joshua in. He is bound and gagged.*)

GRAND WIZAR: Oh, Mary—is *that* it?

FIRST MAN: It's all we could find.

GRAND WIZAR: Dennis, you fool!

DENNIS: There was no one else. We were lucky to find *him*.

GRAND WIZAR: I sent you into the city. It's *filled* with beauties.

DENNIS: The city burnt down.

GRAND WIZAR: Oh come on!

DENNIS: I mean it. *The city burnt down.* We had to stop at the river; there was nothing left. Someone said it started in the ghetto.

GRAND WIZAR: (*Moved*) Thank heaven we left. The Lord moves in strange ways. He's gay, you know—and this must be a sign that He is with us.

DENNIS: We started back, and we saw this boy lying in a field. He must have got out before the fire.

GRAND WIZAR: You silly goose, look at him! He's not presentable at all. Tattoos on his chest. And look at that *face!*

DENNIS: He was beautiful once. You can tell. And his body is still fairly strong. Can't we keep him? Please, Princess.

GRAND WIZAR: Darling, you *do* have a heart of gold. The Knights of Ganymede have to be *strong*. Where did "heart" ever get us? Oh, O.K. If you like him so much, we'll take him along. Guess his face doesn't count, anyhow. Wash him up, Dennis, so we can start rotating him. (*To Knights*) Brothers—volleyball time!

(*The Grand Wizar and the Knights leave. One Knight returns, leaves a basin of water and a wash-cloth, then goes. Dennis is alone with Joshua.*)

DENNIS: You're safe now. I couldn't leave you in that field. You looked so lost. We'll take you with us to New Orleans. We've heard about the new republic there—everyone lives in peace. We thought we'd have a look. (*He wipes Joshua's face*) This may hurt . . . (*Joshua struggles*) Don't. I know it stings, but . . . Oh! (*He pulls off Joshua's gag*) There! That better?

JOSHUA: What's wrong with my face?

DENNIS: You better look. (*He takes out a pocket mirror, holds it up to Joshua*) You *were* handsome once—?

JOSHUA: (*Turns away from the mirror*) Yes.

DENNIS: I knew it.

JOSHUA: (*Softly*) Joanne always caught me looking at my reflection. One time, I passed a store window and flirted with myself. I thought, "Gee, who's that groovy guy?" (*Shrugs*) Oh well—goodbye beauty.

(*Silence*)

DENNIS: Joanne?

JOSHUA: Joanne.

DENNIS: You don't have to play butch with me.

JOSHUA: I'm not playing anything.

DENNIS: Aren't you . . . one of us?

JOSHUA: I'm just *me*. Look, Dennis, can't you untie my hands?

DENNIS: You might run away.

JOSHUA: Why would I do that?

DENNIS: Sometimes our prisoners do try to escape.

JOSHUA: (*Laughs*) I'm not really a prisoner?

DENNIS: Oh yes. You're booty. We're all going to take our turns with you.

JOSHUA: No, no, you don't want to do that!

DENNIS: Oh, yes, yes, we do. Despite your face. (*Joshua winces*) I'm sorry. Don't be sad. I have scars too. See? (*He holds out his wrists*) I've only tried three times. A lot have tried more. Have *you* ever . . . ?

JOSHUA: No.

DENNIS: I don't have to anymore. Now that I belong to something.

JOSHUA: Dennis, untie me.

DENNIS: I can't.

JOSHUA: We can run away. Both of us. No one should ever be alone.

DENNIS: I'm not alone.

JOSHUA: We *both* are. And we could both use some love. Could we ever! We can love each other. Do you understand that? We can be lovers.

DENNIS: No. That's not permitted . . .

JOSHUA: You cared enough to take me out of that field. I knew things weren't as bad as they seemed. There really is hope again. Oh, Dennis, come on. Just the two of us.

DENNIS: No. That never works . . . that never works . . .

JOSHUA: Please, Dennis!

DENNIS: (*Shouts, impulsively*) *Help!* Hey, fellas! Hurry! Come here! Hurry!!

(*Several Knights rush on*)

DENNIS: The—the prisoner's ready. I've washed him. Take him away! Hurry up and take him away!

JOSHUA: Poor Dennis.

(*The Knights start to lead him off; he struggles*)

JOSHUA: What do you want *me* for? Look at my face! Hey, guys, look at my face . . .

(*They disappear. Dennis remains alone. Blackout. In the distance, the Knights of Ganymede are heard singing "We Shall Overcome." The lights rise on a public square. A banner hangs overhead: "Welcome to New Orleans." The singing grows louder, closer. Suddenly there is a rapid burst of machine gun fire. The singing stops. Silence. The Governor of New Orleans enters. He wears a badge and carries a machine gun. He grins and looks back over his shoulder*)

GOVERNOR: Y'all come back and visit us now, y'hear?

(*A New Orleans Trooper brings Joshua in. Joshua's hands are still bound*)

TROOPER: We found this one marching behind them, Governor.

JOSHUA: You've *killed* all of them!

GOVERNOR: I guess my boys overreacted. Happens sometimes. This is a happy city. We keep it pure. Are you one of *them?*

JOSHUA: No. I was their prisoner. See! (*He holds up his bound hands*)

GOVERNOR: Prisoner? Then don't look so unhappy, son. We saved your life.

JOSHUA: Thank you.

GOVERNOR: Don't mention it.

JOSHUA: Can you untie my hands?

GOVERNOR: Be quiet, son. If you talk too much, you get yourself into trouble. (*To Trooper*) We'll keep him for the ceremony. I know just the spot for him. (*To Joshua*) I feel kindly toward you, son. Glad I don't have to shoot you.

(*Residents of the city drift in. They are racially mixed and in festive spirits. Some are masked and costumed. Confetti pours down. A Rock and Roll Combo is pulled out on a small platform. They are a bit grotesque*)

COMBO: (*Sing*)

"See the yellow steps burn
In the valley of madness
See the sinking sun turn
In a tango of sadness
See nothing at all
See nothing at all
See nothing at all."

(*The Trooper holds Joshua at the edge of the crowd. Television cameras are brought in. An Announcer thrusts a microphone at scattered faces throughout the crowd. The Combo continues its song*)

JOSHUA: Listen, can't you untie my hands? I can make better music than that!

ANNOUNCER: And many more are coming to the weekly public spectacle . . .

COMBO:

"Do frozen custard stands

Still sell
Vanilla fudge?
Do ice cream parlor walls
Still ring
With secrets
Forbidden . . . ?"

> (*The Governor puts his arm around Joshua as he greets several members of the crowd*)

GOVERNOR: You see these people, son? See how happy they are?

JOSHUA: They'd be happier if they had better music.

GOVERNOR: Do you know, there's no place else in this vast expanse of land that was once the United States of America where the black man and the white man live side by side in perfect harmony?

JOSHUA: Yes, I noticed. They're a *fantastic* audience. If you ordered someone to untie my hands, I could play for them. I'll do it for free.

GOVERNOR: You see, every human being has an appetite for violence. So once a week, I satisfy that appetite and there is never any need for the people of my city to take it out on one another.

JOSHUA: Don't you know who I am? Don't you *recognize* me? People have my poster on their walls!

GOVERNOR: And today, son, you can take part in this program. Be proud!

> (*The Governor walks on to the platform, raises his hands for quiet. The Combo stops playing*)

GOVERNOR: My beloved people. Welcome! Today, by popular request, in nearby Jackson Square, we are having a giant auto-da-fé. Forty of our neighbors from Shreveport will be burned in a wonderful display, backed by The Rampart Street Light Show *and* The New Orleans Symphony Orchestra. But first, as an appetizer, right here before us, a public flogging. (*The crowd cheers*) And two very special guests . . . (*The Trooper brings Joshua onto the platform*) First, a young man, a newly captured outsider from New York. Let's all give him a big hand!

(*The crowd applauds*)

JOSHUA: Oh my God! Look! I'll give you much more pleasure—*much more*—if you let me sing!

GOVERNOR: Quiet, son. Strip and string!

(*The Guards strip Joshua and string him to a pole as two other Guards bring in a girl of about eighteen*)

GOVERNOR: And next—a young runaway. Isn't she lovely? Let's all give her a big hand. Strip and string!

(*The Guards strip the girl and string her to a pole alongside of Joshua*)

GOVERNOR: And now—a man and a woman—side by side . . . Oh, my people, my beloved people, how *fortunate* we are!

(*The crowd cheers. The Governor steps down. The Combo plays and sings. The people sway in ecstasy. The Guards savagely begin to whip Joshua and the girl in tempo with the music. The Announcer holds the microphone up to Joshua's mouth and then to the girl's. The television cameras swing in for close-ups. Some of the crowd dance, some swoon, others just stand mesmerized*)

COMBO:

"See the yellow steps burn
In the valley of madness
See the sinking sun turn
in a tango of sadness
See nothing at all
See nothing at all
See nothing at all.

Do trolley car riders
Still taste
Of banana?
Do Lucifer's friends
Still plan

To return
The honey . . . ?

See the yellow steps burn
In the valley of madness
See the sinking sun turn
In a tango of sadness
See nothing at all
See nothing at all
See nothing at all."

> (*Some of the crowd are exhausted; others are at a fever pitch. The Governor jumps back on to the platform. The Combo stops playing*)

ANNOUNCER: In a moment, we'll have an instant replay of the flogging . . .

GOVERNOR: We mustn't be late for the auto-da-fé! (*To Joshua and the girl*) Thank you both so very much. (*To Trooper*) We'll let them hang throughout the night; the killing can take place in the morning.

> (*The Governor, Troopers and Guards depart. The crowd disperses. Joshua and the girl are alone, hanging from their poles*)

JOSHUA: (*Shouts*) *Can anyone hear me? Is anyone around?*

GIRL: Just me.

JOSHUA: Oh. Look. You mustn't worry. Maybe we can find someone who's not at Jackson Square; someone who will cut us down.

GIRL: My name is Lisa. What's yours?

JOSHUA: Joshua. *Can anyone hear me?*

LISA: You're not *the* Joshua, are you?

JOSHUA: Yeah. *Somebody help! Help!*

LISA: I have all of your records.

JOSHUA: That's nice. *Help! Help!*

LISA: Even the early ones.

JOSHUA: Fine. *Help! Help!* Even the *first?*

LISA: Yes.

JOSHUA: Gee, nobody has that.

LISA: Well, it isn't very good.

JOSHUA: *What?*

LISA: The others get better.

JOSHUA: Thanks.

LISA: At first, you were structured for thrust but you really had very little counterthrust, but then later you moved to a kind of languid melancholy—especially in your allegorical ballads that ultimately became very plastic.

JOSHUA: Uh-huh. *Help! Anybody!*

LISA: You see, my boyfriend used to be record critic for *Chance.* That was an underground newspaper, but it folded and he disappeared and took all of my records with him and I felt so lost when that happened, I wanted to go home, I really just wanted to go home.

JOSHUA: Why *didn't* you?

LISA: I tried—oh I tried! But my parents wouldn't take me back. They said that every family on their block had at least *one* runaway and they didn't want to be different. So I had to go back to the city but I really couldn't do that either because all the cities are putting their runaways into detention camps and I really didn't know what to do and then I heard about Flower City.

JOSHUA: Flower . . . ?

LISA: The place in the mountains where the Flower People live. I hope I can get there because it's really beautiful, and everyone there is filled with love. Are you going there too?

JOSHUA: I just want to get off of here!

LISA: Oh yeah. Wow! That would be something!

JOSHUA: I thought if we *both* shouted . . .

LISA: Why don't we try some voodoo? I went with a warlock for a whole month and he taught me a lot of things. We could make a Dragons-Blood Stick. That's the greatest for getting out of unpleasant situations! Except that you need some dragon's blood, and it's not likely that we'd find a bleeding dragon . . .

JOSHUA: I thought if we both shouted . . .

LISA: It would be so much more fun if we sang! I love to sing and we could do some of your songs and some of mine because I set all of my poetry to music and it would be really groovy under the stars . . .

JOSHUA: For Christ's sake, will you shut up for a minute!

LISA: (*Starts to cry*) I thought you were gentle.

JOSHUA: I am. I'm *very* gentle.

LISA: You are not!

JOSHUA: I am too!

LISA: You just want to bring me down! I was feeling so good. I was high on speed. Don't bring me down . . .

JOSHUA: Look. They're going to kill us in the morning unless we do something.

LISA: So let them. What does it matter?

JOSHUA: It *matters*.

LISA: Why?

JOSHUA: I have no idea. It's just a silly instinct of mine.

LISA: It isn't *my* instinct! So what if someone cuts us down? Something *else* will happen that's awful.

JOSHUA: Nonsense. Things will get better. Come on, let's make some noise.

LISA: I'm too depressed.

JOSHUA: Just do what I do. *Help! Help!* Like that.

LISA: Big deal. *Help! Help!* See? Nothing. This whole thing is a bummer.

JOSHUA: Come on. Again. *Help!*

LISA: *Help!*

JOSHUA: *Help!*

LISA: *Help!*

(*A loud roar. The sound of racing motorcycles*)

JOSHUA: Listen! Listen!

(*A man drives in on a motorcycle. He wears a leather*

jacket with Hell-Riders emblazoned on it. He reaches up with a knife and cuts Lisa's bonds)

LISA: Oh! Wow!

(The man on the motorcycle laughs, pulls Lisa down from the pole, puts her behind him on his bike and roars off)

JOSHUA: I knew someone would come, I just knew it!

(The roar continues. Headlights flash on and off. Two other Hell-Riders enter on foot. They cut Joshua down. A third man enters on a motorcycle. The first two chain Joshua to the end of it. The Cyclist drives off, dragging Joshua behind him. Blackout. The roar continues. Men are laughing. The lights come up on a field. The Hell-Riders are standing in a circle. Lisa can be heard from within the circle, moaning. Then she is silent. The Cyclist enters, pushing Joshua ahead of him. Joshua's hands still are bound, but he has recovered some clothing. The Cyclist directs him so that he does not see the circle. They both sit on the ground, some distance from the others)

CYCLIST: Joshua, huh? Hmph! *(He takes out a harmonica, plays and sings)*

"Will we be here when another moon rises
Will the days to come be filled with surprises?
I really don't know
I really don't care
Our love
Is not to analyze.
Who thinks about another moon
When the old one so slowly dies."

(He puts down the harmonica)

You sang that for us one time in California. Bet you don't remember. I almost didn't recognize you. Man, you look awful. *Everyone* sang for the Hell-Riders. We were the biggest thing going then, before everything went crazy. We split that scene; now we wander, place to place—every day another town—it's wild. And, man, wherever we go, *we rule!*

JOSHUA: Why don't you untie my hands?

CYCLIST: "Another Moon" is a pretty good song, but you stole it, man, from Shakespeare.

JOSHUA: I *what?*

CYCLIST: Stole it. "Four happy days bring in another moon; but o, methinks how slow this old moon wanes." . . . "A Midsummer Night's Dream," baby.

JOSHUA: How did you know?

CYCLIST: I know a lot of things!

JOSHUA: Why don't you untie my hands?

CYCLIST: And have you try to stop my buddies?

JOSHUA: From what?

CYCLIST: Taking on your girl.

JOSHUA: She's not my girl.

CYCLIST: Well, she's sure being raped.

JOSHUA: (*Turns swiftly; sees the circle*) Jesus! (*He tries to twist himself free*)

CYCLIST: Easy, easy . . .

JOSHUA: She's just a kid!

CYCLIST: All the nicer.

JOSHUA: Why don't you *stop* them?

CYCLIST: I like my friends happy.

JOSHUA: What are you doing with these . . . these . . . you're too intelligent!

CYCLIST: (*Laughs*) Oh, baby.

JOSHUA: No, *why?*

CYCLIST: If you're as smart as I am, the only sane thing you can do with your life is end it. Let's face it, it's not *your* world. Well, I figured there was one alternative—and that was to jump in with both feet and live in the worst possible way. You sensitive ones make me sick. Singing your songs, strumming your guitars—man, where's that get you? You should rape a little and rob a little; ride free in the night air and be king wherever you go!

JOSHUA: That's awful.

CYCLIST: Nothing's awful.

JOSHUA: What about . . . love?

CYCLIST: Balls! It's how many times you score, that's what counts. (*The men in the circle laugh*) That and a sense of style. You got to have style. And, man, we've got a lot of it!

(*The circle breaks up; the men move into small groups*)

CYCLIST: Whoops! Party's over! Here, free again! (*He unties Joshua's bonds. Joshua glares at him, then dashes to Lisa who lies on the ground, whimpering.*)

JOSHUA: Lisa! Are you all right?

LISA: (*Sits up*) Sure. What's another rape? That's the first thing you learn when you leave home: rape grows on trees. . . . No, don't touch me! Boy, for a culture-hero, you're really out of it. I told you we should have stayed hanging up there. They would have killed us very gently, quietly and softly in the morning. I wish they had! Where's my bag? They brought my things, didn't they? Where's my bag?

(*She searches through a pile of clothing, finds a rumpled pocketbook. She removes a bottle of pills, empties them into her hand*)

JOSHUA: What are you doing?

LISA: Checking out.

JOSHUA: Oh no . . . ! (*Joshua grabs the pills, stuffs them into his pocket*)

LISA: Come on, they're mine!

JOSHUA: That isn't the way!

LISA: Why not?

JOSHUA: Because. Just because.

LISA: I'm tired. Life's a rotten trip; I want out. Give them back to me. Please! (*She reaches for his pocket*)

JOSHUA: No! Keep away. Look. I've lost everything I've ever loved in my life. Even my face. Whenever I find someone who's really beautiful, they leave. Or they're taken away. But I keep on looking. I keep on loving. Somehow, I always feel that something good is going to happen. It's around the corner. You just got to get there.

LISA: I think you're crazy!

JOSHUA: Maybe. But if it weren't for all of this we wouldn't have met.

LISA: So?

JOSHUA: So—just a few hours ago we were both alone. But now we have each other. And a place to go. There's Flower City, remember? We can go there together and we don't ever have to be alone again.

LISA: Do you mean that?

JOSHUA: Try me. (*He kisses her*) Just try me.

LISA: Oh gosh! That *would* be great. You know, in Flower City everyone is so gentle, they share things and they play music . . .

JOSHUA: Shh! Come on. Let's go!

(*They embrace. Suddenly, the Hell-Riders rise and surround them, menacingly*)

FIRST HELL-RIDER: Look at the lovers.

SECOND HELL-RIDER: Yeah, they're gonna . . .

THIRD HELL-RIDER: Hey, guys, a free show!

JOSHUA: Come on, Lisa!

(*He grabs Lisa's hand and starts to pull her away. The Cyclist steps in front of Joshua, takes out a knife and examines it*)

CYCLIST: Don't move. We're gonna have some more fun . . .

JOSHUA: Cut it, will you. Let us go!

CYCLIST: *Don't move!* Come on, guys, form a circle . . .

LISA: Not again!

JOSHUA: (*Reassuringly*) Don't worry. We'll get out of this. Somehow.

(*The Cyclist signals the men by raising his knife. The men grab Joshua and Lisa. Suddenly there is a loud war cry. An arrow strikes the Cyclist in the back of his neck. He falls to the ground. A flurry of arrows shoot through the air*)

LISA: Oh my God! Indians!

JOSHUA: You see! There's *always* something.

(There are whoops and cries. The Hell-Riders start to flee in all directions; some rush off, some are struck down by arrows. Lisa is bubbling with excitement)

LISA: Oh that's beautiful! Indians!

JOSHUA: Get down!

LISA: Oh wow! What a scene! Beautiful! Beautiful!

(An arrow strikes her. She falls. Joshua grabs her)

JOSHUA: No!

LISA: *(Softly)* It hurts.

JOSHUA: Of course it does.

LISA: You've got to go to Flower City!

JOSHUA: O.K.

LISA: Promise?

JOSHUA: Yes.

LISA: Groovy.

(Lisa dies)

JOSHUA: Don't . . .

(He lowers her to the ground, and kisses her. Two Indians emerge. They throw a huge lasso around Joshua)

JOSHUA: Oh, what *now*?

(The Indians come before Joshua and bow down to him)

FIRST INDIAN: Man-with-Scar . . .

SECOND INDIAN: You are god.

FIRST INDIAN: You shall lead us . . .

SECOND INDIAN: Against the White Man . . .

FIRST INDIAN: Who destroyed our tribe.

JOSHUA: But *I'm* a white man.

FIRST INDIAN: You are god.

JOSHUA: That's irrational.

FIRST INDIAN: Man-with-Scar . . .

SECOND INDIAN: Shall lead us in battle.

JOSHUA: I don't fight.

FIRST INDIAN: Or else we kill him.

JOSHUA: You can't kill a god.

SECOND INDIAN: We always do.

FIRST INDIAN: Find new god.

SECOND INDIAN: We worship you . . .

FIRST INDIAN: To a point.

(*A rustling is heard nearby; the sound of men talking*)

JOSHUA: What's that noise?

FIRST INDIAN: White man returns.

SECOND INDIAN: White man will kill us.

FIRST INDIAN: God protect us.

JOSHUA: I can't if I'm tied up.

VOICE: (*Offstage*) O.K. Now!

(*A mist is sprayed onstage. Joshua and the Indians rub their eyes*)

FIRST INDIAN: We can not see.

SECOND INDIAN: Man-with-Scar help us!

FIRST INDIAN: Man-with-Scar rescue us!

JOSHUA: Man-with-Scar is as blind as you are, you ninnies . . .

(*Joshua and the Indians fall to the ground, completely immobilized. A Policeman enters, wearing a gas mask. He surveys the scene and calls offstage*)

POLICEMAN: O.K., men. Cut the Mace. (*He takes out a pad and pencil*) Let's see. What's in *this* batch? A few motorcycle creeps, already dead. One little hippie girl. Dead. Two Indians . . . Didn't know there were any left! Hey, guys, two Indians! One long-haired bum. Right. Shoot the Indians and send the bum to the chain gang. O.K. Let's clean this mess up. We gotta keep our countryside clean.

(*Blackout. In the darkness, a male voice is heard singing*)

VOICE:

"I don't want to be on a chain gang.

That's not the life for me.

Who wants to be on a chain gang?

I just want to be free."

(*Lights rise on another field. A group of Young Men are chained by their legs, in pairs of two. They are digging with shovels. Their heads have been completely shaved. A Guard holds a rifle and watches them. One prisoner, a black man, has been singing)*

PRISONER:

"I don't want to be on a chain gang.
That's not the life for me.
Who wants to be on a chain gang?
I just want to be free."

(The other prisoners look at him and make occasional incoherent sounds. Another Guard brings Joshua in. The Guard carries a rifle. Joshua's head also has been shaved. The Guard chains Joshua to the black prisoner)

GUARD: O.K. bright boy—get to work.

(Joshua starts to shovel with the others. The Guard joins his fellow Guard; they sit on the side, smoking)

PRISONER: Hiya, baby. You're beautiful.

JOSHUA: *(Laughs)* Stop. Not like this.

PRISONER: Don't worry. It will grow back. What was yours like?

JOSHUA: Long and straight.

PRISONER: Mine was a bush. Basic African. Hey, where you from?

JOSHUA: New York.

PRISONER: No—what school?

JOSHUA: I'm not a student. I used to sing.

PRISONER: Yeah, you know, you look a little like Joshua?

JOSHUA: I *am* Joshua.

PRISONER: Really? I heard that entertainers were sent to the salt mines. You're lucky, chain gang's better.

JOSHUA: I'll remember that.

PRISONER: We're all students. We took over our campuses. Changed everything around. Man, it was wild—things began to *mean* something. Then the Union fell apart and everything went with it. Armies, police, guards—the schools were the first place to get them. They killed . . . they killed most of us. The rest they sent here. Well, it could be worse. They have the peace-marchers down in the pits. Doesn't matter much anyhow. We're going to break our way out of here. We got to. You and I only have one day left.

JOSHUA: What do you mean?

PRISONER: Look at the other guys. They can't speak.

JOSHUA: Why not?

PRISONER: No tongues.

JOSHUA: *What?*

PRISONER: Every Friday a doctor comes and removes the tongues of the new prisoners. That's you and me. *We're* the new ones.

JOSHUA: *That* is ridiculous. That is absolutely ridiculous! Come on—they've cut my hair, my face is ruined, I have this stupid brand on my chest . . .

PRISONER: Yeah, you sure do! What does it stand for?

JOSHUA: (*Embarrassed*) Oh. Do I have to tell you?

PRISONER: Yeah.

JOSHUA: (*Smiles*) Nigger-Lover.

PRISONER: Oh, baby, that's beautiful!

(*They both laugh. The other prisoners make sounds*)

JOSHUA: What are they trying to say?

PRISONER: They want me to tell you about our escape plan.

JOSHUA: Thank God! How *do* we get out of here?

PRISONER: Simple. As soon as they call a rest period, we rush the guards.

JOSHUA: And then?

PRISONER: That's it. We rush the guards.

JOSHUA: With *what?*

PRISONER: Our shovels.

JOSHUA: They have *guns.*

PRISONER: Well, that's an uncomfortable fact. Most of us will be killed.

JOSHUA: Gee, how nice!

PRISONER: But a few will get away. It's the only chance we have.

JOSHUA: (*Amused*) With our shovels?

PRISONER: Yeah.

JOSHUA: Against their guns?

PRISONER: Yeah.

JOSHUA: That's very funny.

PRISONER: It is not.

JOSHUA: You led a campus revolt, huh?

PRISONER: That wasn't very practical either.

JOSHUA: It's a shame we don't have sling shots.

PRISONER: It's not funny.

JOSHUA: I know.

PRISONER: Stop laughing.

JOSHUA: You first.

(*They both continue to laugh. The other prisoners try to talk; again the incoherent noises. Joshua and the Prisoner sober up immediately*)

JOSHUA: What is it?

PRISONER: Almost time.

JOSHUA: We're crazy.

PRISONER: We got to be free, baby!

JOSHUA: I know. (*Shrugs*) Shovels.

GUARD: (*Goes to prisoners*) O.K. Rest period!

PRISONER: *Now!*

(*The prisoners rush the Guard, battering him with their shovels. He screams and falls beneath their blows. The other Guard fires his rifle and hits many of the men. A few strike him with their weapons, but he continues to fire*)

PRISONER: Come on, let's get out of here!

(*Joshua and the prisoner start to run. A bullet hits the Prisoner in the back. He falls. His chains pull Joshua down*)

PRISONER: That's unfair!

JOSHUA: Hold on! Hold on! You're with me, baby, and we're getting out!

(*Joshua crawls off, dragging the Prisoner with him. Blackout. Lights rise on another field. Joshua slowly crawls on, pulling the Prisoner with him as gently as possible. The Prisoner speaks with some difficulty*)

PRISONER: . . . And we were making it like crazy and then her dog climbed into bed just as I was about to come and I told her that was it, I'd had it.

JOSHUA: You mustn't talk anymore.

PRISONER: It's going out of me; I feel it going out of me . . .

JOSHUA: We'll rest.

PRISONER: Did I tell you about the time . . .

JOSHUA: Save your strength.

PRISONER: No. Did I tell you about . . . ?

JOSHUA: Don't . . . (*He holds him in his arms*)

PRISONER: *Listen* to me. Please, baby, listen! Did I tell you about the time a pigeon chased me down the block? A lousy pigeon! It went crazy. Kept pecking at my head. Wouldn't stop. My old neighborhood. I wanted to act like a big man and there I was—running from a pigeon! (*He gasps*) Things like that happen to you.

JOSHUA: Sure. Once an egg fell on my head—in the middle of a crowded street . . .

PRISONER: And no one paid any attention . . .

JOSHUA: How'd you know?

PRISONER: Because that's the kind of thing that always . . . (*He reaches out in pain*) Oh no! It's leaving me!

JOSHUA: Don't worry. We'll find help somewhere . . .

PRISONER: What *kind* of egg?

JOSHUA: I don't know. Regular one.

PRISONER: I like my eggs . . . I like them poached on . . . *oh God!* . . . I like them . . .

JOSHUA: It's going to be all right.

PRISONER: You're beautiful!

JOSHUA: You too.

PRISONER: . . . on toast, that's how I. . . . (*He clutches Joshua's arm*) I can't breathe! Make me breathe! Don't let it leave me . . . I can't . . .

JOSHUA: You can! You can! You're not going to die. You're not going to die . . .

PRISONER: Hey, man, give me a great big kiss. (*Joshua kisses him*) Yeah. That's beautiful. (*He dies*)

JOSHUA: Come on. Don't you dare die. No! I don't even know who you *are*. I don't even know your *name*. What was your name? Don't die! Don't leave me alone! Don't . . .

(*Joshua starts to cry. He cradles the body in his arms. A drum is heard. A group of strange, gnarled people enter. They are mutations—a limb is either added to or missing from their bodies. They speak in high, breathless voices. Some carry tambourines, others colored streamers. One is banging a drum. They are dancing and singing*)

MUTANTS:

"Sing tra
Sing la
Sing heigh
Sing ho
Sing lee
Sing loo . . ."

(*They dance around Joshua*)

FIRST MUTANT: Look! A man! *A man!*

SECOND MUTANT: He has no hair and he has scars. He's ugly, he's ugly!

THIRD MUTANT: Did his parents take those drugs too?

FOURTH MUTANT: No, silly. He's a different kind of ugly. He's not one of us.

FIRST MUTANT: (*To Joshua*) Where are you going?

JOSHUA: Flower City.

THIRD MUTANT: Oh, that's in the hills. We know where that is.

JOSHUA: Is that where *you're* going?

FIRST MUTANT: No. We're marching to the sea.

JOSHUA: What are you doing there?

SECOND MUTANT: Marching *into* it.

THIRD MUTANT: It's the nicest way.

FOURTH MUTANT: We're tired of being ugly.

FIRST MUTANT: But we're going to make it a happy thing.

THIRD MUTANT: Even though it was scary when *they* came for us.

JOSHUA: Who?

FIRST MUTANT: Armies. To the marshes, where we lived. They're going everywhere. Finding everyone who's strange.

THIRD MUTANT: You have to be careful, because *you're* ugly too.

FIRST MUTANT: We'll take you with us.

SECOND MUTANT: We'll take you to the sea.

THIRD MUTANT: Come with us . . .

JOSHUA: No! I have to go to Flower City. Why don't *you* come with me? Why don't . . .

FIRST MUTANT: We have no time to argue.

SECOND MUTANT: We have to hurry.

JOSHUA: But . . .

FIRST MUTANT: Let us be *happy,* please.

THIRD MUTANT: We're going to dance to the sea . . .

FOURTH MUTANT: With flowers and streamers and drums . . .

FIRST MUTANT: Come with us!

THIRD MUTANT: No one will want you—you're so ugly.

SECOND MUTANT: Come with us!

FOURTH MUTANT: No one will have you—you're so strange.

FIRST MUTANT: Come with us!

THIRD MUTANT: Follow the path of the moon . . .

SECOND MUTANT: Into the sea.

JOSHUA: No. I can't. I won't! I have to get to Flower City. It's a place to *live.* I have to get there!

FIRST MUTANT: That's a shame.

THIRD MUTANT: You're very sad.

FOURTH MUTANT: Even though you're not one of us . . .

FIRST MUTANT: . . . We'll show you the way to Flower City. (*He unties Joshua's chains; Joshua holds on to the Pris-*

oner's body) You'll have to leave him here. We have no time.
Come on.

    (Joshua is dazed. They take his hand)
    FIRST MUTANT: Follow us.
    THIRD MUTANT: We'll show you the way.
    MUTANTS: *(Sing)*
"Sing tra
Sing la
Sing heigh
Sing ho
Sing lee
Sing loo . . ."

    *(They dance away. Blackout. Lights. Joshua marches
across bridges, through rivers, over mountains. He reaches
a sign with an arrow pointing straight ahead. The sign
reads Flower City. Blackout. The lights rise on Flower
City. A mountainside, with hills beyond. The city is filled
with giant wooden crosses. A Flower Person has been
nailed to each crucifix. Some move their lips. Some are
humming. Some are silent. Some are dead. The ground
is littered with guitars. A Cameraman films the scene. An
Announcer is behind him with a microphone)*
    ANNOUNCER: . . . Left as a warning by Concerned Cit-
izens everywhere that they will not tolerate the kind of life led by
the Flower People . . .
    *(Joshua enters. He stumbles on a guitar, stoops down and
picks it up. Then he looks up—and sees the crosses)*
    JOSHUA: Oh no!
    ANNOUNCER: Other forces are being mobilized to find
the remaining dissidents hiding in the mountains . . .
    *(Joshua walks beneath the crosses. He looks up at a girl.
It is Joanne)*
    JOSHUA: Joanne! Joanne! *(He looks at the other people
on the crucifixes. He seems to recognize them)*
    ANNOUNCER: Some people have fled to the hills, but
the armies are on their way . . .

JOSHUA: Everyone I've ever loved . . .

ANNOUNCER: They have pledged to destroy . . .

JOSHUA: Everyone I've ever loved! Everyone who was beautiful. Everyone who had something to say, to give, to share! *Everyone!*

(Joshua cries out and runs off. Some of the Flower People call out, very quietly)

FLOWER PEOPLE: Joshua . . . Joshua . . . Joshua . . .
(Blackout. Lights rise on a mountaintop. It is late evening. Joshua enters, still holding the guitar. He sits. He is silent for a long time. Gunshots can be heard far in the distance)

JOSHUA: *(Finally; to himself)* Well, shmuck, here you are. Joshua the Great! Three cheers! Oh baby, you were wrong about *everything.* You kept turning corners and there wasn't anything there. *(Silence)* I'm alone. I knew it. I knew someday I'd be alone. It isn't fair . . . *(Silence)* Listen to those guns. Someone's gonna be coming for me. *(Silence)* Why don't they hurry? *(He remembers something in his pocket)* Hey! *(He reaches in and removes the pills he took from Lisa)* Well—why not? It's better than letting the creeps get you. O.K. Let's see—there are red ones, green ones, brown ones. Which is which? Maybe they don't mix. Suppose they make me sick? Oh Joshua, if you're going to die, what does it matter? Just take them! *(He raises the pills to his lips)* I don't want to vomit. I haven't vomited since I was five years old. I'm not going to vomit. I'm just going to sleep. Take them! *(He looks at the pills)* They're awfully big. How am I going to get them down? There isn't any water. I might choke to death! Oh shit . . . Maybe I can crush them? No, then they taste horrible. Joshua, come on! *(He puts one on his tongue)* Suppose I just fall asleep—and sleep—and then *wake up* three days later? Yeah, that's what would happen. That would just be my luck! I can't even commit suicide. *That's not even going to happen right!* I can't even die. But I mustn't live. Come on—take them, take them. There isn't anything, anything, anything to even *think* of living for. Take them, Joshua! You're not going to choke, you're not going to wake up. Take them! (*He drops the pills*) I can't. *Why the hell can't I do it?* (*The shooting grows closer*) It's getting noisy. (*Weeps*) I don't have any hair. They took away my hair. What will I do without hair? My beautiful hair. (*Silence*) Shmuck. It will grow back. Oh what the hell, I've made it this far. I might as well stick around to see the sun come up! Who knows, something good may happen. (*He picks up guitar*) What do *you* have to say? (*He plays a few notes*) You're absolutely out of tune. (*He adjusts the strings*) People don't know how to take care of their instruments. There. Let's see. (*He plays a melody and sings*)

"There are moments in time
And you have to . . ."
(*He stops, adjusts the strings again*) Come on. That's right. (*Resumes:*)
"There are moments in time
And you have to grab them
Before they turn to dust.

I found the sea in Babylon
And dreamt a dream of Babylon
Bright golden dream of Babylon
(And what is wrong with that?)

I want to stay in Babylon
And sing my song in Babylon
For hope lives on in Babylon
(And what is wrong with that?)
Ain't nothing wrong with that."

> (*He continues to play. The noise grows closer and louder. Marching sounds. Bombing sounds. Screams. But he continues to play, as:*)

Curtain

The Editor

Stanley Richards is a man of wide and varied experience in the theatre. He has written 25 plays, among them *Through a Glass, Darkly; Tunnel of Love; August Heat; Sun Deck; O Distant Land;* and *District of Columbia.* He is the editor of the following anthologies and series: *The Best Short Plays 1970; The Best Short Plays 1969; The Best Short Plays 1968; Best Plays of the Sixties; Best Short Plays of the World Theatre: 1958–1967; Modern Short Comedies from Broadway and London;* and *Canada on Stage.* Twelve of his own plays have appeared in the prize annuals *The Best One-Act Plays* and *The Best Short Plays.* His television play *Mr. Bell's Creation* holds a record: it has had more live network television productions (both here and abroad) than any other play.

Mr. Richards' latest play, *Journey to Bahia,* adapted from a prize-winning Brazilian play and film, *O Pagador de Promessas,* premiered at The Berkshire Playhouse and later was produced in Washington, D. C. under the auspices of the Brazilian Ambassador and the Brazilian American Cultural Institute. (It also has been published in book form.)

His plays have been translated for production and publication abroad into Portuguese, Afrikaans, Dutch, Tagalog, French, German, Korean, Spanish and Italian.

In addition, he has been the New York theatre critic for *Players Magazine,* and a frequent contributor to *Theatre Arts, Playbill, Writer's Digest, Writer's Yearbook, The Theatre, Actors' Equity Magazine,* and *The Dramatists Guild Quarterly.*

As an American theatre specialist, Mr. Richards has been awarded three successive grants by the United States Department of State's International Cultural Exchange Program to teach playwriting and directing in Chile and Brazil. He taught playwriting in Canada for over ten years and in 1966 was appointed Visiting Professor of Drama at the University of Guelph, Ontario. He has produced and directed plays and has lectured extensively on theatre at universities in the United States,

Canada and South America. Mr. Richards, a New York City resident, is now at work on a collection of *Mystery and Suspense Plays of the 20th Century Theatre; Best Short Plays of the World Theatre: 1968–1973;* and *The Best Short Plays 1971.*